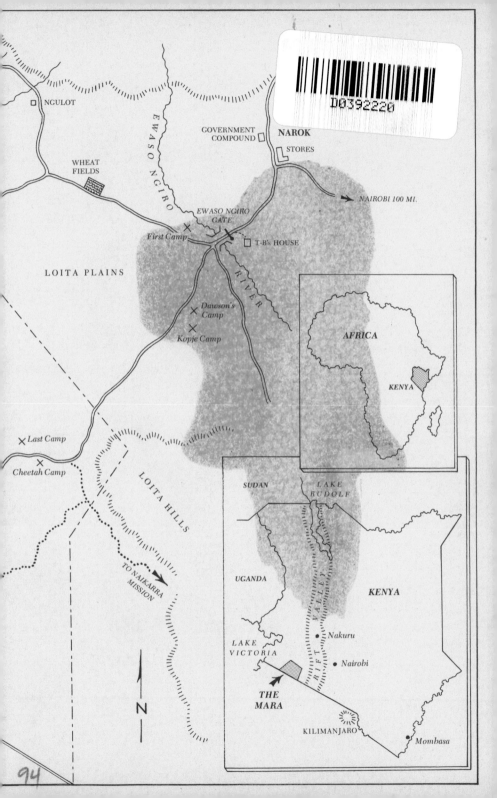

Also by Colin Fletcher

The Complete Walker

The Man Who Walked Through Time

The Thousand-Mile Summer

THE WINDS OF MARA

THE WINDS

OF MARA

by Colin Fletcher

ALFRED A. KNOPF   New York   1973

THIS IS A BORZOI BOOK
PUBLISHED BY ALFRED A. KNOPF, INC.

Copyright © 1972 by Colin Fletcher

All rights reserved under International and Pan-American
Copyright Conventions.
Published in the United States by Alfred A. Knopf, Inc.,
New York, and simultaneously in Canada by Random
House of Canada Limited, Toronto. Distributed by
Random House, Inc., New York.

Library of Congress Cataloging in Publication Data:

Fletcher, Colin.
    The winds of Mara.

    1. Zoology—Kenya—Mara.   2. Mara, Kenya—
Description and travel.   I. Title.
QL 337.K4F54   591.9'676'2   72-2237
ISBN 0-394-47091-5

Manufactured in the United States of America

FIRST EDITION

To Michael Magzis, Editor

I think I could turn and live with animals, they're so placid
 and self-contained,
I stand and look at them long and long. . . .

They bring me tokens of myself, they evince them plainly
 in their possession.
I wonder where they get these tokens,
Did I pass that way huge times ago and negligently drop
 them?

WALT WHITMAN

The cultural influence of the West European civilization
upon tropical Africans [among many others] *. . . is so recent*
a ferment that it is not possible to predict whether it will
evaporate without permanent effect, or whether it will turn
the dough sour, or whether it will successfully leaven the
lump.

ARNOLD TOYNBEE

Et in Arcadia ego!

Contents

Prelude   3

SEARCH   15

CONFIRMATION   80

Interlude   164

EXPLORATION   174

DISCOVERY   283

Postlude   330

Bibliography   339

THE WINDS OF MARA

Prelude

You can become aware that something has stirred at the back of your mind long before a shape emerges. And after it is all over and you can look back down the floodlit tunnel of hindsight you may well see that what finally emerged was big enough and solid enough to deflect the tide race of your life. But all you know at the time, to begin with, are the minutes and hours of another day.

That first morning at Keekorok we left the lodge early and drove north across the pale savanna. At least, I think we went north. It is something of a surprise, the way I know that corner of the Mara now, to find that I am not at all sure where we were, just after sunrise, when I touched our driver on his arm and nodded toward a big herd of zebras. But I can still remember the grass, all around us, when he swung the Volkswagen minibus off the track and up an open slope. The grass was long and dry and it glowed golden in the slanting sunlight.

We stopped sixty yards from the zebras and stood up, heads and shoulders out above the sliding roof. The air was still cold but the sun struck warm and welcome where it found bare skin. The other three vehicles of my party pulled up alongside so that we formed an impromptu little grandstand out there in the open. I could smell the grass now, with its blend of dust and life. It rustled, very faintly.

The sunlight, slanting forward over our shoulders, fell full on the zebras. Their stripes stood out sharp as test patterns on a TV screen. There were eighty or a hundred of them, bunched tight, midway between us and a wedge of dark trees. We stood watching them through binoculars.

And then the lions came out of the trees.

They came in loose line abreast, making no attempt to conceal themselves. They walked slowly and lazily, low-slung bodies dark gold against the pale golden grass, all twenty of them moving steadily toward the zebras.

The zebras bunched tighter still, every animal alert and facing the danger. The lions kept coming. The zebras edged away to the left, out of the lions' path. The lions held course. The zebras, reassured, halted.

The lions continued their slow and lazy passage, directly toward us. Once a lioness stopped and turned her head to look briefly at the zebras, then walked on. A trio of cubs began to romp and tumble; an adult cuffed them into order. The gap between us narrowed. Soon we could see magnificently self-assured expressions on golden faces; then rib cages showing faintly, sculpturally; then muscles rippling beneath powerful haunches. Eventually it seemed as if we could see each hair adjusting to the animals' slow and lazy movements. Before long the whole pride, somewhat scattered now, was threading its way among our vehicles. Several of the beasts passed so close that you felt you could reach out and touch the long, lean, golden bodies. Then they were moving away from us, into the sun, and the detail had gone. I could almost hear my people let out their collective breath.

It would be difficult, I think, to say just what had held us. After all, there had been no drama—no ferocious snarling, no skirmish in the dust, no sudden slaughter. And the quiet scene had lasted, I suppose, less than ten minutes. But there had been more to it than the lions' perfectly timed entrance. More to it than their languid and graceful and arrogant passage across the stage. More to it, even, than the vivid morning sunlight. But perhaps the light was the essence: it touched the scene with a freshness that seemed to have been distilled from the dawn of more than one perfect and passing day.

We drove slowly after the lions, taking care not to disturb them. All of us, I think, were conscious of that warm sense of privilege you get when you are lucky enough to watch, close up, as truly wild animals go about their quiet business. And something may have stirred in my mind, even then.

Soon we were watching the pride drink in small groups from a grass-fringed pool. We were so close that we could see their tongues curl into pink, flexile ladles that lapped up the water with the same deft and astonishing motion by which a house cat's tongue annexes milk. When they raised their heads from the pool we could see water glistening on pale whiskers.

An old male, ignoring our vehicles in the extraordinary way that lions nearly always do, walked slowly over to the bus I was in. He moved with an aloof, languid kind of arrogance that is rarely achieved anywhere outside England. Still ignoring us, he lay down in the bus's shadow. His huge, regally maned head was less than six feet from mine and I could see the outline of every scar on his broad nose, the mottled inlay of pink on the black skin of his nostrils, and the parallel lines of neat black dots along the roots of his whiskers. When he deigned to look up at us—with an uncomprehending and curiously inefficient kind of stare—I found myself looking down into golden eyes with pupils that were not large and elliptical but small and round and quite uncatlike.

We stayed with the lions for more than an hour. But we left at last—depriving the old male of his awning—and drove slowly back toward the lodge. A line of wildebeest, or gnus—bearded and unbelievably outdated-looking creatures—galloped past like an animated frieze on a caveman's wall. A herd of buffalo, several hundred strong, flowed black and powerful through distant trees. Beyond them the savanna rolled westward—grass and trees and grass again—toward a hazy blue escarpment. And in everything we saw there was the same early and unspoiled harmony, fresh and clean and simple. At least, I think I had recognized the harmony by then. Hindsight certainly contends that by the time we got back to the lodge for breakfast my mind was already stirring. But perhaps the day was still just another day.

Yet I suppose it was never what you could call an altogether ordinary day. I had not been to the Mara before, either during the years I lived in Kenya or in the two months since I had come back, and I was there now only because I had signed on to guide twenty Americans on a game-viewing safari. I had taken the job with misgivings, mostly because I needed money, but my party had turned out to be a lively and open-minded crowd and I was soon enjoying myself. We had sampled the cream of East Africa's game areas, and a new world had begun to open up for me. Then we came to the Mara—and it was different. So perhaps it is not just hindsight after all when I suggest that by the time we went into the lodge for breakfast that first morning I felt the promise of something more incisive than ordinary enjoyment.

Between breakfast and lunch most of my people sunned themselves beside the swimming pool, out in the crescent of mown grass enclosed by the lodge and the visitors' cottages.

All the buildings were low, with simple lines, and built of gray-brown local stone and rough-hewn beams. So they fitted in. And the place had a quality that few game lodges attain: comfort of the standard most tourists demand, without the kind of walled-in sumptuousness that holds Africa at too hopeless an arm's length. Through wide windows you looked out past a line of trees onto rolling grassland and thick, scattered bush. In the distance rose hills that were sometimes green, sometimes black, and sometimes a pale, ephemeral blue. If you were lucky you saw a herd of gazelles or a hyena or a group of browsing elephants. And always, even with the amenities of the lodge pillowing your senses, you could, if you made the effort, halfway feel the savanna's raw reality.

In the afternoon of that first day in the Mara I took my party to see a Masai village, or *manyatta*. It lay just outside the ten-by-twenty-mile Game Sanctuary that surrounds the lodge, the sanctuary that is the core of the Masai Mara Game Reserve, the sanctuary in which not even the local Masai people may live, the sanctuary in which no man may camp or sound a car horn or drive after dark—a sanctuary, that is, from man's harsher world, a place in which the other animals come first, always.

Just outside the Sanctuary we passed a group of six men walking across the open plain. They strode along in single file, fifty yards to the right of the road. The sun shone full on their tall, lithe figures and we could pick out every detail of men and clothing. I pointed out the pigtailed hair and—conscious of the thinness of my knowledge—explained that it was a style worn only by Masai *moran*, the members of the warrior age group.

In some ways the moran looked more like early American Indians than Africans. And the resemblance went beyond their faintly aquiline features. Red mud coated their pigtailed hair. Red dye, rubbed into their bodies, gave them a warm and almost glowing sheen. The dye, I explained, was made of red ocher and animal fat. The men's only garments were lengths of red-brown cloth, knotted at one shoulder. These cloths, called *shukas*, hung loose and swung partly aside with every step. Under his shuka each man wore a waistbelt with a short, leather-sheathed sword thrust into it. Each wore above his right wrist a small, brightly colored bead bracelet. And each carried in his right hand a long, slender, broad-tipped spear.

Our driver slowed down. The moran strode on, easily and lightly and unhurriedly. They ignored the dust cloud that billowed out behind our vehicle and drifted over them. They ignored our very existence. And they walked with heads held arrogantly high. But their arrogance was the natural, self-assured arrogance of a lion, not the kind it had been sad to find in Nairobi. You would never accuse a Masai of carrying a chip on his shoulder. The land he walks is his land. He is one of the Chosen People. No one—and certainly not a flabby white man or woman gawking out of a minibus window—can come close to being his equal.

Our driver accelerated and the moran slipped back out of sight.

Soon afterward we came to the manyatta. When the village elders and I had finished our inevitable but mutually demeaning haggle over a collective admission fee, my party walked into the manyatta through a gap in its dense thornbrush fence.

The circular enclosure measured about a hundred yards across. Scattered around inside the fence were a dozen rectangular, flat-roofed, mud-encrusted huts. Otherwise the place was empty, dead, a mere arena of trampled earth. The hump-backed cattle, the pith of every Masai activity and thought, were somewhere out on the savanna. They only came into the manyatta at night, for protection against lions and hyenas. Then, warm and noisy and jostling, they no doubt injected vigor and meaning. But all we saw was the lifeless enclosure, its surface trampled into gray-brown, dung-littered dust.

The emptiness of the place was accentuated rather than broken by the women and children who stood stiffly in line waiting for their photographs to be taken. (The men had vanished as soon as money changed hands.) The women wore enormous necklaces and earrings and bracelets, all neatly constructed of gaily colored beads. Silver bangles encased their calves in gleaming, Michelin-like cocoons. But they stood sullen and resentful in the hot afternoon sun, ignoring us almost as successfully as they ignored the flies that swarmed around their faces and shaven heads and bare arms and shoulders and around the pendulous breasts that often hung outside their loose, red, togalike upper garments. There was the same now-you've-got-your-pound-of-flesh phoniness about it all as there is about a visit to a commercialized Indian pueblo in Arizona. And at such times it does not help at all to tell yourself that you, the voyeur, are the maggot, buying your way into strangers' lives and unable to comprehend the signs that give meaning to those lives.

Eventually I persuaded the line of women to break up. We mingled among them and their children and bought some of their finery, and things began to go a little better. But when we left after half an hour of it my people looked sad and disappointed.

We drove slowly back toward the lodge. A couple of miles inside the Sanctuary, in a sloping meadow, we found a small concourse of animals. A ram impala flung back slender and superbly curved horns, then moved protectively between us and his harem of twenty Bambi-like ewes. Nearby, four brown kongoni mingled with a herd of their purple and pewter cousins, the topi. Beyond them a lone wildebeest and two giraffes stood stalk still. Off to the right, three small groups of zebras grazed slowly forward. They mingled with the impala, passed through, mingled with the topi and kongoni, passed beyond them too. Nothing else happened, really, but we sat watching the scene for half an hour. The sun sank lower. The light sharpened. Soon it was as vivid as the morning light had been. And once again the grass glowed golden. The animals ebbed and flowed across it. Group blended with group, then disengaged, each going peacefully about its business, independently but in harmony with its neighbors. Only patterns persisted.

We did not drive on until after the sun had set. By then the grass was once more the pale straw-brown it had been when we left the lodge that morning before sunrise.

The morning and the evening had shared something, I decided. Something more than the grass and the light. That final concourse of animals had had something in common with the pride of lions coming out of the dark trees beyond the zebras. Something in common, too, with the tall red men striding loosely across the plain, at one with their land. There was the same early, unblemished freshness about it, the same feeling of rightness that you sometimes get and can never really explain when everything fits together, piece meshing with jigsaw piece so naturally and so easily that you wonder why the world is not always so simple and so beautiful.

By the time we saw the lights of the lodge, twilight was slipping down over the savanna. And with it came the coolness. When we pulled up outside the lodge at last it was good to get out of the minibus and go in past the sign that said KEEKOROK LODGE, KENYA—5256 FEET ABOVE M.S.L—105 MILES SOUTH OF THE EQUATOR, and to turn into the warm, crowded lounge with the bar already its seething center, and then to walk over and stand for a few minutes beside the blazing log fire.

After dinner I had a drink at the bar with Steve Joyce, the young assistant manager.

Steve was cheerful, Irish, serious. "Yes," he said, "but things don't always change for the worse, you know. Take this lodge, now. One of the few places in Kenya that anyone has persuaded Masai men to work inside. Certainly the first lodge it's happened in. We've got them as porters, waiters, cooks, the lot. If only . . ."

A group of people surged out of the dining room and homed on the bar. Their hubbub washed over our conversation, cutting its threads and leaving us side by side but alone, each with our thoughts. When the noise receded at last I found myself saying, quite unexpectedly, "This is a good place, Steve. Yes, a *good* place." And then, surprising myself again, I added, "Hell, even the porters are happy."

Steve looked at me quickly. Then he smiled. "Thanks," he said. "I hope you're right."

Soon afterward he was called away. I sat on at the bar, alone in the pit of the crowd.

The afternoon before, when we drove in from Nairobi, hot and tired and dusty, four Africans dressed in the standard porters' uniform of khaki shorts and shirts were sitting on a bench at the lodge entrance. As we got out of our vehicles all four men stood up and came forward to greet us with broad smiles. They helped our drivers unload the baggage, then carried it into the lobby and finally out to the various cottages. And they seemed to do it all as if they enjoyed doing it, not just because they enjoyed the thought of the tips that would infallibly follow. I think I must have noticed that, even at the time. After all, porters are not exactly renowned, by and large, for their spontaneous good spirits, and if you find such a hopeful sign when you arrive in a new place I suppose a part of you always registers it and is grateful.

I finished my drink and stood up and walked across the lounge to the big glass sliding doors. Outside, floodlights poured down onto the swimming pool. The mown grass around it was bright emerald green, like the outfield at a night game. I stood at the door, looking out across the grass, trying to cut off the noise that filled the room.

The surface of my mind worked away at the floodlights: at this altitude it was always cool after sunset, and often cold, so not many people would use the unheated pool after dark; the lights, then, would be mainly to discourage other animals from wandering into our human territory. But underneath I kept worrying at something else. All day, because I was leading a safari, it had been a rush. Even when I sat at the bar, briefly alone in the crowd, there had been no calm. Perhaps, I decided, that was the reason I had walked to the big glass doors that looked out onto the savanna. And then, carrying this thought to its logical conclusion, I slid back one of the doors and stepped out into the night.

It was cool outside, but not cold. I closed the door behind me and walked toward the pool. The din inside the lodge faded and the sounds of the African night took over—the nightsounds that are always there, thundering away in a kind of subdued bedlam. But the insects' instruments are so subtly orchestrated that you rarely notice them: you filter them out and register only unusual noises. And so, most of the time, you hear only the silence of the night.

I walked on across the soft green grass. Somewhere far out in the blackness beyond the floodlights, a lion proclaimed dominion over his territory. The proclamation was half roar, half grunt, wholly regal. It had a slow, diminishing cadence to it, and the final notes came faint and almost ghostly. As they died away I reached the pool.

The pale blue water fitted its edges like glass. I stood looking down into it. The floodlights cut through so cleanly that I could see the veins of a small brown leaf that lay on the bottom. Behind me, a muffled hum still seeped out from the lounge. It only amplified the silence.

My eyes began to trace the detail of the leaf's vein pattern. It was very beautiful. Each branching intricacy fitted into the harmonious whole. But although I continued to stare at the leaf, my eyes did not really pass along their information. For from the recesses of my mind a solid mass had begun to press forward. I could feel the tension now, feel it growing, like the pressure of water building behind a dam. The shape that was emerging had something to do with this place. Something to do with the herds of free, unknowing animals. Something to do with lions emerging from dark trees at sunrise. Something to do with tall red men striding loosely across open spaces. Something to do with a corner of Africa not yet whipped raw by harsh winds of change.

Out in the darkness, the lion roar-grunted his proclamation again. The sound diminished, died. Once more there was nothing except the silence and the insects' orchestra and the muffled nightsounds from the lodge.

I stood looking down at the leaf that lay brown and still in the pale blue water, letting myself drift at last with the sounds and the silence, with the floodlight and the darkness. I floated above the leaf.

And then the dam across my mind disintegrated. The mass of hints surged forward. The waves met, mingled, paused—and exploded upward in a tall and joyous fountain.

I am almost sure I laughed aloud, out across the pale blue water of the pool.

All day it had been staring me in the face. Here in this unspoiled corner of Africa, where I had found harmony between animals and land, between men and land, between men and animals, here in this sanctuary, here in this place where for the first time in two months I had forgotten that I was looking for something, I had found it. Next day I would have to take my party down into the Serengeti. But within a week I would be free. I would be free, if this new elation lasted, to return to the Mara and set in motion the things that so clearly had to be done.

Wildebeest

SEARCH

Two weeks later, on the last afternoon of August, I drove out of Nairobi, alone. Out to the Rift Valley Escarpment I drove, and down past the little red-roofed chapel that was built during World War II by the Italian prisoners who made the highway. The Italians had selected such an apt niche for their offering and had worked with such quiet distinction that when I first saw the chapel, two years after the war, it had already become a Kenya landmark.

A dozen miles beyond the chapel, out on the floor of the Rift Valley, I turned left onto the dirt road that cuts westward to the Mara.*

The Mara road was imperfect, even by Kenya's tolerant stan-

---

* "The Mara" (which rhymes with Connemara) is a somewhat vague and malleable term. This book uses it in the restricted sense of "the Mara Plains": a thousand-square-mile expanse of savanna that lies between 5,000 and 6,000 feet above sea level and is bounded (see map) on the south by the Tanzanian border, on the east by the Loita Hills, on the north by rising

dards. My little rented car began to flounce in protest. Behind us, dust billowed out in a towering cloud but the wide sky and waving grass consumed it without effort or contamination. Soon, a herd of Thomson's gazelles frisked and gamboled beside the road, black tails metronoming over clean white butts. A Grant's gazelle stood quiet, statuesque. And all around me now the grass stretched golden. But because I had so recently left the city an invisible screen hung outside the car's windows, cutting me off from the reality of the savanna. It would take time, I knew, to break through this screen, and I would hardly begin to do so until I had camped at least once in the open savanna, unsurrounded, in touch, alone. There was another thing too. That afternoon my eyes were fixed on a human target with a solid reputation for elusiveness, and I knew that a lot hung on the way our first meet-

bushland beyond Narok, and on the west by the Isuria Escarpment.

The Mara and the much larger Serengeti to the south form a single ecological unit. It is a significant unit. Sir Julian Huxley has written: "The Serengeti-Mara . . . is the home of the richest and most varied population of large wild animals left in the world. It is indeed an exemplar of the Pleistocene climax of biological evolution, before man began to make his drastic and often ruinous alterations in habitats, and to spoil so much fine scenery."

ing went. On it depended, almost certainly, the kind of cooperation I could expect in the things I had made up my mind to do.
So I drove in a state of mild anxiety. This anxiety set up a second
screen. But behind the double impediment surged elation. For I
knew that when I drove out of Nairobi I had made a fresh start—
and I felt sure that this time I was on the right road at last.

I had landed in Kenya two months earlier—twenty years almost to the day since I had arrived in the country to settle, nearly
fifteen years since I had left. I had come back primed and expectant, eager to see the people savoring their new independence.
But I had also come back looking for ghosts and echoes that
would serve as sounding boards, and at first I returned, naturally
enough, to the up-country farms I had worked on. But I found
nothing that would echo true down the tunnel of fifteen years.
And I barely caught a glimpse of the man who had once flickered
about that stage under my name. Perhaps I tried too hard, over-
consulting my feelings, like litmus paper, at every turn. Or perhaps a screen is bound to fall between the shadows you remember
and the new reality. Anyway, after a month of it I gave up and
went back down to Nairobi.

I had never liked the place. Now I grew to loathe it. Even
more than in colonial times, it seemed cut off from the realities
of Kenya. And there were other things too.

Yet I hung around the city for almost a month. Because I had
lost my way, I found plenty of good, solid, unwriggleable pre-
texts to keep me there. And for a time I went on trying to pick
up the old threads. I met an ex-wife and we communicated and
got loads off our chests without tears and without reproach. I
met an ex-houseboy, a Luo whom I remembered with respect
and affection, and although my Swahili had by no means thawed
out yet from its years in cold storage, that was good too. But
eventually the truth caught up with me. The Africa I had known
and half remembered was dying, fast. And the Africa that was
alive, and stretching, I had never known.

There was also another barrier. In planning what I would do
when I returned to Africa I had, with extreme but human stupidity, forgotten that I too had changed, radically. But now at last,

in going out to find the new Africa, I put away my preconceived targets.

I attended an international conference on wildlife management, held in Nairobi. And I began to visit game parks and to watch the wildlife that I now recognized as East Africa's true wealth—though not necessarily in an economic sense. But the shoestring on which I was running my trip soon began to fray and I took the job as a safari guide. Ten days later I stood looking down into the floodlit swimming pool at Keekorok, seeing the simple harmonies of a small brown leaf and of much more besides. And since that moment I had never doubted that I was on the right road at last.

For twenty-five miles the dusty, potholed road cut westward across the floor of the Rift Valley. Then it angled up the first of the escarpments that form the valley's flank. I drove on across rolling bushland. The day's clouds came with me, cruising serenely westward like colossal cotton icebergs. I crossed a stream, climbed a second escarpment, swept through more miles of rolling bush. And a little after five-thirty I came to Narok, the administrative center for—and the only town in—an area the size of New Jersey.

My permit to visit the Mara said, "Report to District Commissioner/Police in Narok on arrival." I drove past the line of uninviting wooden stores that are the commercial "town" and went on up the hill to the government compound.

At the police station a tall and amiable *askari* validated my permit and entered particulars in a much-thumbed book.

"Major T-B?" he said. "*Ndio, anakaa Ewaso Ngiro. Milu kumi na mbili tu, kwa njia ya Keekorok.* Yes, he lives at Ewaso Ngiro. Twelve miles only, on the road of Keekorok."

"Is he at home today?"

The askari hunched his shoulders and spread his hands in eloquent helplessness. "I am not able to know," he said. "That one, he comes and goes. There is no man who knows his road. But the ranger at the barrier at Ewaso Ngiro will know if he is at home. The house of T-B is very close to the barrier."

Perhaps, I said, I would meet T-B on the road. And it was

essential that I be able to recognize him. "I hear that he always drives a Land Rover, and that he is very tall."

The askari looked surprised. "You do not know him?"

"My eyes have never seen him, not even one time."

The askari surveyed me, head to toe. Then he smiled, teeth white, ear to ear. "*Lakini yeye hapana ndugu yako?*" he said.

I went back out to my car. The askari's words, literally translated, meant, "But isn't he your brother?" Like most languages, though, Swahili does not always translate literally. *Ndugu* can signify not only "brother" but also, more loosely, "a relation" or even "someone with whom you have something markedly in common."

By the time I had filled my tank at the gas pump outside one of Narok's stores and then had headed out on the Keekorok road, it was almost six o'clock. I urged the car forward. In Kenya, where it is dark by seven-thirty all year long, six-thirty is about as late as you can call unexpectedly on a man you don't know—even if all you want to do that day is set up a later meeting, and even if he does not have a phone and you can say in all honesty that you have been trying for several days to get a message to him. At least it seemed to me that six-thirty was about as late as you should call if you were heavily conscious that a lot hung on the way your first meeting went.

The Ewaso Ngiro road turned out to be another obstacle course. Dust jarred up from the car's floorboards and settled over everything as a coarse, red-brown film. In the roughest sectors, the car complained *fortissimo*. I eased up on the gas pedal.

The little right-hand-drive car was the cheapest I had been able to rent: a faintly comic piece of tinmongery called a Renault R4. It had been built with two eyes riveted on economy and would, I felt sure, have failed to pass U.S. safety standards with something to spare. But it had been designed with flair and cunning. I had already found that its front-wheel drive and independent suspension wafted me across country that sleek, road-hugging cars would only whinny at from the fringe. It did forty miles to the gallon, fast. And it made a very passable house. The square white box of a body might be an architectural lament, but by uprooting and casting out all its furniture except the driver's seat I could fit in half a cabinfull of gear and still leave room, with only minor rearrangements, to roll out a sleeping bag full length on the floor.

The Renault R4 is marketed in East Africa under the name Roho, a Swahili word that means "heart" in the sense of "spirit" or "soul," and as my ugly little Roho looked like being just the kind of trusty steed I needed to take me tilting at whatever windmills I might find in the Mara, I duly christened it Rohosinante.

By the time Rohosinante and I reached the Ewaso Ngiro road barrier—a checkpoint for all traffic entering and leaving the Mara proper—the light had begun to fail.

"*Hapana iko*," said the game ranger. "*Aliondoka jana*. No, he is not here. He went away yesterday."

"When do you think he'll be back?"

I think I knew, even before the ranger began to hunch his shoulders and spread his hands, that it was a foolish question.

"Oh, but do you know where he went?"

"Yes, he went to Mara Bridge. Perhaps he is in the Triangle."

"Ah," I said, "the Triangle."

The Triangle is the least accessible part of the Mara. It lies tucked away in the southwest corner, a two-hundred-square-mile enclave wedged between the Tanzanian border, the Isuria Escarpment and the Mara River. My map showed no roads leading into it—only one thin-dotted-line of a track that petered out almost at once. For ten days, ever since I had begun to ferret out information about the Mara, the idea of the Triangle had been strengthening its grip on my mind like a benign but irresistible tumor, and the moment the ranger mentioned it I knew where I would be going first thing next morning.

That plan meshed with other ideas too. Even before I left Nairobi I had decided that if I at first failed to find the Senior Game Warden of the Mara—the elusive Major Temple-Boreham, whom everyone called T-B—I would go scouring the countryside for him. It seemed to me that if I managed to track him down far out in the bush somewhere he could hardly fail to see that I was both determined in my aims and also able to look after myself. Searching for him would also give me a mildly plausible excuse if I had to wander around the countryside for longer than my two-day camping permit authorized. So one way and another I had been more than halfway hoping I would be forced to go out and look for T-B. And now here he was in the Triangle. Some days, your goddam cup just brimmeth over.

The ranger confirmed that it was about sixty miles to Mara Bridge. The road, he said, was "not bad." No, there was nothing there except a bridge over the Mara River. But T-B would be somewhere around. Within twenty miles or so, probably.

I wrote my name in another well-thumbed book. The ranger saluted and lifted the barrier. I urged Rohosinante forward into the Mara.

Dusk slid over into darkness. Soon, starlight and headlight suggested open country to the right. I turned off the road and drove across pale grass. A line of small thorn trees swam up into the headlights. I circled, tight, to check for lions, then stopped and switched off.

At once it was different. And familiar. Now the long pool of grass in the headlights stretched calm and unshifting. Orchestrated nightsounds surged in through the open window. Somewhere out in the darkness an owl hooted. I felt my shoulders begin to relax. Almost as physically, the day's driving sank away into the past. And with it went the taut memory of Nairobi.

After a while I took the flashlight from the glove shelf and probed the darkness through the windows on both sides. The grass was still unoccupied. I think I smiled at my caution. But this, after all, was my first camp in the Mara. And that made a difference.

I got out and went around to the back of the car. The door that formed its entire rear surface was coated, thick, with red-brown dust. I twisted the handle at the bottom of the door and banged. Dust slid down in a red-brown avalanche and at once the door was halfway white again in the pool of my flashlight beam. I swung the door high and locked it in position. It formed a ridiculous and ineffectual little roof against the immense star-studded sky; but it established an immediate and comforting sense of residence.

I leaned inside the car, lifted the butane pressure lamp out of its cardboard box, and set the lamp down in a small open space at the rear of the dusty, rubber-covered floor. Then I struck a match, opened the control valve, and pushed the match up into the glass globe until the flame touched the mantle. The lamp hissed into brilliance, canceling the starlight and swamping the silence.

At once, everything was different again. The big, smooth, bulging blue cylinder of the lamp stood at the unvarying center of the circle of white light. Now there was only that circular hissing world of light, with the blue lamp and me at its center. Beyond the circle, only darkness. Within the circle—dust or no dust—everything was clean and simple. And I knew that wherever I created that circle the hours and minutes and seconds would all be mine. I would have to share them with no one, would have to depend on no one.

I picked up the lamp, walked back to the driver's door, leaned in and switched off the headlights. It made no real difference.

I went back under the little roof and set the lamp on the ground. Very carefully, I pulled out the two groundsheets that covered everything in the back of the car. When I shook them a cloud of dust rose red-brown in the glaring light. Slowly and silently it drifted out beyond the circle and into oblivion. I watched it go.

Quickly, then, I set up the folding wooden table and chair close beside the car, under the little roof, facing out into the night. And when I had put the lamp on the table and had added the butane pressure stove and then the two cardboard boxes of kitchen things and had unpacked the boxes so that everything stood on the table beside the hissing blue lamp, my sense of resi-dence had ripened into a spurious but immensely gratifying sense of ownership.

I opened a bottle of beer and began to cook dinner.

While I cooked, insects kept zooming in and out of the darkness and crashing against the lamp and falling, stunned, onto the table. One pale brown moth nosedived into the stainless steel Sierra Club cup and lay there kicking concentric waves across my beer. I fished it out, remembering other moths I had fished out from that same cup. For the cup was an old backpacking friend. And beside it stood other old and familiar friends: the two nesting cooking pots, comfortably dented from many years' use and misuse; the Boy Scout spoon with the two little lugs on the handle; the old sheath knife, its leather scabbard bound with bright red tape. I stood looking down at them, feeling the familiarity and valuing it.

Two vehicles came pounding down the road from the west, headlights probing the darkness, their racket disrupting my noisy white night-silence. They passed a quarter of a mile away, off to the left, and the din began to fade toward Ewaso Ngiro. I stood listening, still looking down at the table.

The new things I had bought in Nairobi would soon become familiar too: the three white plastic water canteens, the shining knife and fork, even the frying pan with the spatula that was too big but which I knew I would never get around to replacing. And once they were familiar they would become more than mere useful articles. It is ridiculous, of course, the way familiar camping gear latches on to your affection. But that is what happens, I find, always.

The vehicles' din had almost died away. I stood listening, waiting, still looking down at the varnished tabletop. Its grain was very clear. A big whorl, almost dead center, had the kind of contour that on a topo map would have meant a hill that you just had to investigate. The grain showed clear, too, on the wooden arms of the chair; and because the arms were further away from the lamp than the tabletop, their waving brown lines looked warmer, even more comforting. The canvas of the chair's seat and back was emerald green and very bright.

The sound of the vehicles died at last. My lamp and the insects reclaimed the night. It would be all right, I decided. It would not be quite the same as backpacking, perhaps. Not quite the same as camping on a mountaintop four days from a road and leaning back against my pack as it stood propped up on the walking staff. Here, the trappings would always be with me, the machined reminders of that other world. But once I got used to them they need not get in the way.

Steam began to drift up from the stew in the familiar, dented pot. I stirred it, then turned down the stove. The stove had the same kind of big blue cylinder as the lamp. The two stood side by side on the table, smooth and bulging, like Tweedledum and Tweedledee. Above me and a little to the left I could see one corner of Rohosinante's ridiculous little rear door, tilted up against the stars. Otherwise, beyond the table, there was only the circle of grass, pale as straw in the hissing lamplight. And beyond that the enfolding blackness.

Yes, it would be all right. Not much doubt about that, now. It would be very good indeed.

The sun, striking warm through the car window, nudged me awake. I eased up on one elbow: blue sky, golden grass, trees black against distant blue hills.

I fought a rearguard action with the guilt endemic to those of us who are sluggards by constitution but achievers by culture, lost, fumbled out of sleeping bag and car, urinated, wiped dew off the table, put a pot of water on the stove, lit the stove, took food boxes out of the car, put them on the table, and sat down and waited. To describe me as awake would have been hyperbole. But in the due course of creeping time the water boiled. I made tea. I drank. The day began to pull itself into focus.

It was, I saw, no ordinary day. It was one of those mornings that is all sunlight and shadow and cutting edge of contrast, one of those mornings when the air tastes, and you haul huge reserves of it down into the cobwebbed cellars of your lungs and hold it there while you smile and roll it around your nerve ends, the way you would a clear, cool, vintage Liebfraumilch. The morning, in other words, was a typical Kenya highland morning.

I seeped awake. All around me stretched open grassland. The road still ran east and west, I felt sure, a quarter of a mile off to the left, but it stayed in decent hiding. There were other things in sight: the line of small thorn trees that had swum up into my headlights the night before; a darker line of trees and undergrowth that marked a dry watercourse, less than a half a mile away; and beyond them broken bushland. But none of these things corrupted either the grass or the openness. There at my little table, alone in the sunlight, with the car out of sight behind me, I seemed to sit at the center of a world that was endless, open grass. Or perhaps I mean just "endlessly open." For this time it was not the grass that mattered, I think, so much as the sheer openness. The openness and the sense of freedom. This time there were no animals. But the rest of it was already there, just the way it had been the morning we drove out from the lodge, the way I had hardly dared hope I would find it again: simplicity, cleanness, a sense of almost moral rightness, the conviction that this was the way the earth was meant to be—an intimation that here in the Mara I had opened a chapter in the uncensored book of creation.

And as I sat on, content, there in the clean, open, sunlit savanna, lord of all I surveyed, I began to comprehend—or at least to imagine I did—some of the simple, difficult things about the clean and open and sunlit world of the Masai. I began, for example, to understand why the moran strode across their plains with such superb arrogance, unassailable, the Chosen People.

Before the white man came to East Africa, around the turn of the century, the Masai roamed with their cattle over vast areas. If they met men of neighboring tribes they tended to kill them. The women they appropriated. They did these things efficiently and often. Their neighbors therefore lived in constant fear of them, deep into the marrow. So the Masai were, to all intents and purposes, the lords and masters of all they felt inclined to survey.

But the Masai did not, with a few exceptions, kill nonhuman animals. They lived alongside them, in mutual tolerance.

Now most of us have grown used to the idea that we humans are—except for a few isolated, backward, and largely impotent groups—the world's dominant animal, and that every other form of life must give way to us, absolutely. But seventy years ago the powerful Masai, though very much the dominant humans in their land, were by no means the dominant animals. They were, at most, one not very aggressive predator species among many. For they lived in balance with the world around them.

This harmonious condition—exceedingly rare in any situation that embraces *Homo sapiens*—may have been the Masai's strength, the fundamental reason their way of life exerted such a hold on them.

There can be little doubt about the strength of this hold.

When the white man came, the Masai way of life survived, virtually unscathed, its confrontation with the intruders' startling new knowledge and accomplishments. It was very different with the other tribes that came into direct and frequent contact with the new challenge. They quickly adopted at least the rudiments of Western clothing and, often, of Western religion. They learned Swahili—the Bantu language, spread as a coastal lingua franca by the Arabs, that the white man had brought inland. Soon they began to learn English. Above all, they began to learn money.

The Masai would have none of these things. They rejected them out of hand, with disdain. They preferred to roam, following the grass, with the cattle that provided blood and milk for their Spartan diet, hides and horns and hooves for their clothing and utensils and ornaments, impetus for almost every activity they undertook, and meaning for their lives. The mesh was total. As a Masai you could not say "the cattle" without at the same time meaning "my people, the Masai."

But under the Pax Britannica the Masai could not go on roaming far and wide, unrestricted. The newcomers wanted some of the "empty" land they had discovered. (To them, it indeed appeared empty: the Masai had never done more than pass from time to time through vast tracts of their far-flung command, and at that time they and their cattle seem to have been at an unusually low ebb.) Indirectly, the British created other restrictions too: neighboring tribes such as the Kikuyu soon recognized the value of the new alien shield and began to edge cautiously forward from the hills and forests that used to protect them from the warlike but plains-dwelling Masai. And there began, all over the country, the slow building of new pressures that Pax Britannica would create: an African human population that more than doubled; a population of African-owned cattle that increased eightfold. Before long the Kenya Masai signed a series of agreements with the British. And eventually they found themselves penned into a fairly spacious but rather arid southern sector of the country. Within this enclave they continued to reject most Western ways and went on living their old, satisfying life. At least, that was how it had been when I lived in Kenya. But now, people said, things were changing.

Things were bound to change, I knew that. The wind was blowing keen across "changeless" Africa. New ways of life might evolve, strong and healthy, from the old; but failing that the Western ways would be imposed or slavishly copied and would therefore remain, in all probability, both superficial and corrupt —not necessarily because the West was itself corrupt but because the new wind blew too hard and too cold for weak underpinnings. Recent parallels hardly encouraged hope. But in Masailand, as everywhere, the matter would probably pivot on the spirit of the people. And as I sat at my table on the open, sunlit grass, remembering the moran striding across their open, sunlit plain, I dared hope. Perhaps, I thought, the old spirit was still there—the inner strength and the assurance and therefore the humility that come with a life lived in harmony.

I finished my third cup of tea and began to cook breakfast—and remade the always surprising and satisfying discovery that bacon and eggs fried in the open can magnify rather than mar a morning's freshness. I had just sat down to eat when I saw, less than fifty yards away, a man walking toward me across the open grass. He was young and tall and slender and he walked with a loose, easy step. He carried a small bow and a quiver full of arrows. He stopped ten paces away and stood looking at me.

I smiled and greeted him: *"Jambo sana. Habari ya 'subuhi?"*

The young man smiled and said something I did not understand. Then he walked forward and stopped close beside the table. He smiled again. I smiled back.

My breakfast breathed up at me.

I cut a piece of bacon and offered it to the young man. He took it, examined both sides twice, sniffed it, looked at me, smiled, and put the bacon into his mouth. He chewed tentatively, then confidently. Then he looked at me and smiled again, broadly.

I gave him another piece of bacon. He took it, squatted on his heels within arm's reach of me, and put his bow and quiver on the ground. As he did so he turned his head and I saw that his long hair had not been plaited into a pigtail. He was too young, I assumed, to have graduated yet to the moran, or warrior, class.

In due course my guest accepted a third piece of bacon. And after that he accepted, subjected to grave inspection, sampled, devoured, and clearly approved of a piece of fried egg, a cup of tea, and a slice of bread and butter and marmalade. I think it was canned pineapple that I offered him next, though I am no longer sure; anyway, whatever it was, he got as far as the sampling and then rejected it with a wry half-smile and handed it back to me.

I tried speaking to him in Swahili again but we drew another blank. It did not seem to matter, though. We went on eating breakfast, each sitting at ease in our accustomed style, out in the middle of the open, sunlit grass.

Now I have not said, I know, what my young Masai guest looked like, or even what he wore. The trouble is that I am not sure. Usually I remember such detail clearly. Or I have notes that I jotted down soon afterward, or photographs. But for some reason my writer's note-taking habit failed me that day. And to lay hands on a camera and point it at the young man squatting beside me and sharing my breakfast was, of course, unthinkable. So I do not have the details. And yet, although I am not sure why, something about that first breakfast in the Mara remains sharper in my memory, even now, than do other scenes I carried away from Africa on celluloid and emulsion.

Come to think of it, a few minor details are still there. The young man's arrow quiver was, I am almost sure, made of red-brown leather. He wore some simple and suitable garment that can hardly have been anything else except the same kind of red-brown shuka, knotted at one shoulder, that the six striding moran had worn. And I know in a diffuse sort of way that the young man's face was long and faintly aquiline. There is nothing else I can remember about him, physically. But I know, as if I could still see every detail of his face and as if I had talked to him earnestly and for a very long time, that he was easy and unafraid and almost naively innocent—and also that, although he understood that there was still a lot for him to learn, yet he was already sure of himself. But above all I know, rather differently, that he was free, and that he fitted in with the sunlight and the golden grass.

He stayed there beside my table, squatting on his heels, for perhaps half an hour. Then, without warning, he picked up his bow and quiver, stood up, smiled good-bye, and went on his way.

I cleaned and packed away the breakfast things. Then, remembering the two vehicles that had pounded past at dinnertime, I drove back to the Ewaso Ngiro barrier.

"*Ndio, alirudi usiku,*" said the ranger. "Yes, he returned in the night."

And all at once my anxiety was back.

I drove a hundred yards up the road and then, following the ranger's directions, turned right onto a narrow track. The track meandered through scattered bush. Grass grew thick along its center strip. In places the grass had even colonized the wheel ruts. After the broad, dusty road everything looked very green and private. Around one corner I surprised a pair of dikdik—tiny gray-brown antelopes with long mobile noses, creatures so delicate that they look like hares on stilts. The dikdik wobbled noses at me, then faded away.

Half a mile, and the track forked. Down the right fork I could see a small administrative compound: a square wooden building and two or three round, whitewashed huts with thatched roofs. They stood, widely separated, in a big grassy clearing. The place looked neat, functional—and sterile.

I drove down the left fork. At first the bush pressed close. Then, without warning, I came out into another clearing. The track circled around on itself, and off to the right I glimpsed a red roof and gray stonework.

There was nothing sterile about this second clearing. Fifty feet above the ground spread a green canopy. Supporting it— standing out sharp and yellow, as if coated with mustard powder —were the trunks and branches of the huge, stately, umbrella-shaped thorn trees that suffer from the local name of "fever trees." Among the trees grew clumps of sisal, so artfully arranged that you had to look twice to make sure they had not really been planted at random. The pinelike tufts of their poles gave a suggestion of understory, and grass and low plants carpeted the ground. Beyond the trees, a meadow led to a small lake. Beyond the lake, the bush took over again.

I parked beside a young sisal plant and switched off. There was birdsong too; and behind it, silence. My nervousness finally ebbed away.

I got out of the car. Gray stonework, red roof, circling red-brown track, the patterns of graded greenery—they all fitted to-gether. And everything about the clearing was quiet, unpreten-tious, protected, with just enough of man's hand in it to hint at order, not nearly enough to scar. It would be a good place to come home to, I decided, even if you often came back late at night and caught no more than shadowy intimations of the whole as your headlights swung around the circling driveway.

I began to walk toward the house.

"Can I help you?" said a voice.

In dappled sunlight beneath a thorn tree stood a table and two chairs. A woman sat in one of the chairs. I walked toward her. She was small, blue-eyed, perhaps forty-five. We introduced ourselves.

"He's up in the office at the moment," said Mrs. Temple-Boreham. "And he's terribly busy. Perhaps you can tell me a bit about what you want."

"Well—"

"I'm afraid I can't ask you into the house, though. They're

painting it and the smell's awful. But would you care for a cup of tea out here? I was just going to order some. I hope you'll forgive me if I'm not very bright this morning, but I haven't been too well."

So we sat there beneath the yellow-trunked thorn trees, looking out over the meadow with the little lake at its far end. A slate-gray heron planed in to the lake. A servant brought tea. Dappled shadows drifted across the table. Their patterns dissolved, regrouped, dissolved again.

I explained, briefly, what I wanted to do. "And people tell me," I ended, "that if I can get your husband on my side everything will be all right. I gather that he's still a sort of local viceroy."

Mrs. T-B did her best not to look pleased. "Oh, I don't know about that. But he's been here in the Mara for thirty years, you know—and, as you may have heard, the Masai have given us some land so that we can settle on it when Lyn retires."

We finished the tea and went on talking. We talked about T-B and then about the Masai and the Mara and Kenya and the future of the animals, and then about the heron up on the lake and how the Masai cattle kept the meadow cropped short so that it always looked neat, as if it had been mown. We talked for over an hour.

We were back to the future of the animals when Mrs. T-B put a hand to her forehead and let out a long, tired breath. "Oh dear," she said. "I do hope you'll excuse me, but I think I'd better go and rest. I've been in bed for a while and this is my first day up and I'm still feeling pretty weak.

"But about seeing my husband. . . . The trouble is, he's always terribly busy and it's difficult to fix up time with him. He's had quite a few writers around here these last few years, too, and . . . well, some of them didn't work out too well. But you seem to have a feel for the place already, and . . . Look, I'll have a word with him at lunchtime. If you can come back about two o'clock I might just possibly have some news for you."

I murmured appreciations. "Tell him that if I have to wait

I'll be perfectly happy to go and sit in the bush for three days. More if necessary."

"With luck we'll do better than that," said Mrs. T-B.

I drove back partway down the track, swung off into the bush, and parked in a small grassy clearing. I sat in the car and thought through, yet again, all the things I wanted to say to T-B. Then I wrote the main headings and some of the words on a sheet of yellow paper. And for the rest of the morning I went over and over and over my script.

When I went back to the house after lunch Mrs. T-B was smiling and I knew we had won.

"If you can be up at his office in the compound at ten o'clock tomorrow morning," she said, "he'll be able to talk to you. It's the square wooden building."

By nine forty-five next morning I was waiting outside the office. Some things are enough to provoke anyone to punctuality.

It was very quiet and peaceful, there in the big, neat, still sterile-looking clearing. I leaned against the car. This time I felt no nervousness. After all, I had done my homework. And the omens looked good. There had been the relaxed hour with Mrs. T-B. And the "*ndugu*" business with the police askari at Narok. And back in Nairobi a white hunter had said, "Not everyone finds T-B easy to talk to, but I think you'll get along with him all right. Yes, I think you'll get along." So all I had to do, really, was to remember the words on the sheet of yellow paper in my shirt pocket.

A few minutes after ten a man in drill slacks and jacket appeared on the far side of the clearing and walked slowly toward me. I felt a moment's mild shock—and the edge of a new anxiety. Several people had mentioned that T-B was tall, but this man was a mammoth: six feet five or six, broad-shouldered, broad-beamed, with hands like catcher's mitts. When he came close I saw that even his features were monumental. And his face was all folds and creases, like a bloodhound's. There was something bloodhound, too, about the weariness that invested him, as if half the woes of the world had settled on his massive shoulders. The years had weathered T-B, I decided; had even begun to erode some of his prodigious strength. But he was still a rock of a man.

"Good morning," I said.

T-B looked me over. "Morning."

There was a brief silence. I tried to tell myself that it was absurd to feel nervous. "Thank you," I said, "for sparing the time to talk to me." Before I had half the sentence out I knew I was trying too hard.

T-B looked over my head and gave a sort of sublaryngeal grunt. I think his shoulders moved, just a half shrug.

I tried again. "I don't think it need take too long."

But T-B was already halfway up his office steps. I followed.

Now in my more sententious moments I am fond of proclaiming myself so detribalized as to be "a terrestrial"; but on occasion I admit to being not only Welsh but also irreparably English. And I know I am still horribly capable, when I need to protect my feelings, of erecting the traditional English barricade of frost. So it would seem reasonable that I should have no trouble, when other Englishmen do the same, in diagnosing and understanding and ignoring the chill, and so in penetrating their defenses. But it rarely seems to work out that way. As I followed T-B's huge bulk up the steps and into his office I was thinking, "Oh, Jesus! He's one of those men who still believes that God speaks English!"

T-B motioned me to a chair and sat down on the far side of a broad desk. He picked up some papers, put them down again, picked up a pencil. In his fingers it looked like a toothpick.

"Well, what can I do for you?" he said.

I took a deep breath. "As your wife will have told you," I heard my voice say, "I'm another bloody writer." But that came out wrong too. Sitting in my chair, obviously, was a second-rate actor who had learned his lines and nothing more.

T-B's pencil tapped the desk.

I stuck to my script. But I felt myself rushing it, so that everything sounded false. First I outlined my background: British birth and upbringing, Kenya interlude, a dozen years' American residence. "And now I'm a writer by trade and . . . well, I don't mean that I came back to Africa looking for a book to write. Not really. But what I want to do and what I want to write are always hopelessly mixed up. Anyway, I think I've found what I'm looking for at last, here in the Mara. And I smell a book."

T-B sat like a statue, staring to his left, out of a window and across the sunlit clearing. I found myself wondering if his graven features ever moved.

"The book'll be mostly about animals," I said. "But I've also got a kind of idea that what goes on out here may actually have more to do with the future of Africa than all the political nonsense in Nairobi."

Just for a moment, T-B was looking at me.

I began to tell him about the book. T-B was back with his window, but after a while I got used to it and began to shake clear of my script.

T-B stayed with the window. Occasionally his pencil toothpicked at the desk. Otherwise he sat like stone. Like a statue of an aging bloodhound. I had no way of knowing if he were really listening, and although I kept talking I found myself having to suppress continual little uprisings of anger.

"Of course, people will come into it as well," I said. "The local Masai, obviously. And you and Simeon Tipis too." I knew that Simeon Tipis, the Masai game warden at Keekorok, was a protégé of T-B's.

Next I tried to outline some directions the book might take. Before long, though, I began to bog down again. "But it isn't really the facts that matter, not at the beginning like this. They come later. Anyway, the whole thing'll probably turn out quite differently from the way I see it now. It usually does. There's got to be excitement, though. That's always what gets a book started. And this time, as I say, it hit me down at the lodge. It's still there, but the only way to find out if it'll last or if it's going to die on me is to give it a chance."

I took a deep breath. And all at once the yellow script was there again in my shirt pocket, hot. Trying to forget it, trying to remember it, I launched into my peroration. "So what I'm asking for is permission to wander around the Mara for three or four weeks, starting now. Then, if the excitement's still there and I can still smell a book, I'll come back for at least six months, sometime next year probably, and do the real research." I paused. "And I'm asking if I can do all this without the usual camping and entrance fees. Frankly, I just can't afford them right now. But I'll offer the local Masai five percent of all royalties I get from the book—not to mention some damned good free publicity for the Mara."

My voice died away. It was very quiet in the little office. The statue in the chair, still staring out of its window, had not moved for several minutes.

I waited. At one point I found myself wanting to stand up and say, "Oh hell, let's forget the whole thing." But I went on waiting. I knew I could not, at this point, allow myself the luxury of self-indulgence.

I was still waiting when the hum of a vehicle filtered into our silence. The sound swelled; homed on the office door; died.

"Damn," said T-B. He stood up and went outside. Soon his voice floated back, faint and muffled, through the half-open doorway.

I sat looking at the empty chair on the other side of the desk.

The white hunter in Nairobi had said, "You'll find you can never tell what T-B's thinking. Sometimes you wonder if he's thinking at all. Don't kid yourself, though. No flies on T-B." But it still wasn't easy to reconcile the man who had sat in the chair with the man everybody had told me about: the man who loved the animals above all things, the man who exercised immense influence over the Masai, the man who was almost single-handedly responsible for the Masai Mara Game Reserve, the man who could have been Chief Game Warden of Kenya many times over but who preferred to stay on, year after year, in his beloved Mara.

I heard the vehicle drive away. T-B came back inside. "A hunter," he said to his desk. "Had to talk business with him."

He stopped behind the empty chair and stood there, huge, staring at one of the many maps pinned to the office wall.

And all at once he began telling me how busy he was. There

were all these damned meetings in Nairobi for one thing. He had
to go to them. Otherwise there wasn't a hope in hell of government approval for the things he wanted to get done. Even here at
home he was always being interrupted by someone or other. It
left precious little time for the things he really wanted to do, for
all the things that still had to be done. And time was getting
short. In a couple of years he would have to retire. . . . His voice
went on and on.

At first I had to hold myself on a tight rein. Genuinely busy
people, I told myself, can never spare the time to explain how busy
they are. But as I listened, really listened at last, I began to understand—to grasp some of the responsibilities and frustrations that
were eroding this huge, tired, dedicated man. I felt myself beginning to relax.

Without warning, T-B sat down. He looked directly at me
across the table and said, very quietly, "If I were you I don't
think I'd offer the Masai a percentage of your royalties. I don't
mean that they don't want money, but they'd smell a rat. I'd just
be inclined to say that you can give the Mara some good publicity."

And from then on it was all freewheeling.

When I made another attempt at explaining why I could not
know at this stage just what I might write about, T-B heard me
out and then nodded, very slowly. "I think I understand," he
said. "Yes, I think I understand."

Once, when I mentioned my conversation with his wife, T-B
frowned. "Yes, but she shouldn't have been out there yesterday.
Hardly out of bed after a bad go of pneumonia." Then his heavy,
sculpted features rearranged themselves into a warm and engaging
smile. "But you just can't keep her indoors, not even when she's
sick."

Mostly, we talked about the animals.

He was pushing hard, he said, for a game lodge in the Triangle. It was the only way to stop the poachers. They were non-
Masai and they came from over the Tanzanian border. He managed to catch a few now and then with ranger patrols, but it was

a losing battle. You simply couldn't do the job without roads and a permanent base. So, little as he liked it in some ways, he was pushing for a lodge.

"The poaching's bad?"

T-B glared at me across the table. It was an industry, he said. A damned industry. Done purely for money, not food. Mostly they took zebra skins and wildebeest tails and rhino horn and other items that they could sell to the middlemen, who in turn sold them to exporters. "Murderous, I tell you. Bloody murderous. And now, by God, we've got the wheat."

The local Masai, it seemed, were turning to agriculture. That year they had put in six thousand acres of wheat. Next season they were going to plow fifteen thousand.

T-B's bloodhound features sagged even further. "Historically," he said, "wheat has always meant the end of the game. Look at Eldoret and Nakuru and the Kinangop. All magnificent game country at one time. And then the settlers came, after the first war, and today it's all fences and plowed fields and not an animal left alive."

I nodded, remembering the man with my name who used to manage a farm near Nakuru and who used to say, "You can't farm in a menagerie." I had always felt vaguely sad when I said it. But I had said it, often.

Now, I made an attempt to explain how it had been, but T-B did not really seem to hear.

"The only way we'll save the game," he went on, "is to show the local people that they can make money out of it. Most of us have come around to that now, I think." He had just managed, he said, to get the hunting fees increased. Most of the money went to Narok County Council, and it helped, even with ordinary hunters. "Then there's controlled cropping. Like that fellow I was talking to outside—he's got a license to shoot eight hundred zebra. Carefully selected animals, of course. To be honest, I'm not too happy about it, but he's almost finished now, and at least it may help to show the county council that game can pay better than wheat."

T-B leaned forward. His massive hands gripped the desk. I

saw his knuckles pale. "Frankly, this wheat scares me stiff," he said. "We've got to do *something* about the stuff. And quickly, too. Don't forget what I said—historically, it has always meant the end of the game."

The best way to fight the wheat, he felt almost sure, was game-viewing. Most of the entry and camping fees went to the county council, and a good slice of the lodge profits too. And every year more and more tourists were coming to the Mara. "But a good book about the place would do one hell of a lot of good. That's why I think you ought to make a big thing out of the publicity."

We discussed my next steps.

I did not, I said, expect to write a popular ecological study of the Mara, but I had to know the scientific facts and I had heard that some research was being done down in the Serengeti.

"Indeed there is," said T-B. "Some of it's darned good stuff too. You'd do well to go down there. Serengeti Research Institute. Man to see is Hugh Lamprey."

T-B leaned back in his chair. Later on, he said, I would probably have to put my case in person to the county council. For the time being, though, waiving the camping fees was all right—as far as he was concerned, anyway. But it was Simeon Tipis's baby, really, and I would have to talk to him, down at Keekorok. "You may find him a bit nervous to begin with. You may even think the poor fellow's only got one eye. But don't worry, it's just a part of his nervousness. Frankly, he's had a long struggle with himself. He's well on top now, though. Quite a man, in fact. Once you get talking to him I'm sure you'll find it's all right. . . . Oh, but I'd forgotten—he went to Nairobi yesterday. Won't be back till Monday at the earliest."

I felt my back straighten. "That gives me two days," I said. "If it's really okay about the camping fees, I think I'll go out to Mara Bridge, and maybe down into the Triangle. Somehow that place intrigues me."

T-B smiled. "I don't think you'll be disappointed. But I don't think you should go down there alone, not in that little Roho." It was pretty hard country on vehicles, he said, even on Land

Rovers, and if I ran into trouble I might sit there for a week and never see another soul. But it would be all right to go as far as Mara Bridge and that would give me a good idea of the country. "Look out for elephant, that's all. Our lion are very quiet, but I'm damned careful with the elephant. Charged twice by a cow the other day. It's the cows you've got to watch, especially when they've got calves. Keep your eyes open, all the time."

T-B stood up. "Later on," he said slowly, "you'll need a Masai to show you around. I think I can fix that up for you."

I thanked him.

He came to the door of the office with me. We shook hands in sudden, slanting sunlight.

"I'm sure I'll be seeing you again," said T-B. "But in the meantime I hope everything moves along all right." His massive features refolded into their unexpectedly warm smile. "You have my blessing, anyway."

Half a mile beyond the Ewaso Ngiro barrier I stopped for lunch. While I ate, private in a little clearing, the day's clouds began to gather into squadrons. I took to the road again, following them westward. And soon I came to the place at which I had turned off two nights before and driven across open grass to the camp where the young Masai had joined me for breakfast.

I had been waiting for that turnoff place, of course. Beyond it the road would be new: it would taper away ahead, unseen but luminous, all the way to Mara Bridge, riddled with possibilities, vaguely disquieting, utterly irresistible. It is infantile, I know, to feel this way about almost every road you travel for the first time. God help me if I ever grow too old for the game.

The afternoon revealed no hint of senility, and as I drove on westward there was more than the rose-tinted road to titillate me. More, even, than the Triangle. For I drove with the firm, warm, brainless conviction that I was striking out at last on "a survey of my domain."

At first the road offered meager encouragement. It undulated through monotonous, restrictive bush. I saw no animals. No distant prospect rose up to beckon me. And the sun shone no more than fitfully: the cloud squadrons had by now massed into flotillas.

Then the road dipped. The bush thinned and fell back. And then I was out in the open, free, and all around me was light and space and the grass stretching pale and rolling and endless. Across the grass raced cloud shadows, squadron after squadron, flotilla after flotilla. Far ahead, the clouds themselves had begun to gather in a dark and threatening fleet; and beneath this fleet— where the grass ended at last, you had to suppose—a pale blue line now humped and rolled and folded and refolded. And this line beckoned—for I knew without checking my map that it must be the lip of the Isuria Escarpment and that it therefore marked the far limit of the Triangle.

I drove on. A pair of Thomson's gazelles trotted lazily away from the roadside, then stopped to watch me with casual interest. Otherwise, I still saw no game. But now the grass was cropped short. Twice, off to the left, Masai manyattas squatted dark and secretive.

A dozen miles of rolling grassland. And then, still far ahead, a big, dark slab beside the road—square, eyesore, ominous. Clouds almost covering the sky now. And down on the plain, only beleaguered little patches of sunlight racing across gray grass.

I reached the square of plowed land. Its fence cut arrowlike across the open savanna—strict, rigid, alien, incompatible. It had occurred to me before, in beautiful and unspoiled country in America, that prehuman nature drew no straight lines. Not on a large scale, anyway. But here on the Mara Plains the discord struck even harsher. It was, after all, a very new note. The straight line did not invade this part of Africa until about seventy years ago. Even today, if you fly over its wilder regions and ignore the road ribbons that we newcomers are beginning to unroll, you still see only curve and coil and harmony. For the man-made trails all snake and wind, just as the trails of the other animals do, just as country footpaths still do in unwrecked corners of Devonshire and Vermont. Most African buildings are circular, too. Even the rectangular Masai houses are all curves and rounded edges—and the thornbrush fence that encloses a manyatta forms a rough circle. But the fence enclosing this square of plowed land cut across the plain like a sword slash across bare flesh.

I got out of the car. The wind blew cold now. A sign on the fence said, in neat professional signwriting: NAROPIL AND GORIGORI WHEAT FARMERS LTD, P.O. BOX 4, NAROK. In the lower right-hand corner was painted, like a signature, a small Masai shield. Beyond the sign, the bare earth stretched flat and gray beneath the gathering clouds.

I walked through a gap in the fence. The work had been well done. Fifteen years earlier, the young farm manager from up near Nakuru would have stood and looked with approval at the neatly turned furrows. But now I saw only the fragile soil and the gathering gloom and the past and the present and the future. I saw man, the day before yesterday, plowing thin Carthaginian soil and creating a North African desert. I saw him, yesterday, in America, scraping away at the topsoil of the fragile western prairies and then watching half of it blow to kingdom come. And I saw him today, with different aims and different tools but the same arrogance, preparing to crucify the fragile North Slope of Alaska and create a different but even more criminal desert.

I walked a few paces into the plowed field.

He was still at it too, everywhere—individually and corporately and nationally. He still imagined, because he had paid somebody a few of the paper baubles of some passing human civilization for the passing human title to a lasting patch of land, that he had acquired the right to slash and savage that land without thought for the living world as a whole. And more and more often now he did these things not in an effort to produce his own vital food but merely to accumulate more and more of the paper baubles. Modern man stood guiltier, too, because he understood that he was only one species among many. At least, he understood it intellectually.

After a while I turned my back on the dark furrows, walked slowly to the car and drove on westward.

I had barely cleared the far end of the plowed land when I saw, far ahead, a small herd of Thomson's gazelles grazing close to the road. Their bodies showed dark against the gray and somber grass. Off to their right, a thin band of sunlight was sweeping across the plain. I watched idly, wondering if the brightness would pass over the herd. I was still a quarter of a mile away when several of the gazelles raised their heads and looked in my direction; and then the whole herd had bounded across the road and was streaking over the open grass, directly away from me. By chance they ran toward the moving band of brightness. They moved inside it. For a long and beautiful moment they were racing in unison with the sunlight, held by it and protected by it and even transformed by it. Throughout that long and fateful moment they seemed to be racing in order to keep pace with the moving sunlight, in order to hold on to its bright promise of safety. But then the shadow that covered the wheatfield and most of the open plain was pressing in on the band of brightness, squeezing it toward extinction. The band narrowed; faded; vanished. And then the little herd of gazelles was left racing on its own across the doomed gray grass.

At a movie, I might have felt that the director had overdone his symbolism. But out on that intensely real and three-dimensional plain I saw, all too vividly, more than that one little band of gazelles racing in terror from a car that was still a quarter of a mile away. I saw, almost as clearly—just a few miles back, where no wheat grew, where no wheat had to be protected—a pair of gazelles trotting a few yards from the road and then standing to watch me pass with only casual interest. I saw, too, back a little further, whole herds of them near the lodge—deep in their sanctuary, where they had not been hunted for years—grazing confidently around our dazzle-painted minibuses. I also saw T-B gripping his desk, knuckles pale, and launching once more into his dirge: "Historically . . ." And then, back down fifteen fleeting years, I saw the young farm manager from Nakuru and heard him say, yet again, "But you can't farm in a menagerie!"

The racing gazelles vanished over a ridge. I drove on. The plowed land slipped away behind and at last I could no longer see it in my driving mirror.

Soon I turned right up a side road and drove eight or nine

miles to the Indian-owned store that the map called Ngulot.
There, I confirmed that I could buy gasoline and provisions. It was
useful knowledge: later on, when I camped in the Triangle, it
could save me an extra thirty miles back to Narok. But the detour taught me something else too. The country around Ngulot
was rough and broken bushland, and the people I saw were not
Masai but Kipsigis. And when I came back down onto the plain
again I understood that because I had been up the side road to
Ngulot and seen the country and the people with my own eyes I
had established—far more surely than any map could have established it—the northern boundary of "my domain."

By the time I turned westward again, toward Mara Bridge, it
was almost seven o'clock. Clouds covered the sky, pressing the
night forward.

Seven or eight miles down the road, a couple of buildings
showed faintly, off to the right. The map said "Lemek." A few
yards more, and a white sign announced the start of the photographic block that forms a de facto outer skin to the Masai Mara
Game Reserve.*

* With no more than a pinch of imagination—well, maybe two pinches—
you can visualize man's administrative arrangements for the other animals of
the Mara as being a small half-onion. The cut edge of the onion lies along
the Tanzanian border. Northward, skin on skin, radiate four distinct zones.

First, surrounding Keekorok Lodge, the Sanctuary.

Next, surrounding the Sanctuary, the balance of the seven hundred-
square-mile Masai Mara Game Reserve. Here the Masai live and their cattle
graze and a limited number of tourists may camp, at four dollars per head
per night. But no man may shoot another animal.

Next, beyond the reserve, "photographic block 61." All game areas of
Kenya were long ago divided into "hunting blocks" that anyone can reserve,
at a fee, for his pleasure. Most blocks still cater for those who find pleasure
in killing other animals. But times are changing. In certain blocks in various
parts of the country you are now permitted to shoot with nothing more
lethal than a camera. Block 61 is one of them. A game department order
could rescind its photographic status overnight, but for the time being it in
effect doubles the size of the game reserve.

Finally, beyond the photographic block, an ordinary hunting block. Here,
hunters may seek trophies or may even, under license, crop eight hundred
head of carefully selected zebras. But this outer zone is no more than a
patch of rough skin on the peeled half-onion of the Mara.

Almost at once, beyond a line of trees, I found exactly the kind of place I was looking for. I turned off left, across open grass. Three giraffes were browsing along the edge of the trees. In the last of the light I could just make out a ram impala grazing quietly and alone.

I camped west of the trees, out in the open.

I lifted my head. A film of moisture coated the inside of the car window. I rubbed a hole in it. The grass stretched pale and dead, almost gray. Above it, gray clouds drifted slowly westward. Two or three miles away, their keels scraped a line of low hills.

I lay back again on my air mattress, conscience at rest. I dozed. But before long—ten minutes later, perhaps, or an hour—I gave up trying to deny that the hole in the window had begun to grow uncomfortably bright. I sat up and opened the car door. And at once the achiever in me was angry at my criminal laziness.

Only scattered clouds remained, scudding after the broken fleet. Eastward, nothing but flotsam fragments cruised the shining blue sky. And all around me the grass was glowing its morning gold. Scents and birdsong interwove.

I got out of the car and put water on the stove.*

Ten yards from my table, a column of bare earth thrust up six feet above the grass, its red-brown surface sculptured by the sunlight with black caves and canyons. The column was stark and strong and living. A few yards beyond it a sad little grass mound, a mere swelling on the surface of the plain, marked the place that an earlier anthill had reached the final stage of its crumble back to unstructured dust.

---

* When my literary agent, Carl Brandt, read the first draft of these pages he reminded me with a glint in his voice that I did not belong to a tea lobby. "This tea-brewing business could develop into an annoying stylistic quirk," he said. And he's probably right. The trouble is that no day in my life begins to revolve—or, later on, to sustain its revolutions—without adequate infusions of tea. So if I am to describe with accuracy just what went on in the Mara, particularly in early morning, it will often become necessary to brew and pour a verbalized cup or two. So I face, you must admit, a grave dilemma.

Apart from the anthill, the place was empty.

I shambled a few paces from the table, began to irrigate a random patch of Africa, and found myself standing beside a whistling thorn, or gall acacia—the common savanna tree that the Masai like best for building the thornbrush fences around their manyattas, the fences that protect their homes and cattle from lions and hyenas and other dangers. The tree I was standing beside seemed even more thickly studded than most with the round black galls that swell up on their branches like burned chestnuts. With my free hand I reached out and flicked one of the long gray thorns and then watched like a smug puppet master as out of the holes that perforated the shell of each nearby gall—the holes that make the tree whistle in any kind of a wind—there poured an army of small black ants. They were very angry animals and their tails kept flicking up like scorpions' tails as they rushed furiously over galls and branches and thorns, clearly intent on protecting their homes from whatever unknown danger now threatened. But within a minute or two their alarm subsided and they went back indoors to whatever was their normal business. I finished mine and walked back to the breakfast table, almost awake.

I drank the day's first and most catalytic cup of tea. A bush slid into sharper focus. On its summit sat a small bird, immobile in white shirt and black tuxedo, his dignity marred only by the flag of shirt protruding between jacket and long black tail, his character betrayed only by the rapacious hooked beak, black against golden grass, and by his red and roving eye. When I had cracked an egg beside the bacon in the frying pan I consulted my bird book and confirmed "long-tailed fiscal shrike." Applying labels was something new for me and I still felt with some surprise the satisfying pleasure of matching bird and book.

I began to eat, and there was time to look around.

The place turned out to be less empty than it had seemed. Most of its inhabitants, I found, were intent on breakfast, each in our own niche. The shrike swooped from his bush, annexed something in midair, landed in the grass, consumed his morsel, then flickered back to his vantage point. Half a mile away, two giraffes browsed beneath tall, umbrella-shaped thorn trees. A pair of small brown birds, name unknown, scurried past my table, absorbed in their hunt for something else I could not name.

I finished my bacon and eggs and picked up the binoculars.

Into my field of view swung the heads of two ram impala. They stood close together, three hundred yards downwind, alert and suspicious, lyre-shaped horns held high. When I first saw them, half concealed behind tall grass, they were peering directly at me. But soon they began to watch something off to my right. I swung the binoculars around. Two hundred yards away, back toward Lemek, a ewe impala came running around a patch of scrub. Almost at once she stopped, solid. Her long, delicate, hornless head pointed directly at me. Another female joined her. They stood side by side, stock-still, slender brown bodies warm in the sunlight. Their bodies, like those of most antelopes, were white on the undersides; but their brown flanks were dark above and pale below, and the dividing lines between these two sections looked so unnaturally sharp that it was as if a car painter had sprayed their coats on and used masking tape to keep the two tones apart. After a while the ewes relaxed. They began to chew the cud, and so lost the fine edge of their beauty—though the loss was far less severe than when a pretty girl begins to chew gum. Five minutes passed. Ten. From time to time the animals' heads moved slightly as they looked first at me, then at the distant males. Once, one of them lifted a delicate foreleg and shook it with an undeniably feminine air. Otherwise they stood motionless.

At last one of the rams began to trot forward. He was bigger and more muscled than the ewes and his superbly curved horns with their deep-cut, spiraling rings gave him an altogether different presence. He was totally masculine, almost regal, assuredly not to be denied his fancy.

He advanced across the open plain, moving closer and closer to my breakfast table but keeping his eyes fixed on the ewes. At the closest he would come to me—less than fifty yards—he stopped. His head turned toward me. Through binoculars I could see the fire in his dark, moist, smoldering eyes; and just for a moment I felt the excitement he felt—the hot, compelling drive that was thrusting him across the open plain, the wild, animal excitement surging through the loins and then outward through the whole body. Then his head turned away and he was moving forward again. He moved faster now, more urgently. As he closed on the ewes he thrust his head forward in an exaggerated smelling attitude and his tongue came out and licked his moist black nose—just the way I had seen bulls smell and lick, back on the farm, when they approached cows in heat. The ram broke into a canter and began to give a low, almost bull-like call. The call's tempo rose, step by step, to a medley of hard, excited grunts. Then there were only a few yards left and the ram was bounding through the air.

He reached the ewes. They stood fast, just looking at him. The ram paused, uncertain. The ewes, still side by side, moved a few paces backward. There was a deliberate and delightful insincerity about the movement that I find myself unable to describe without using the word "coy." The ram moved forward, took a few circling steps, and made a half-hearted attempt to mount one of the ewes. She moved away. The ram lowered his head and began to graze, or at least to pretend to graze. Minutes passed. I waited. But the ram went on grazing, apparently content, as if the only thing on his mind all morning had been breakfast. After a while the ewes began to graze too. I lowered my binoculars.

A piece of paper blew off the table. Automatically, I jumped forward and grabbed it. Out of the corner of one eye I saw the shrike slant off in alarm from his bush. And when I looked up, paper in hand, the three impala were bounding away behind a patch of scrub. And then the place was empty again. Empty, that is, except for the anthill and the thorn trees and the wide, golden grass.

I sat down, cursing my carelessness. When you move among wild animals you can get away with almost anything provided you do it slowly enough (a rule that also applies to domesticated species, of course—witness politics and seduction), and I have for many years been aware that if you break the rule regularly among

wild animals you will spend a lot of time watching birds slant
off in alarm from bushtops and mammals bounding out of sight
behind patches of scrub. But after a term in the man-driven world
it always takes time to slow down your tempo, and I had clearly
not yet slowed mine down, here among the wildlife of my new
"domain."

I began to wash up the breakfast things.

It was disconcerting to look back and remember that the
young farm manager from Nakuru had not been aware of the
gulf between the man-driven world and the animal world. Not
really aware. Not so that he understood it all the time, un-
shadowed, up there and available in the forefront of his mind. He
had thought, rather, in terms of "a menagerie." When his crops
were green and tender he would have an African patrolling with
a shotgun to protect them, and every now and again this guard
would bring in an antelope of some kind and the farm labor would
flock around for the meat. The manager did not even know the
names of the different antelope, except once when it was a new-
born dikdik, found trembling in the grass after its mother had
been shot. He had christened the frail, wobble-nosed little creature Tom Tom. ("No ordinary Tom Tom, Dik Dik or Harry
Harry.") But within three days it was dead. "Yes," somebody at
the club had said. "It's a pity you can never rear young dikdik.
They always die on you." That had been all right though, really.
After all, the manager had done nothing wrong, not personally.
But there were also the baboons. They had lived on the cliff, up
behind the house, and occasionally they came down and raided
the maize field at its foot. Once, the manager went out into the
little meadow below the maize field—the sloping meadow with
the big granite boulders strewn around it—and took the guard's
gun and shot at the baboons as they escaped up the rocks at the
foot of the cliff. And later one of the African milkers came and
reported gleefully that he had found blood on the rocks, and the
manager had felt, even then, as if he had committed a crime.
There had been other things too, not all of them to do with wild
animals. There were bound to be such things, I told myself, if you

looked back over enough years. Anyway, that life on the farm near Nakuru was fifteen years dead now. Dead and gone.

I finished washing up the breakfast things and sat down, content merely to be there, out on the open, empty plain.

Fifteen years. But the trouble was, the things you did never died. And now, looking back at the young manager, there was the quick, easy, routine temptation to label him "bad," the way you find yourself, unless you are very careful, labeling as "bad" everyone whose values run contrary to your own. And yet, although I could not honestly say that I any longer knew the young farm manager with my name, I knew that this was not how he had been. He had been a decent enough fellow, by his own lights. It was ridiculous to call him "bad." He had done no evil deeds. At least, I hoped not. But you could never be sure, because as a rule it is not evil men who do evil deeds. It is simply unaware men.

That got nobody off the hook, though: we are all of us at any given moment, to some degree or other, pitifully unaware. It can happen even if you manage to avoid the holier-than-thou trap and the true-believer trap, both of which certainly get you right back in there, strong, among the evil deeds. You can be momentarily unaware, for instance, in something simple and harmless, in something you are perfectly aware of, really—in something like forgetting not to move quickly when a piece of paper blows off your table as you are watching a trio of impala. . . .

I glanced up. There was a whole herd of them now—a ram and perhaps thirty ewes, out in the open, close to the same patch of scrub. Most of the herd were grazing. All were ignoring me. I grabbed my binoculars, which I had hung on the back of the chair while I washed up the breakfast things. And once again I moved too quickly. Out of the corner of my eye I saw the shrike, whose return I had also missed, slant away once more from his perch. And over by the patch of scrub the impala herd rippled. It was not that they had been really alarmed. Not this time. Not quite. But they were no longer at ease. They began to retreat. Soon, the last of them had vanished behind the scrub.

For perhaps a minute I swung the binoculars in vain. Then I found, to the left of the scrub, above a palisade of long grass, a

line of neat brown heads: white-flecked muzzles, delicately mobile; big, outspread ears, white inside, with small black imprints;
and a single pair of curving, authoritative horns.

For a moment the whole herd stood behind their palisade, uncertain. Then a ewe broke from the left of the line and began to
race across a gap between the long grass and a wedge of dark
bush. I swung my glasses, following her. All the way across the
wide, unshielded gap, she bounded and swerved as if striving to
throw off a pursuer. And yet, for all this evasive action, her whole
going was a single, glorious, liquid, flowing motion. She reached
the wedge of bush. And in the moment she was about to disap-
pear, she leaped. She leaped, I suppose, for the mundane purpose
of clearing some obstacle. But in her leaping she built an archway.
It was an archway of flowing brown motion that seemed to go
on and on, curving up and up and then pausing, suspended, and
then curving down and down, very slowly, as if reluctant to
come to an end. The impala landed; and in the same instant she
vanished. But I found myself still staring at the dark and empty
bush, binoculars gripped tight, as if the warm brown archway that
she had built still curved up and over.

Something made me swing the binoculars back to the gap. The
whole herd was surging across, each animal bounding and swerving with the same wonderful liquid motion, yet each blending
and merging with its neighbors so that the herd became a single,
swirling mass of warm brown bodies flowing through and over
the grass. I waited. The lead animal reached the wedge of bush.
And then, as I had hardly dared hope, the archway was there
again, even surer than before, built by animal after animal after
animal leaping with the same casual but catapulted grace. I held
my breath. The archway went on and on. Sometimes, three or
four brown bodies were curving through the air at once. And
then it was all over and there was nothing to see except the dark
and earthbound bush.

I lowered my binoculars. Once again, all around me, the place
was empty. Empty, that is, except for the anthill and the whistling
thorns and the shrike back on his bush and the distant giraffes still
browsing under their umbrellas. Empty, except for the sunlight

and the grass and the gentle breeze and a few scattered wisps of cloud still cruising slowly westward toward the Triangle.

That is the way it stayed for almost all the rest of that long, relaxed day.

I do not mean that it was like the archway: such movements do not come to you very often, anywhere, anytime. But almost all day there was the illusion of empty savanna, the same sense of a land unsoiled by man.

It is a shade surprising, I suppose, that the day turned out to be, until its very end, a relaxed and leisurely affair. After all, the Triangle lay just ahead, beckoning, and that should have been enough to maintain pressure. But this authentic lure was more than offset by my first chance to ramble through the new domain without an eye on any strict, distracting target. And so I felt free to dawdle, hour after hour, relishing every peaceful minute of it —until almost the very end.

After the impala had built their archway and then removed it I began to break camp. For a while there was only sunlight and silence and birdsong. But soon a faint lowing drifted down on the wind. It came from the direction of Lemek, from beyond the line of umbrella trees where the giraffes were browsing. The lowing grew louder. The giraffes slow-motioned away to the left, vanished. A bell began to tinkle accompaniment to the lowing. And finally, just about the time the first of the densely packed, dust-shrouded mass began to pour out of a gap in the trees, I heard the herdsman communicating with his cattle. He delivered his message in whistles and words, in chants and incantation, all strung together in an unbroken flow. It was a high-pitched sound, eerie, almost ritualistic.

The herd continued to pour out of the gap in the trees. There must have been a hundred head—some black, some brown, some white, some brindled. The dust that they raised enveloped them in a dense, barely translucent cloud.

The herdsman appeared at last, red-brown in his flowing shuka, almost a part of the swirling, red-brown dust cloud. When he came out of the trees he was already looking toward me. I signaled a greeting with wrist and forearm. He moved his spear, just a few inches. Then he was following his herd westward into another line of trees. Soon, only the dying, red-brown dust cloud showed where they had passed. Then the dust had vanished too and once more I was left alone with the grass and the sunlight and the silence and the birdsong.

I am no longer sure what time it was when I started the car at last. But I know that it did not matter. My map showed that it was little more than twenty miles now to Mara Bridge, and when I swung back across the grass onto the red-brown road and turned westward once more, toward the beckoning blue line that was the Isuria Escarpment, I drove slowly. The sun was already warm and I drove stripped to the waist, windows wide.

I drove through empty, sunlit paddocks.

Now I am obviously not talking about man-made paddocks. But in typical Mara savanna you often feel as if you are driving through well-kept ranchland. The landscape is not always so candid: at times trees and bush may crowd in on you, thick as thieves in a prison. But much more often grassland stretches wide and clean and uncluttered. Yet your eye can rarely look far across open grass before it meets a dark, obstructing wedge of vegetation. The obstacle may be just an isolated patch of bush (sometimes called "lion bush," because that is where the Mara's lions like to lie up during daylight); but more often your line of sight has been blocked by trees and bushes that line a *donga*, or dry watercourse. In much of the Mara, these dongas divide the savanna into large, irregular, natural pastures. The dongas rarely form very serious barriers to animals not equipped with vehicles, and they tend to peter out; but your eye, failing to detect the gaps, sees them as hedges, and as you drive through the rolling countryside you seem to be passing through a succession of large, well-kept paddocks.

That morning the paddocks that lined the road to Mara Bridge looked empty. But I knew now that "empty" savanna can be a busy place; and when, a few minutes down the road, my eye caught a flick of distant movement off to the left, I stopped. The movement came from the far end of a natural avenue that cut directly away from me between parallel dongas for almost a mile. I lifted my binoculars. There was definitely something there, down in scattered bush at the end of the avenue. Something pale brown. Many things pale brown. And then, just for a moment, one animal of the half-concealed herd moved into an open space and I saw the distinctive rectangular outline of its body and a hint of big, backward-sloping horns.

I thrust down the binoculars, swung off the road, and drove as fast as I dared down the open, grassy avenue.

Everybody, I suppose, has his favorite wild animal—one that makes his heart beat faster than logic would seem to demand. Almost always, I think, his heart is responding to old echoes.

One day when I was the young farm manager from Nakuru taking a fishing holiday at the base of Mount Kenya, I was driving down after dark from the upper reaches of a river when I swung around a corner and saw, no more than two or three car lengths ahead, impaled on my headlight beams, half a dozen antelope, big as oxen, peering at me over low roadside bush. I braked to a stop. The antelope held their ground. I switched off the motor. And then—for a silent, mesmeric interval that may have lasted ten minutes or twenty minutes or even thirty but was not really something to be measured in such cloddish units as minutes—for this suspended interval we stood and sat there, those antelope and I, twenty feet apart, surveying each other, with the night drawn black around our floodlit confrontation. My headlights picked out every detail: narrow, sensitive brown faces; moist, twitching noses; big, soft eyes; and heavy, spiraling horns that swept back and up, straight and strong. Through all our private, floodlit interval, nothing happened. We just stood and sat, looking at each other. Occasionally an antelope moved a yard to one side, trying to peer past the headlights. But that was all. I sat very still. But at last the antelope turned, one by one, and slid away into the night and I drove on down into the mundane world.

That was my only meeting with eland while I lived in Africa. But its echoes carried safely down the years: since coming back to Kenya I had seen several eland herds, and each time my heart had begun to beat faster than logic demanded. I had never managed to get very close, but at least I had learned how the pendulous dewlap gives a distinctive rectangular outline to these, the largest of all African antelopes.

We had better pause, I think, for a look at this word "antelopes." It is no longer a strictly scientific classification; but many zoologists still find it a convenient term for all ruminants, or cud-chewers, that have hollow horns and are "deerlike" (excluding, that is, oxen, sheep, goats, and goat antelopes). The American "pronghorn antelope" is a distant relative: it sheds its horns annually, whereas true antelopes never shed theirs—and in case of breakage cannot grow new ones.

In Africa, antelope are often called "buck" (exceptions: wildebeest, and perhaps one or two of the largest species). The word is not, as in America, reserved for males. Generally speaking, the males of large species are called "bulls," those of smaller species, "rams."

Africa has about seventy species of antelopes. The Masai Mara Game Reserve, according to one reliable authority, has nineteen. In rough order of size, they are: eland, roan antelope, defassa waterbuck, wildebeest (or white-bearded gnu), topi, knogoni (or Coke's hartebeest), impala, bushbuck, bohor reedbuck, Grant's and Thomson's gazelles, oribi, steinbok, klipspringer, bush duiker, red duiker, blue duiker, Kirk's dikdik, and suni. The size bracket is broad. A big bull eland may stand six feet at its humped shoulder, measure eleven feet from nose to root of tail, and weigh close to a ton. Suni, like dikdik, are mere "hares on stilts": both species stand about thirteen inches at the shoulder and probably average around seven pounds.

And antelopes' diversity does not end with size.

Some species graze, some browse, some do both. (Grazers eat grass; browsers eat herbs, shrubs, trees.) Wildebeest, kongoni and topi are normally classified as grazers, bushbuck as browsers, and impala as the classic example of browser-grazers. But diet seems to be one of those cheerful fields in which classification is honored less by the animals than by their classifiers.

Some antelopes need water every day. You never find waterbuck very far from a river or lake. (The extreme in water-loving antelopes is the rare sitatunga: it lives in swamps, has splayed-out hooves for bog-traction, and when alarmed often submerges, leaving only its nostrils exposed.) But Grant's gazelle and klipspringer (and many dry-country species such as gerenuk and oryx, which are not found in the Mara) seem able to subsist indefinitely on the traces of moisture they find in their solid food.

That morning I drove westward from Lemek toward Mara Bridge, I had yet to learn that each antelope species also seems to operate under a different, idiosyncratic set of social rules.

Halfway down the grassy, mile-long avenue at whose foot I had seen the eland, I stopped and checked through binoculars. Once more I glimpsed straight, powerful horns slanting back above humped shoulders and dewlaps swinging brown beneath delicate, restless heads. But it is one of eland's attractions that in daylight they tend to be timid, and by the time I came close to the bush that blocked the foot of the avenue the herd had melted away. Even before I knew for sure that they were gone, I had seen, beyond a gap in the donga that formed the avenue's left-hand boundary, a mixed convocation of animals; and when I found that the bush ahead was too thick for me to follow the eland, I swung the car left and drove through the gap.

Beyond the donga, something was different.

The Law of Inverse Appreciation, which I have promulgated elsewhere, states: "The less there is between you and the environment, the more you appreciate that environment." The law applies to both what you travel in and what you travel over. And that morning, just beyond the donga, I formulated a corollary: "The further you go from any impediment to appreciation, the better it is." It had been better the moment I turned off the dirt road and began to drive down the grassy avenue. And when I turned left and crossed the donga—thereby cutting off the road in some additional way—I became aware of a new edge to my senses.

Now this may well sound like nonsense. It would seem reasonable to assume that once you have turned off a road's man-smoothed artificiality and surrounded yourself with the grass and the trees and the dark, obstructing bush, all free and strong in their rich abandon, then the thing is done, closed, unimprovable. But it does not seem to work out that way. As the man-made road sinks away out of existence, so the savanna grows richer. Which is another way of saying that your senses, titillated, grow keener.

I do not think I am really trying to imply that by the time I crossed the donga I was a mite scared. For that would be ridiculous. When you turn off one of the Mara's little dirt roads I suppose you do increase real dangers a notch or two: long grass may conceal a wheel-clasping ant bear hole or even a resting but uncertain-tempered buffalo; you no longer have the road as a fast, untrammeled escape route; and you have just about waived what chance there was of being bailed out of trouble by a passing motorist. But I doubt that I am talking about any of these things. In part anyway, the vague sense of unease that had mounted as I drove deeper and deeper into the donga-lined avenue could probably be chalked up to inexperience: I had not yet grown used to the Mara—or to Rohosinante. Later on, come to think of it, it made almost no difference to me whether I was on or off a road. Almost no difference. Note that I have hedged. Perhaps there was always, right to the end of my time in the Mara, a vague stirring somewhere way down in my gut if I drove more than about half a mile from the last vestige of man-signature that could reasonably be called a road. And the further I went, the greater the titillation. Anyway, that morning beyond Lemek, when I drove through the gap in the donga into a very large, long paddock, my appreciation of the place had definitely been honed to a fine, rewarding edge.

There was nothing very exciting to see, really: just another of the Mara's routine convocations. Off to my right, less than a hundred yards away, stood half a dozen giraffes. Thin-necked and wizen-faced but lording it high above the other animals, they looked like elders forgathering on a rostrum—defensive, already anxious for their authority. To their left—front and center, as it

were, in the body of the auditorium—waited a herd of wildebeest. Gray and bearded, standing quiet and sober in a solid body,
they suggested safe support for the Establishment. But the zebras
hinted at trouble. Their dazzle-dress would have been enough
in itself, but they had also clumped into small, self-contained
groups. And their relaxed postures, with heads often lolled affectionately over each other's backs, boded ill for discipline. Beyond
them—in the public gallery, no doubt—was a wedge of slim,
youthful-looking Tommy (as Thomson's gazelles are popularly
called). They already showed signs of restlessness. In the rear,
though—out in the lobby—the Establishment had marshaled a
posse of topi, stalwart in purple and pewter uniforms. On the
fringe of the posse, one topi stood guard, forelegs up on an anthill, surveying the scene, very calm. Almost a quarter of a mile
beyond the topi, half hidden in a clump of trees—no doubt lurking there in readiness, waiting to see which way things would go
—an impala herd looked almost suspiciously casual and innocent.

I drove slowly forward until I was sixty or seventy yards
from the wildebeest. They began to show signs of restlessness. I
stopped, switched off. And all at once it was very quiet. I could
hear grass tap-tapping on the side of the car. The sun beat in
through the driver's window, warm and pleasing on my bare
shoulders. I took off moccasins, shorts, undershorts. Even in a car,
it helps to live as naked as the animals you are watching. With the
clothes you seem to cast off some of your civilized veneer as well
as your inhibitions. As often as not, you can soon begin to tell
yourself that the Adam-like simplicity is allowing you to feel the
way the other animals feel.

Before long, sure enough, I saw that it was blind and arrogant
to picture a peaceful animal convocation in terms of a modern
human confrontation. The giraffes were not in the least like men
past their prime, fumbling for the familiar reins of power. Not
really. And the zebras and Tommy were not like fractious members of an unspanked generation, asking all the right questions and
coming up with all the wrong answers and then seeing just how
far they could go while they had a ball under the comforting ban-
ner of a good cause. They were not like that at all. Given the urge

for simile, I decided, it would be better to think of the Tommy as minnows. For their restlessness had suddenly boiled over. Individuals fidgeted, pivoted, skipped, frolicked. And each time an animal changed direction its texture changed too. Face or butt or bulging belly would flash white in the sunlight; then back or flank or neck or haunches glowed warm and brown; then tail or lateral stripe sheened rich and black; and then a flank would slew into the softer blackness of unexpected shadow. For a minute, perhaps two minutes, the little herd was all flash and glitter, its beauty like the beauty of a shoal of minnows as they scatter in sunlit shallows. Then the restlessness had died away.

Off to the right, a zebra knelt down in a circular patch of soil laid bare by ants, then rolled over on its back. A cloud of fine dust squirted outward. The zebra wriggled happily, just the way I had seen its cousins the wild burros wriggle when they took dust baths in Grand Canyon. A red-billed oxpecker that had been perched on the zebra's back until it rolled over, and which had for a moment fluttered overhead, began to fly toward the giraffes. I swung my binoculars, following it. And then, halfway, I stopped. Out beyond the oxpecker, near the dark and curving line of trees that marked the far end of the paddock, almost two miles away, something was moving. Even before I saw the colors of the shapes inside the dust cloud, I knew they were not game animals.

Now it would seem reasonable that the sight of cattle being herded along in a tight, controlled mass, raising their red-brown dust cloud as they went, should have shattered the illusion of Eden that had built as I drove further and further from the man-made road. Yet no rupture even threatened. Perhaps I did feel a brief jab of regret; but the needle immediately withdrew. And afterward it was almost better than before.

I do not mean that distance protected me by hiding all human presence and consuming all sound. In fact, it was the unseen man and his unheard voice that made the moment. For once I had calculated time and distance and confirmed that there was no logistic barrier, it was almost as if I could see the man, red-brown shuka against red-brown dust, and hear once more his eerie, high-pitched ritual of whistle and chant and incantation. And in that sight and sound of a contented man communicating with his cattle I could detect no discord.

The cattle began to dissolve into the dark trees that sealed the far end of the paddock. Soon the trees had absorbed them and I was left with only the fading dust cloud; and then—very quickly this time, because of the distance—the dust had vanished too.

I went back to watching the wild animals. The sun climbed higher. It angled down through the windshield—hot now, almost fierce. I applied a bandanna as figleaf.

I sat on, a member of the convocation. And by degrees my mind began to mesh with its rhythms. I became conscious of the same ebb and flow among these animals as we had seen in the group we stopped to watch on our way back from the manyatta, that first afternoon at Keekorok. But after a while I decided that the words "ebb" and "flow" were too active, too busy. Animals were always moving, or almost always moving; but their movement was a gentle, haphazard kind of thing—a slow and subtle drifting, barely perceptible, that might reverse itself without any reason I could detect and that would do so with such languor and sleight of hoof that the change had taken place and the slow drift back begun, sure and steady, before I woke up to the fact that anything at all had happened.

Within this slow flux, events occurred, of course. A zebra foal lay down, spread-eagled on its side. Several adults rested on their bellies, upright, legs tucked under, the way ordinary domestic horses will rest. The pairs with heads lolled across each other's backs would from time to time groom each other—nibbling mouth to black stripe, white stripe. Once a pair of adults drew back their lips at each other, then rose on rear legs and briefly shadowboxed. I could not decide if it was quarrel or play. Once there was even a mild disturbance among the staid wildebeest. The giraffes lost an early curiosity about the car and began to browse on a clump of small thorn trees. Up and down their necks, oxpeckers quested for ticks. The topi guard relinquished his anthill; another replaced him. The impala herd faded back into the trees, reemerged.

Outside these low-key, widely spaced events, nothing happened. Nothing dramatic, I mean. But by now I was beginning to realize that, contrary to our common expectations, this is how the savanna works, almost all the time.

The canker behind our aberrant expectations is the camera. Nowadays we are bombarded almost from birth with photographs of wildlife, and especially of African wildlife. The stills are bad enough. They give you, safe and soft in your armchair, a far closer look at the wonderful detail of a leopard's paw or an elephant's eye than you are likely to get in person, even through binoculars. Movies are worse—or better. They can capture for you, superbly, the beautiocomic canter of a giraffe, liquid yet ludicrous, and the way its sloping back makes you wonder, when it puts on the brakes, whether it will slide ignominiously down onto its butt. Good movies can even capture an impala archway or the poetry of a cheetah's breathtaking burst of speed as it closes on its chosen prey. Of course, movies are not a substitute for reality. Not even for isolated vignettes of reality: unless mud clogs your arteries you will still be astonished, somehow, at your first sight of a dusty, leatherbound elephant picking its five-ton, delicately elephantine way through tangled bush. But photographs inoculate you. They reduce the varieties of experience left for the real thing, even for real, isolated vignettes. Worst of all, they tend to transmit only the bizarre, the stunningly beautiful and the dramatic. And that, most of the time, is not how the savanna really is.

There is another thing too, less obvious but just as damaging: photographs isolate. Even the best animal movies cannot encompass the whole. They cannot really capture such subtleties as the kind of slow flux I watched that morning near Lemek. And so they tend to leave you looking at rhinos and elephants as no more than curiosities that move without meaning across a beautiful but meaningless landscape. Perhaps that is why some people grow bored with game-viewing safaris, even on the rich East African savanna. Unless you are total poet, you cannot watch isolated vignettes forever. To keep interested, your mind must keep moving on, must begin to grasp meanings. And that morning as I sat naked in the sunshine watching the slow flux of the animal convocation and the small events that made up the lives of its members, as I began to grasp the way each individual went about its business—alone or interacting, yet always in harmony with its neighbors—as I began to sense more surely the slow rhythms that throbbed almost imperceptibly through this open, sunlit life of the savanna, so I began to understand how much there was for me to learn.

The savanna had its dramas: lions killed, buffalo stampeded, elephants charged. Such events were necessary, perhaps even important. But as I sat watching the convocation I saw that the essence of savanna life lay in the quiet, harmonious scenes—and that the components and wiring of such scenes were what I must strive to understand if I was to catch even a glimmer of how it felt to be a zebra or a topi or a Tommy on the Mara. It would be quite a task. In my preliminary three- or four-week reconnaissance I could hardly expect to do more than stake it out. Even in the six months when I came back—assuming I came back—there would be one hell of a lot to learn.

But for a start I must never forget how stupid it was to look at animals in human terms, the way I had first looked at this convocation. You could do it for fun, of course; or to explain how things looked, so that people could picture a scene vividly. But you had to be careful. Most of the time, you could with advantage look at men as animals—which they are. But you could very rarely look at animals as men—which they are not—and make much sense of it.

I do not know just how long I sat watching the convocation, but at last I became aware that lunchtime was almost on me and that since leaving camp I had advanced barely three miles toward the Triangle. I drove back to the road and turned west again, toward the beckoning blue line of the Isuria Escarpment.

To my left, the checkered savanna fell away toward Tanzania. Wedges of dark bush thrust across the landscape. But mostly I crossed open grassland, paddocked by dongas and studded with isolated thorn trees and gardenia trees and candelabrum euphorbia.

Because they are big and tend to stand alone, gardenia trees and candelabrum euphorbia are, next to thorn trees, the Mara plants that most often catch your eye. The gardenia is a broad-leaved, oaklike tree, and the base of its ballooning foliage is often shaved off flat, six or eight feet above the ground, by the backs of animals that have exploited its shade in the heat of the day. The candelabrum euphorbia is a striking plant. A big one will grow forty feet high. For almost thirty feet it may rise as solid and woody and many-trunked as a defoliated elm. Then every branch explodes into clusters of succulent arms that reach dark green toward the sky, like a jumble of candelabra that have been stored for so long in the attic of a damp junk shop that every surface has been verdigrised, thick. The effect is stylized, sculptural—vaguely reminiscent of a sahuaro cactus. (Euphorbia, also succulents, are the African equivalent of cacti, which are not natives. But back near Narok I had seen whole banks of prickly pears growing thick along the roadside—for when we Westerners colonized East Africa we introduced various cactus species, and they also found the land to their liking and in places showed more vigor than local life forms. So they too, in colonizing, had disturbed existing balances. It is tempting to look on all such disturbances with regret, even horror; but—whether or not you happen to like colonists and cacti—that seems to be the one way the world gets stirred.)

The road climbed through trees to a gap in a line of low hills, sideslipped onto the floor of a natural amphitheater, three miles across, and debouched through the amphitheater's open end. I drove on, racing cloud shadows across the open plain. The day's first cloud galleons had floated by while I sat watching the convocation. The squadrons followed. Now whole flotillas were cruising westward to join the fleet already massing above the faint, blue Isuria Escarpment.

Just beyond the last road junction that the map showed before Mara Bridge (the other road cut south, past "Aitong Tsetse Survey and Control," to the Talek Gate entrance to the Sanctuary), I pulled into the shade of a big candelabrum euphorbia.

I took my time over lunch: it was barely fourteen miles to the bridge now.

During lunch, the faint blue line of the escarpment grew even fainter. At first I assumed that only the massing clouds obscured it; but then I saw, billowing up from near the foot of the escarpment, down where the Triangle must lie hidden, four or five columns of smoke. The columns rose slowly, fused into a gray screen, then merged with the gray cloud fleet. Soon the bases of the columns had fused too. Before long the whole western sky was a tarnished gray screen of smoke and cloud. By the time I drove on, the escarpment had vanished; yet all around me, except when a squadron passed overhead, the sun still shone.

For a mile the road surface turned black and its cracked and fissured surface bore the deep, erratic, dried-out tracks of a vehicle that had slipped and slithered along it after rain. It is fiendish stuff after rain, black cotton soil. A few drops, and your tires spin like roulette wheels. A shower, and they begin to plow. In a downpour they dig furrows so deep that you soon bog down on crankcase or axles. Failing that, your spinning tires centrifuge the viscid mud and pack it between wheels and chassis, tighter and tighter, until it glutinates you to a halt. Even wildebeest are said to avoid black cotton soil after rain because the mud balls up on their hooves. Although the stuff dries out like rock and I drove on westward without check, I knew that if it rained at all heavily while I was at Mara Bridge I could forget about coming back out for a day or two.

Soon, soil and road surface reverted to red-brown. Since the junction near Aitong, the road had narrowed until it was little more than a graded track, almost compatible with the rich savanna. Now the savanna seemed richer too. The grass grew taller, thicker. The landscape—its road aside—began to look as if Homo sapiens had not yet been thought of. And all at once, remembering "Aitong Tsetse Survey and Control," I understood. Somebody had told me of a continuing project to drive the tsetse fly westward and so extend the Masai's grazing land (most tsetse flies are lethal to cattle, though only a few kinds affect sheep, goats and men). Clearly, I had moved into "fly" territory. I drove on westward through the tall, waving grass, understanding as I had never understood before why the tsetse fly and the malarial mosquito have been called "the saviors of Africa." Often, they alone have held man's greed at bay.

For all its new richness, the savanna still looked "empty." I saw no big herds. From time to time, though, I passed "minor" animals.

A band of small gray vervet monkeys scuttered across the road. Another mile, and a black and white male ostrich angled away over open grass, running effortlessly yet faster than Rohosinante was running, with a gait that managed to be at once both comic and ballet-graceful. Off to the left, a wildebeest taking his siesta under a gardenia tree stood up to watch me pass. A kongoni scanned the horizon, forelegs planted on an anthill to give him a better view, just the way his cousin the topi had mounted guard in the convocation lobby. Soon, a pair of warthogs twinkle-legged across the road, tails erect. They vanished into the tall grass. Vanished, that is, except for their tufted tails, which continued to cut through the grass like submarine periscopes festooned with seaweed. Once, a hundred yards ahead, at a wooded donga, a posse of dark figures bounded across the road on all fours. When I reached the place, the troop had vanished. But in a gray-limbed roadside tree, gravely people-viewing, sat a single gray-limbed baboon—a study in natural camouflage, protohuman curiosity and blatant masculinity.

I drove on. Ahead, the curtain of smoke and cloud thickened.

Four or five miles short of Mara Bridge I stopped to photograph a group of giraffes. There were seven of them ambulating along in scattered single file, almost half a mile from the road, across flat, open grassland. Their lone prop was a stylized candelabrum euphorbia at left center stage. Near the euphorbia the group paused and stood looking me over. They were bunched close now, with their spindly legs and sloping bodies and serpentine necks—several of them craned around neighbors to get a clearer view—all silhouetted against the flat gray backdrop of smoke and cloud. The hornlike protuberances on top of each inane, compressed head stood out like a snail's eyestalks, and for some unpinnable reason put the finishing touches to the line of seven etched and eloquent question marks.

The giraffes moved on beyond the euphorbia. Soon they were strung out again, moving gravely at a deliberate, rocking walk, still silhouetted, all their necks raked forward in neat visual unison, stylized as euphorbia. The effect was Japanese seascape—and at the same time Jurassic swampscape. For that line of huge, slow-moving animals with their long, slender, supple necks had flicked up before my mind's eye a half-forgotten picture of brontosauruses lifting their necks in inquiring curves as they wallowed, a hundred and fifty million years ago, in some immense swamp that stretched flat and featureless beneath a gray and vapor-filled sky.

As I finished photographing the giraffes a Land Rover appeared on the road ahead. I put on a pair of shorts. The Land Rover pulled up alongside.

A weather-beaten man of about forty was driving. A woman sat beside him. Four children packed the rear compartment.

When we had exchanged travelers' greetings I asked if they had been down into the Triangle.

"Afraid we only had time to go a couple of miles beyond here," said the man. "Not much to see, anyway. Whole place is covered in smoke. And we ought to be in camp by dark, back near Ewaso Ngiro. We're working the country around there. Shooting zebra on license."

I asked if he had by any chance called in at T-B's office the day before. The man said he had.

"I was inside when you talked to him."

The man nodded. "Yes, I remember your car now. Standing outside." His name, he said, was Jock Dawson. He introduced his wife and children. When I mentioned a family of Dawsons I had known in Kenya in the old days, he said he was a distant relative. We dredged briefly for common ground. Then Dawson glanced at his watch. "Look, I'm afraid we've just got to get going," he said. "But why don't you drop in at our camp sometime? We've almost got our zebra quota now, but we'll be there a few days more. Till Friday, anyway." And he marked their campsite on my map.

Two more miles and the ground began to drop away. Fingers of bush reached out into the grassland. The bush thickened, took over. But soon there was an opening. I stopped. Through the opening I could look down a steep valley. The map had shown that this valley opened onto the northern end of the Triangle.

There was very little to see. The smoke blurred all distinctions. Even the Isuria Escarpment, which the map billed as steep and dramatic, was no more than a flat, dull, cardboard wall set somewhere far back in the flat, gray gloom. Beneath it I could make out only a suggestion of plain, a mere thickening of the gray pall. I might almost have been approaching Los Angeles on a bad day.

I drove on. The grade steepened. For half a mile I had no time to notice anything except the gullied bedrock and casual stones that were the road's surface. Then the gradient slackened, the road reverted to road, and I found myself looking over the line of greenery that hid the river. Beyond it the steep face of the escarpment—suddenly close and clear—was a blank of blackened grass and dark boulders. Scattered and beleaguered trees offered only token relief. The fire had also passed through gently sloping bush at the foot of the escarpment. But there, before updraft had fanned it into holocaust, it had spared many trees and bushes, and they stood green and confident. Between them, patches of pale, unburned grass softened the blackness.

The road curved right, flattened out, became bridge.

It was a concrete bridge, gray and meager. Its plain parapets were no more than eight inches high, presumably to offer minimal resistance to flash floods, and along them had been daubed a line of white paintmarks. But when I drove out onto the bridge the river was broader than I had expected, and stronger. It must have averaged forty or fifty feet across. Upstream, rapids gleamed white. Just above the bridge was a deep, swirling pool, and the whorls and waves and glides that eddied its surface kept bending the smoke-filtered sunlight into restless, wayward patterns. On both banks, clear down to the water, trees and bush pressed green and virgin.

I reached out and turned the ignition key. The motor died.

In through my open window floated the music of the river: the rapids' deep and constant bass, the lively treble of swirls and whorls and glides. A finger of breeze brought me a sweet, Daphne-like scent. My eyes began to search for its source. I could no longer see the scorched earth behind the bank of greenery that lined the river's left bank, but my mind remembered, and my eyes searched only to the right. I knew that there, behind the greenery, the grass still grew long and pale and whole.

Suddenly, at the fringe of my vision, out in mid-river, I glimpsed a small black incongruity. It was just a half glimpse, really, of a round, smooth something on the surface of the river. I faced around toward it. Nothing. Nothing but the dance, light and shade, of a swirling ripple.

I waited, hoping. The hope lost its buoyancy; began to settle; settled; began to sink. And then I saw, just for an instant, a few feet above the ripple—small and black and round and smooth and quite undeniable this time—a mammal's head.

Another wait. But this time no need for such hard hoping. And then it was there again, briefly, over to the right; and then once more, back out toward mid-river. The second time it made a long appearance, facing me, so that through binoculars I saw the mouth open and close. And even after the head had gone and once more there was only the shimmering river I could still see the way beads of water had formed moving strings along the fine, black whiskers.

A long wait then, and the beginning of a need for more hoping. But at last, so quickly that I missed the moment when only a head was showing, the whole animal out onto a little rock promontory, slim and lithe and black and gleaming and never still. And then, almost before it was definitely up on the promontory, off it again and back into the water and in the same motion, or absence of motion, out of the water still further up, beneath a curving canopy of grass, and working its way toward an overhanging bush. And in that same moment, while the wet little body was still quicksilvering along beneath the grass canopy, another head, out in the current. A bigger head. But then, almost at once, before I could be quite sure they were looking at each other, both gone.

I reached for my mammal paperback: "Clawless otter: Total length about 5 feet, of which the tail measures about 2 feet. Weight up to about 40 lb. as a rule." So they were far from full grown. The slim little body that had flickered over the rock promontory could not have been more than three feet long, tail and all. Even the one with the bigger head . . .

I looked up. The two of them were sitting on a flat stone, up under the overhanging bush. There was not much difference in size after all. They sat side by side, half awash, grooming each other with deft little paws. Even in that quiet domestic pose they were fluid, flashing, mercurial. For perhaps five seconds they sat cleaning each other. Five seconds, I already understood, was a considerable spell in their quicksilver world: I even had time to see, through binoculars, the expressions on their faces.

Then, without detectable warning, back into the river. Back through its shimmering surface in perfect, arching unison, still side by side, the two tails disappearing parallel, like a pair of sucked-under water skis. Almost at once, out again onto the stone, still as if bound together. No cleaning this time: without pause, another arched duet of a dive.

But now that I have time to think about it, I see that "dive" is far too static a word. The whole process of change from quiet domestic scene to total immersion had, like the river itself, been a single flowing entity. There were no discrete parts. It was as if a single idea had touched those two small heads and with the speed of light had sent the sleek, wet bodies arching over into the river like parallel currents. And the water had seemed to accept them as something less than solid, with hardly more commotion than you would expect to see when you stood watching a battery accept a booster charge.

After that second return to the river there was a long pause.

wo heads surfaced briefly, still side by side, out in mid-
ouths opened and closed. I stifled with difficulty the
t they were laughing. An even longer gap. Then, close
far bank, one head, alone. For an instant it seemed to
be looking back toward me. Then it had vanished.

I sat quiet. Seconds ticked by. Minutes. My body began to
signal for afternoon tea. But the book had said, "It is always a
matter of luck to catch a glimpse of an otter during the day." So
I went on waiting. But at last I drove slowly over to the far end
of the bridge and parked the car at the foot of the sloping road
on its far side and set up my wooden table and chair on the last
couple of feet of the flat concrete surface of the bridge. That
way, there was room for another car to pass and I could see all
of the river but none of the escarpment's blackened slope, nothing
of the gray pall that hung over the Triangle.

I must have sat there for a long time, taking my afternoon tea
at the end of the bridge, feeling mildly foolish in my wooden
colonial splendor but keeping very quiet and looking hopefully
out over the river. It definitely helped, facing the river. Its music
lilted on. The surface patterns changed and persisted. They
filigreed the flat, smoky sunlight. Part of the trouble, anyway,
had been that I had expected too much. It was always happening
when you looked forward to something too eagerly or for too
long: you built an expectancy barrier. Most often it was a movie
you had been told about, or a friend of a friend. But it could
happen with anything—and it could ruin everything. It had
definitely happened this time. Without quite knowing it I had
built a picture of the Triangle as an open, pristine place crowded
with huge herds of huge animals—a kind of wide-screen version
of the Keekorok savanna with a towering Beethoven score. After
the vision, reality had been something of a comedown, I had to
admit that; but the shock was already dying away. The otters
had helped. They had been Mozart rather than Beethoven, of
course; Brubeck rather than the Beatles. But I could still see the
expressions on their faces, still feel their sheer delight in everything they did. Yes, they had definitely helped. Without them I
would not be sitting quiet and content, already halfway at home

in this injured but forgiving place. Perhaps, come to think of it, the otters had been enough.*

The otters did not reappear, and when I had finished tea I stowed everything back into the car, drove a dozen yards up the road, and turned right along a rough track. T-B had said I would find campsites up the track, in beside the river. I found two. But one, inside the river forest, was oppressive and man-trampled; the other, out in the open, was a man-mown square of short, green grass surrounded by black, annihilated stubble. And even if the smoke had cleared by morning, neither campsite would have commanded more than a flat sliver of a view down over the Triangle. I drove back to the bridge. The map showed that after three miles the road angled up the escarpment. With luck I would find a camp high up, overlooking the Triangle.

The pall of smoke and cloud had already doused the sun, and as I drove the smoke thickened and the lowering clouds sagged another notch. Three raindrops patterned the windshield. For the first time, I noticed the thick dust that coated it. I leaned forward, peering ahead. The afternoon seemed, as if by the flick of a switch, to have become evening. I glanced at my watch: five forty-five. But the leaden light said six forty-five.

The road suffered a relapse. I negotiated a rocky crest, found myself confronted by a small stream, surveyed its boulders with horror, offered up thanks for the steel shield that protected Rohosinante's differential and crankcase, prayed to Something or Other, eased forward in low gear with clutch slipping, ground my teeth as steel grated over bare rock, felt relief and then pride swell up as those astonishing little front wheels pulled us up the far bank onto something once more recognizable as road, let out my breath, and changed into second gear.

The road angled gently up a slope. Black stubble pressed in on either side. It deepened the gloom.

---

* I am aware that certain lean-faced gentry will cluck superior zoological clucks over the way I attribute to the otters a "sheer delight in everything they did." But such people enjoy the support of by no means all their fellows. Not long ago a young biologist wrote me: "Many animals have a great time of it—dolphins, otters and wolves, for example—and this has long been ignored or denied by professionals."

Then, droppings on the road: solid, unmistakable dollops, like miniature brown igloos. Above them, cutting obliquely down from the escarpment, a trail two feet wide and six inches deep. And beside the trail, two small trees with wounds showing white where branches had been wrenched off. I stopped. The wounds looked very fresh: I could almost see gray trunks stuffing the branches into big, recessed mouths. Below the road, the trail plunged on down into the gloom. I had a clear view out over the plain now, but there was still nothing to see except a thickening of the grayness.

When I drove on, a voice began to speak from somewhere down among the road noises. "It's the cows you've got to watch," said the voice. "Especially when they've got calves. Keep your eyes open, all the time."

I accelerated.

"Charged twice by a cow the other day," added T-B.

At a corner, a track swung off to the left; but it was not where the map said the track into the Triangle should begin. I drove on. The grade steepened. To the left, I could at last make out the broad patterns of the Triangle. Just as the map had promised, the line of greenery that was the river angled away from the escarpment and snaked down toward Tanzania, segregating the Triangle from the rest of the Mara. But across the pale meadows of the Triangle spread fingers and hands and arms and even torsos of dark vegetation. The gloom snuffed out all detail, but the wedges wrote something unexpected.

I could see the fires now—some of them close under the escarpment, others far off, down near the Tanzanian border. None looked very big, and even through binoculars I could see no flames. But from each fire rose a column of smoke, sickening the air.

Soon, the top of the escarpment. Still no campsite. And the light fading fast. Against its evidence, my watch insisted six-ten. Two hundred yards into the suddenly flat country, I found a place to turn. I was back on the escarpment slope again before I registered that in some way I had not taken time to identify it had been a different world up there, and that I had established another boundary of "my domain."

Halfway down the escarpment, the road swung left around a spur. Down to the right, the spur flattened into an almost level terrace that in morning sunlight would command a panorama of the Triangle. And the roadside bank was conveniently low.

Crossing the bank, Rohosinante's breastplate rasped briefly on a hidden stone. Then we were over and plunging into long, pale grass. It was like fording a river and finding, unexpectedly, that the water came up over your navel. Feathery grassheads rippled toward me, higher than the hood. The invisible bumper thrust at their stalks and they wavered, fell back, then subsided, down and away. As I eased down the slope, the surface of the grass lapped at my right elbow. To the left it rose in a forbidding wave.

Thirty yards and we were on even keel again, safely at anchor on the terrace. In the morning there would indeed be a panorama of the Triangle, but now there was nothing to see except a flat, blank grayness.

When I had succeeded in pushing open the door against the pressure of the grass, I stood up, waist deep. Behind Rohosinante, the way we had come, a square-cut trench slanted up the slope. Its floor was almost as neatly thatched as if the grass had been cut and not merely bent flat. The floor, I decided, was the only truly solid looking thing about the trench: by not flowing in to fill the gap, the vertical walls seemed to defy the most basic laws of physics, and for a long, uneasy moment I understood the kind of distrust the Israelites must surely have felt as they walked across the rolled-back Red Sea at deliverance time.

Outside the trench, the sea of grass spread calm and even to the lip of the terrace. But even as I stood there beside the car it occurred to me that a lion could with no difficulty at all slink unnoticed to within bad-breath range. An elephant fortunately could not; but beyond the terrace the spur fell away so sharply that a whole herd of them could easily arrive on its windward lip, unannounced and barely twenty paces from the car.

I glanced out over the Triangle. It looked very dark down there now. Along the foot of the escarpment, where the smoke had been, flames flickered. They injected the fires with a new reality. I looked again at the thick, dry grass surrounding me

—and remembered the black stubble of the escarpment above Mara Bridge, where updraft had fanned a fire into holocaust. Here, for the moment, the air hung calm. But the Mara's prevailing east wind could send flames roaring up the escarpment's steep, dry slope. I peered down again. Some of the flames were directly below me. Already they seemed bigger and stronger, even closer. I glanced back at the pale grass that surrounded me. It no longer looked liquid. Here on the escarpment, obviously, the only safe place to camp was where the grass had already been burned.

And then, as I stood there in the gloom, undecided, it began to rain. I do not mean that a storm broke. But the gathered clouds at last gave themselves up, like overtaxed mourners at a funeral, to silent lamentation. And the big raindrops, falling cold on my bare shoulders, made up my mind for me. Wet grass might reduce the fire hazard, but it would also reduce Rohosinante's powers of traction. If it rained hard during the night we might not even make it back up the slope to the road.

I pulled on a shirt and sweater, got back into the car, started engine and windshield wipers. When the blades had wiped holes in the mud that had so recently been dust, I drove carefully forward, circling left, tight as I could, praying fervently against boulders and ant bear holes and all other perils of the deep. The circle seemed endless. But at last the grass drained away from in front of the hood and I was left fitting neatly and comforted inside the square-cut trench, facing back up the slope. Inside the trench there could be no new submerged perils. I gunned the engine.

As it turned out, the grass was the easy part. Only once did the wheels begin to slip, and even then it was no more than a hint of how things might have been in the morning. But as we broke clear of the trench and tilted up onto the roadside bank, we jammed to a halt. Twice I backed off and attacked from a new angle. The third time, the breastplate grated briefly on stone. For a moment we hung, poised. Then all four wheels were over, safe on the road.

I drove down the hill fast, trying to race the light, trying to ignore elephant-size shapes that kept looming up out of the dusk and then resolving into clumps of roadside bush. Soon I had to switch on the headlights. The rain slanted down in silver links. The road gleamed. Blackness hid the elephant shapes.

In spite of the dark, the stream crossing was easier this time, the way anything is once you know it can be done. And suddenly the rain stopped. Then I was turning left up the rough track, a dozen yards short of Mara Bridge. Before long my headlights swept around the last blackened bend onto the square of mown grass. This time, it looked a splendid camp. Three minutes more and the blue lamp was hissing white on the grained brown table and the chair canvas stretched green against the green grass and the black night, and I was back inside my own territory. I leaned into the car and groped in a cardboard box for the bottle of beer I had insulated among clothes. I felt it, hard and round. My fingers found a way through the clothes and touched smooth glass. It was still pleasantly cool. I lifted the bottle out and stood there holding it, accepting the moment, feeling my shoulders begin to relax. The air was sweet with the smells of wet earth, and overhead a wedge of stars already thrust deep into the blankness.

In the morning the smoke and clouds had perished and the world shone. Southward, my line of sight across the Triangle was too flat for me to see much except the dark arms of vegetation reaching out from the base of the escarpment and a line of flat black hills that the map showed were halfway down to Tanzania, where the river made an eastward jog. During breakfast I considered driving up the escarpment for a clear view. But I decided against it. After all, I would be back. Anyway, I ought to be at Keekorok by around lunchtime: T-B had said that Tipis might be back from Nairobi by then. There was the black cotton soil too.

After breakfast I drove slowly down to the river and crossed the bridge and went up the far side of the valley. I am no longer sure if I admitted to myself at the time that coming up out of the valley was a relief; but I know that on the edge of the plain I stopped and looked back. The line of sight was still too flat for me to see much except the dark arms of vegetation and the black, flat-topped hills halfway down to Tanzania. But now the whole Triangle basked in sunshine, and that made it a different world.

I need not have worried about the black cotton soil: out on the plain little or no rain had fallen. The only serious impediments turned out to be animals—and I quickly learned two lessons: Mara country that looks empty today may be teeming tomorrow; and when it teems you may as well forget about fast, sensible forward travel.

All that morning the savanna teemed. A huge wedge of buffalo drifted through broken bush, placid looking as black Angus cows. Another mile, and a troop of banded mongooses peered at me over an anthill—alert, inquisitive little creatures, almost as lithe and low-slung as otters, and each individual a character. Half an hour later I dragged myself away. Then I bogged down in a paddock that was almost rock-festival crowded: not only giraffes, wildebeest, zebras, kongoni, impala and Tommy, but also several grizzled waterbuck, half a dozen ostriches, two turkeylike ground hornbills, and a pair of jackals that skirted the assembly with noses busy at the earth, ignoring everybody with a dogged, elaborately feigned preoccupation. By lunchtime I had only just turned south at the road junction and passed the little snuggle of huts that was the Aitong Tsetse Survey and Control Station.

After lunch I drove steadfastly toward Keekorok. A manyatta showed faint behind distant trees; but the grass still rolled pale and golden and still the herds of animals grazed or rested or moved slowly and silently across the sunlit landscape. Even the red-brown road struck no real discord.

Ten miles short of the Talek entrance to the Sanctuary, I saw a group of men far ahead, walking. As I came close they moved to the side of the road and began waving their arms. I pulled up alongside.

There were five of them. All wore red-brown shukas, loose over one shoulder. Their hair was plaited and mud-caked, moran style. Each man carried a spear in one hand and a bunch of pale green leaves in the other. They crowded around my window, tall and slender and laughing and shining red. One man pushed to the front and asked in Swahili if I would give them a ride as far as the Talek River.

I explained that the car was already full to overflowing.

The morani scrutinized the car's interior. His eyes moved inch by inch over the camping gear that was stacked high and everywhere, even in the place the passenger seat should have been. At last he nodded. "*Kweli*," he said. "*Hakuna nafasi*. In truth. There is no room."

He turned and spoke in Masai to his companions. Each of them scrutinized the interior. One by one they nodded, comprehendingly. Then, still smiling and laughing, they moved clear of the car and waved me on. For a moment all I could see was red-brown shukas and shining red-brown bodies and gleaming white teeth and arms that waved spears and bundles of leaves.

"*Asante sana*," the spokesman called out. "Thank you very much."

I saluted and drove on. In the mirror I watched the moran re-form into a loose line and slip at once into their long, effortless strides. Then I had turned a corner and once more there was only the red-brown road and the tall, pale grass.

Off to the right, a group of zebras flashed in brief, dazzling horseplay. A lone wildebeest wildebeest-napped under a thorn tree. Then a warthog family, tails up, warthogged it across the road. Here on these pale grasslands, I thought, it was the way the world was meant to be. Man was only one species among many. At least, so this first brief survey of "my domain" seemed to suggest. The Masai remained free of our Western lust to conquer and use every living thing, free of our drive for money. They still drove their multicolored herds across golden grass and into dark trees, communicating by whistle and chant and eerie, ritualistic incantation. They still strode across the savanna, slender and red-brown, with a spear in one hand and an olivelike branch in the other. Their wheat venture was different: that seed blown in on the winds of change might threaten the whole fabric. But otherwise it was all there, just as I had hoped.

When I pulled up at the Talek Gate the two game rangers on duty broke into welcoming smiles. They remembered me, they said, from the day I took my party through to visit the manyatta, two weeks earlier. I asked about the fires in the Triangle. The rangers looked grave. Yes, they said, that was a bad matter. Poachers from Tanzania burned the grass so that it would come up green and attract the game to places they could easily kill them. But sometimes it was Masai sheep- and goat-herders who did the burning: they also wanted fresh green grass. And that was a bad matter, too, to burn even for that. Yes, Tipis had indeed gone to Nairobi, but they did not know if he had returned yet.

The rangers would not charge me the ten shillings entrance fee. "*Leo naweza pita tu*," said one of them, smiling, as he lifted the barrier. "Today you can just pass through."

Half a mile down the road I found a herd of topi in exactly the place it had been when we passed that way the afternoon we visited the manyatta. And as I drove on toward the lodge across savanna that rolled ahead just as it had been rolling all day—and yet was different now, and familiar—I found myself thinking, "Why it's all just as I left it!" I smiled at the conceit, but I made no attempt to cast it out.

And at last I came to Keekorok.

A hundred yards short of the lodge I turned off toward the game warden's office. On the staff soccer field, beside the near goalposts, stood three zebras. Beyond the far sideline—where the playing surface gave way without drastic change to open grass-land—a herd of wildebeest was grazing, a hundred strong, black and ancient against the pale grass. In the distance a lone elephant loomed huge and unlikely.

I went into the game warden's office. No, said the pleasant English-speaking clerk, Mr. Tipis was not back yet, and it was not possible to say when he would return.

I drove down past the soccer field—now repossessed from the zebras by half a dozen men with a football—and pulled in beside the petrol pumps. The pumps were dazzle-painted with zebra stripes. I gassed up, then checked on the stock of food in the little Indian store. Although it was a sparse selection, I took my time looking; and when I circled back toward the lodge at last I drove slowly. You can build an expectancy barrier the second time around.

I need not have worried. The porters greeted me like an old friend, and when we had all shaken hands and I went inside Steve Joyce was at the reception desk. "Good to see you back, Colin," he said.

I went on into the lounge. It was all there: the beamed ceiling, so deftly designed that you did not appreciate how heavy the beams were until you studied them; the big windows and the glass sliding doors; outside in the sunlight, mown grass and the swimming pool; and out beyond the pool, trees and rolling savanna.

On a corner table stood a stack of newspapers. I riffled idly. Most of the papers were a week old and I recognized headlines I had read back in Nairobi: BIAFRANS HOLD ROAD TO LAGOS (secessionist counterattack in western Nigeria); 40 SHIFTA DIE IN BATTLE (Army victory over Somali "bandits" in the unpublicized guerrilla war that had already run on for four years in northeastern Kenya); TEAR GAS USED TO DISPERSE SOCCER FANS (exhibition match in Nairobi between Kenya and Congo-Kinshasa).

I had afternoon tea, then changed into a swimsuit and walked out across the grass. At the edge of the pool I stood looking down into the pale blue water. I think I half expected the leaf to be there, lying in the same place. But its absence did not matter. After all, things had moved on since then.

I dived into the pool. The water was even colder than I remembered. I climbed out and sat in the sunshine. Things had moved on a long way, really. A very long way. In one sense, of course, nothing much had happened. Yet so much had happened that I found it difficult to believe, now, that this was only the fourth day since I had driven out of Nairobi looking for T-B. Then, it had been no more than a hunch that I was on the right road at last. But everything had turned out just the way I had hardly dared hope it would. Well, almost everything. Because I had built an expectancy barrier there had been a temporary setback out at the Triangle—but not here at the lodge, when I was ready for the same kind of trouble. I got up and went and stood above the place the leaf had been. Things had definitely moved on. In a sense, everything had happened.

That night I stayed, by invitation, at the lodge. I had dinner with Steve Joyce and Hans Luther, the Indian accountant—wholly Indian in spite of his highly un-Indian name. Hans's lean, ascetic face and goatee beard made him look vaguely Satanic—until you caught the twinkle in his eye. When a waiter brought our after-dinner coffee tray, Hans picked up the coffeepot and milk jug. "You say you don't take coffee, Colin? Okay. How about you, Steve? Black or white?" He held pot and jug above Steve's cup.

Steve lit a cigarette. "Oh, I think I'll stick to my own color," he said, deadpan.

For an instant the coffeepot and milk jug wavered. Then Hans's slender brown hand had tilted and Steve's cup was full of lily-white milk. And then Hans was studiously filling his own cup with a pale brown mixture.

Steve pounded the arm of his chair with delight. "Bloody Hindi!" he bellowed. "But I'll get level with you yet."

Hans winked solemnly back at him.

Before I went to bed I had a nightcap with Steve.

"Oh, I don't think you need worry too much about talking to Tipis," he said. "First-class fellow. We're lucky to have him here as warden. For one thing, I doubt if there's anyone else could persuade the local Masai to keep their cattle out of the Sanctuary. And a lot of the credit for our good labor relations is due to him too."

On the way down to my cottage, on the path that skirted the floodlit grass, I met an armed askari who was patrolling the buildings, protecting our human territory. We chatted briefly. When I walked on through the bedlam nightsounds I found myself waiting for the lion to proclaim his own dominion, somewhere out in the blackness.

I came to my cottage. No, there was not much doubt, now, about being on the right road. It was all there still—the harmony I had sensed from the beginning in this quiet sanctuary, between animals and land, between men and land, between men and animals. It even seemed to exist, rarest of all, between men and men. I must not get overconfident, that was all. I still had to see Tipis—and the Serengeti researchers. But Tipis was the big one. I would be careful this time, though. The omens had looked good when I went to see T-B, but things had very nearly gone wrong. So this was no time to relax. Not yet.

I went into the cottage and closed the door on the floodlit grass and opened the window to the nightsounds and went to bed.

Impala

CONFIRMATION

Next morning Tipis had still not returned from Nairobi and no one at his office would even make a guess at when he might show up.

Steve smiled at the news. "Yes," he said. "He's getting almost as hard to track down as T-B is."

After breakfast I drove the seven miles out to the main gate of the Sanctuary. The ranger at the gate pointed off to the right. "*Ndio*," he said. "There is indeed a camp over there, in among the trees. Only one complete mile. You can see its road, just here, very near. No, there are not many animals. Perhaps elephant and buffalo, that is all. But it is a very good camp and visitors use it but little."

The track meandered up a rocky slope. The bush closed in. Soon I was among tall trees. Then a small clearing opened up on the left. Its grass was deep and soft and undisturbed. I circled slowly around the edges, checking, then drove to the center and switched off.

Through my open window floated the day's incidental music.

The daysounds of the African bush are altogether different from its nightsounds. They are softer, more subtle—much like daysounds in any part of the world. So you often forget them. But they are there, almost always, when you listen: the caress of birdsong; rustlings in the wind; and minuscule tappings and rubbings that are not much more, really, than different and deeper rustlings. That morning, as I sat in the quiet and protected clearing, they were all there.

And with the daysounds came the daysmells. The smells are always there too, everywhere—a fragile envelope that helps define each place; but, perhaps because they afford too diaphanous an experience to pin down with such clumsy implements as words, they rarely seem to reach the forefronts of our minds. African bush smells are of the subtlest kind, and you tend to overlook them even more often than you overlook the daysounds. But in my secluded little clearing I smelled the smells vividly. That is always a part if it in the simple and still harmonious places. In today's clashing "civilized" world it is necessary for sheer survival that you spend much of your life part anesthetized against anonymous crowds and ugly freeways and the barrages of information. So once you have broken free it is sheer delight to sit back and savor everything your senses can harvest.

That morning, the smells that came floating in through my window were the smells of grass still damp from dew and of sun already hot on dry wood and . . . But you see, even before I begin to build the layers I have run out of words. And I have not really described any smells at all, only two conditions that commonly produce smells we are likely to remember, or at least to think we remember. I know, though, that, as I sat in the car registering this new, quiet place that I had found, my nose reported a solid bank of smells, rich with possibility.

My eyes took more accurate stock: the clearing, perhaps thirty feet across, already mine; the contorted column (itself a melding of six or seven interweaving columns) that was the trunk of the one big, spreading tree in the clearing—a column that was vividly alive, and so gave life and form to my new territory; fifty feet to my left, thrusting up out of a donga, a screen of dense foliage, definitely not mine; beyond this screen, held separate by it as if by a proscenium arch, grassland and bush and spreading trees—a land engraved by avenues that led nowhere, stated nothing, only hinted and suggested; finally, high and distant, the open crest of a hill. When I explored briefly I saw no animals; but about three hundred yards away, deep among trees, I found a big waterhole, dark and still, and I promptly christened my clearing Waterhole Camp. It had the right kind of sound, I felt, for a place that promised to be a personal sanctuary.

Such a retreat was just what I needed. In every journey there comes a time when you feel the need for a pause—to assimilate what has happened and to rest your overworked perceptions so that you will be able to experience the events to come and will not merely pass through them. The need for such a breathing spell may never quite surface: it may just wash around, bumping intermittently against the floor of your awareness. But you are often forced to take a break by the need to catch up with a backlog of chores. After only four days in the Mara I seemed to have accumulated a heavy backlog, and that—on the surface, anyway—was why I had been looking for just such a place.

The chores consumed most of that first day at Waterhole Camp.

They amounted, this time, to more than the regular, recurring mundanities of washing and repairing and catching up with notes:

I had to reorganize the car in response to the experience of the safari's first few days.

It was mid-afternoon by the time I had everything stowed tight and shipshape and convenient: up front, within arm's reach, all the things that had to be within arm's reach—binoculars, camera, clipboard, maps, and one of my five plastic canteens; in the space left by the discarded passenger seat—balancing my weight and also keeping the load forward, on the driving wheels—the four plastic, four-gallon jerricans that replenished the canteens and thereby gave me freedom to wander almost where I pleased; immediately behind my seat, the travel grip containing among other things a clean shift of khaki drill for wear at the lodge and an anti-venin snake kit; in the hold of the car, jammed firmly together, the seven or eight cardboard "grocery store" boxes that acted as food cabinets, kitchen cupboards, clothes closet, booze bin, and a sort of catch-all for the plastic tarpaulin-awning and any other articles that turned up after the cargo had all been battened down under the two old groundsheets that protected everything from dust and covetous eyes; and along the left side of the car, held firm by the mass of cardboard boxes, my aluminum-framed backpack.

It was comforting, I had already found, to catch sight of the pack's bright red nylon bag protruding above the boxes. Down the years, on many long wilderness walks, the pack had been a house on my back. My original plan, in fact, had been to rediscover Kenya on foot. But I had soon been forced to discard it. Under present conditions, I was told, walking would not be safe in populated places, and it was forbidden in all national parks and game reserves. But the pack was still my life belt. If the car broke down in some remote place like the Triangle and I had to walk out to safety I would need a sleeping bag and a tent and a little food and a lot of water, and to carry it all I would need a pack. Mind you, I did not relish the thought of having to walk far. I had been told that even if you were a Masai you selected with some care the places you walked alone in the Mara. And I was no Masai. To a Masai every twig and blade of grass, every sound, every scent, could no doubt signal danger. These signs would be almost as incomprehensible to me, on foot in the Mara, as flashing amber lights and huge green boards with white inscriptions on them would be to a Masai, carborne and terrified, on a California freeway. But if I had to walk in an emergency, the pack would give me range.

When I had finished reorganizing the car I pitched the tent. Each evening so far I had set up camp after dark, and rather than struggle with a new tent I had slept in the car. But even with all windows open the atmosphere had soon grown muggy.

Every hunter and game warden I had spoken to had said that if you slept outside the car in game country, especially on your own, you needed a tent. Otherwise you ran some risk of being taken by lions or hyenas. Almost any kind of tent would do, even a mosquito net. But you had to be able to close it tight. Not long before, a Serengeti lion had dragged a man out through the open door of his tent and killed him.

My new tent was a two-man nylon affair, made primarily for mountaineers. One end had a zipper doorway, the other—for snow use—a sleeve entrance that pulled shut with a drawstring. Both entrances were fitted with mosquito netting, and I felt that if I closed the netting but left the nylon fabric entranceways at least partly open I would be both safe and ventilated. The big fly sheet would help keep the interior cool in sunshine and dry in rain.

By the time I had the tent up it was almost four o'clock. Soon I was sitting naked and content in the shade of the tree with the twisted-column trunk, drinking afternoon tea and looking around my camp with pleasure. The little tent—sheathed in its dark blue fly sheet, with only a modest skirt of the main structure's orange fabric peeking out—had a squat, staunch, confidence-inspiring look. But it was only the beginning. There was the green sleeping bag spread out in the sun to air, and the washing strung out along a white nylon cord, and the bright blue water jerrican standing beside Rohosinante, and the red plastic basin that was bathtub and kitchen sink and laundry, and the heavy ax that had so far come in useful only for hammering in tent pegs but was my sole if not totally trusted protection against lion, leopard, buffalo, elephant, witchcraft and acts of God. Sooner than I had expected, all these mundane and rarely noticed objects had become my familiar friends. For the rest of my time in the Mara they—along with the binoculars and camera and canteens and stove and lamp and cutlery and clothing and flashlight and bird book and alarm clock and all the other very trivial trivia—would underpin my days. Sitting there naked in the shade of the big tree, I celebrated them.

The camp was very quiet. Far above, a wisp of cloud drifted by on the gentle easterly breeze. Trees tossed their heads in mild acknowledgment. But down in my clearing the grass gave only rare and perfunctory nods. Then a tendril of breeze brushed cool and titillating across my body. And all at once my hands reported the chair's wooden arms as warm and smooth; my back and buttocks proclaimed its canvas rough and strong; in front of me, the grained tabletop was suddenly close and beautiful.

The new awareness held, heightened.

A parrotlike touraco flashed overhead—a blur of blue and green and crimson. I looked back down at the grained tabletop. My palms were moist on the chair arms. I sat very still.

And then the springs that had been coiling, building the tension, released: the book could be fiction. Almost before I had grasped this unexpected bulletin, the plot had begun. I had the pattern down inside half a page. Cross-strands appeared, component threads, even single hairs. It was all appallingly untidy, but I was swept along like a matchstick in a cresting river. Then the flood began to subside. Before long it had left me high and dry on the hard stones of reality and I was sitting in the chair and the typewriter was there in front of me, a mere machine. I leaned back and closed my eyes. The tiredness was coming. Under the eyes first. Then down in the jawbones. Then deep in every bone. And with it came the first doubts.

A branch cracked, somewhere up the slope. I opened my eyes. Out beyond one of the donga's proscenium arches, banked in echelon, necks craned, eying me in unison, stood three giraffes. As usual, there was something absurdly comic about them, but I did not think I could have put it into words, even without the tiredness. The giraffes relaxed, began to browse.

They were, I realized, the first mammals I had seen all day.

Even birds had been scarce. And few noises had pierced the day-sounds. Avian schools of music had held a couple of small, sparsely attended classes. Once I had heard, far up the hill, the coughing bark of baboons. That was all. But then, a sanctuary was what I had wanted.

The tiredness ebbed quickly, the way it nearly always did. The sun sank behind trees. I roused myself and put on clothes and washed up the lunch and tea things. A column of ants had occupied the dirty plate and saucepan like a blanket. I looked down into their seething, silent, hidden world—silent and hidden, that is, to us coarse-grained creatures—and as I watched the way each tiny black depository of life scurried about without apparent purpose I felt for a moment, as I had often felt before, the gap that yawned between us. I banged saucepan and plate against the ground and knocked off as many ants as I could, then put everything into the washing-up water. My mild guilt was quickly overridden by the surprise I always feel at the way ants of any kind seem so helpless in water. What did they do, I wondered, in one of the Mara's torrential storms. Did they build underground caverns and waterproof them? Or did they live above ground?

I finished the washing up and put on a sweater and sat down and prepared to watch day surrender to dusk. Something bit my leg; bit again. I bent down. Ants, everywhere. On chair, table, grass, feet. Thick, seething. I picked myself clean and swept table and chair as free as I could and then moved them both a couple of yards and sprayed pyrethrum insecticide in a tight, square, concentrated line around the new dining room. Then I stood and watched the cheated armies advance to the barrier, flinch, and fall back. And this time I felt even less guilt at the casualties left writhing before the barricades. A little self-interest works wonders on your conscience.

To check the casualties, deep down in the long grass, I had to use a flashlight, and when I looked up I found dusk already pressing in on my little clearing. The breeze had died with the sun and the air was very still. I lit the lamp. Outside the sudden white dome, dusk flicked over into night. I opened a beer. Out in the blackness, far up the slope, a lion laid claim to his territory. Perhaps, I thought, it was the lion I had heard that first night at Keekorok, beside the swimming pool. After all, the lodge was only five straight-line miles away. I matched the lion's proclamation—half roar and half grunt—against the Swahili jingle that neatly captures both its diminishing cadence and apparent meaning: *"INCHI YA NANI? YANGU! . . . YANGU! . . . yangu! . . . yangu! . . . yangu! . . . yangu! . . . yangu!* . . WHOSE LAND IS THIS? MINE! . . . MINE! . . . mine! . . . mine! . . . mine! . . . mine! . . . mine!* . . . As the sound faded I found myself holding my breath, striving to capture its last embers, the way you find yourself forced to stand still in an American forest and listen intently for the final drumbeat of a grouse's courtship call. But at last there was nothing to hear except the hissing lamp and the subdued night-tumult beyond it, with frogs now belting out the bass line.

I began to cook dinner. Trying to keep the insects out of the food was a losing battle. Calm nights like this seemed to be the worst, and already the lamp had become an abattoir. Insects of all kinds kept hurtling in out of the blackness and crashing headlong into it, stunning or killing themselves with the impact. Most of them fell around the lamp's base, but some of the bodies stuck on the hot metal globe cover and gave off a faint auxiliary kitchen smell. It was not pretty to look at them and think. But "thou shalt not kill" is a precept you cannot really tackle with the logical sector of your mind. You know, well beyond logic, that "reverence for life" is "right." But where do you stop? You cause death merely by existing. Every time you take a breath you kill a thousand airborne organisms, and you cannot do much about that. At the other limit, it is clearly wrong in most cases to kill elephants or lions or zebras or men. But what should you do about tsetse flies and flesh-biting ants and moths that commit suicide on your lamp? In the end, you do your best by your standards of the moment, and that seems about as far as you can go. As usual, logic is useful for shoring up decisions reached by other means, but it cannot really carry you along.

By the time I had finished dinner, insects lay thick around the base of my lamp. On the smooth, curving blue top of its cylinder, parked like light planes on the edge of a private landing strip, were half a dozen of the small, pale brown moths that all evening had provided most of the casualties. I studied them. They were fluffy little creatures, about an inch long, with antennae that folded back above their wings in an eland-horn position. The fabric of the antennae seemed to be a kind of filigree webbing, incredibly fine; and each antenna was flat and knife-blade-shaped. I let my eye run with pleasure along the parabola of one knife-edge. Then I leaned closer. Closer still. The antenna was not knife-edged after all, its gossamer fabric not webbing. Each antenna was structured like a half feather, with parallel fibers rooted in the "quill" that formed its lower edge. The fibers were so fine that for most of their length they were almost invisible; but at their ends they curled together and formed the pale line that gave the knife-edge impression. I must have sat there, peering, for several minutes, ignorant of how the antennae worked, content to marvel at their delicacy and beauty. At last I leaned back in the chair. And after a while I examined my clumsy fingers and felt suddenly and suitably humble.

A sausage fly came droning in out of the blackness with its specific middle-pitched hum, crashed headlong into the lamp glass, and fell to the table, stunned. I sat looking at the fat, brown, inch-long body and the inadequate wings and the little legs attached in altogether the wrong place, way up front. It was always difficult to believe that these ugly and almost grotesque creatures were the mature, breeding forms of the males of the small and wingless safari ants. And that was another gap between us. Between all men and all insects. We humans, saddled for a lifetime with virtually the same body, naturally find it difficult to imagine a life in which you can, at a single stroke, outside a fairy tale, just by splitting your skin and stepping out, change into something utterly different.

The sausage fly began to twitch. The lamplight caught the shining brown skin of its body segments and suffused them with a faint, blue, almost incandescent glow. The misplaced legs began to drag the cumbersome, bloated body across the table. I watched. There seemed to be no rhyme or reason to the creature's progress. It would head in one direction, deviate, swing clear around, cast off at a tangent, pause, and then take off again on a completely fresh tack.

And then, without warning, it flew.

The flight was a short, convulsive, arching affair, apparently out of control. But it transferred the sausage fly neatly up and into the pot in which I had cooked dinner.

I picked up the pot and put it on my lap. Lamplight flooded down into it.

The sausage fly was climbing up the side of the pot. The little legs, laboring to pull the huge body up behind them, at first found good footholds on fragments of stew left clinging to the lower part of the pot when I had wiped it roughly clean with a damp paper towel. But soon the creature reached the upperworks, where the curving wall of the pot grew steeper and its surface shone clean and smooth. Before long the legs had groped their way past high-stew mark. Almost at once, they slipped. The sausage fly crashed to the floor of its prison. Without pausing it righted itself and once more began climbing. As soon as it reached high-stew mark it fell again.

Six or seven times the creature repeated this operation with little or no variation. Then, apparently by chance, it began climbing that sector of the pot from which I had poured stew onto my plate. I watched intently. If the prisoner held course or swung right, fragments of stew would afford him good footholds all the way to the lip—and freedom. But if he drifted left he would soon reach the edge of a zone that was still clean and smooth and slippery.

The prisoner climbed higher. He passed his previous high point, still on course. But then he began drifting left. The drift accentuated. Barely two inches below the lip of the pot he came to the edge of the danger zone. Just for an instant there was a break in the rhythm of his effort: nothing quite as definite as a pause; but a distinct hiccup.

I found myself urging him on: "Don't be a damned fool!

Swing right. It's easy that way." I'm not sure I didn't speak out loud.

But the legs had already reached up into the clean, smooth, perilous zone. They began to slip. For a moment the big, cumbersome brown body that hung below them was writhing in excruciating effort. Then the legs lost their grip and once again the prisoner was falling. He crashed onto the floor of his arena, righted himself, and without pause began crawling. He crawled in the direction he happened to be facing. And he happened to be facing directly away from the sector he had just attempted. So he crawled clear across the bottom of the pot until he came to the far wall. He climbed laboriously up the wall until he came to high-stew mark. And then he fell.

After nine or ten futile efforts he reattempted, apparently by chance, the sector that had almost brought freedom. This time he hit the danger zone a good three inches short of the lip. He promptly fell. At once, he crawled off in another direction.

I sat watching him, trying to comprehend this apparent inability to learn anything at all from either success or failure. How on earth had such stupid creatures managed to survive?

And then I had crossed the gulf of understanding that had made me ask such a stupid question.

It was a very simple gulf, really. But the sheer and simple climbs—the ones that lack firm handholds of logic—are always the hard ones. On a logical level, in fact, there was no gulf: intellectually, I knew that—although there was now a blurring of the line biologists had once drawn between "instinct" and "learning" —you could still say in at least a general sense that insects, unlike us, lived in a world structured on instinct. Put like that it certainly sounded neat and tidy. It was gratifying too: it meant that we humans lived in a world in which learning power and intelligence played at least some part. And the blind assurance of superiority we normally draw from this knowledge was a help in accepting the distinction and packaging it neatly away, even if the information remained undigested.

But now, watching that fat brown sausage fly learn absolutely nothing from failure or near-success—watching so intently that I had willed it to safety, had perhaps even spoken to it—by becoming so involved I had crossed the gulf even before I recognized its existence. And now I was safely on the far side. The sausage fly would *never* learn, as I could sometimes learn, that when certain actions turn out well and others badly then it is a good idea, next time, to point yourself toward past success. That was all. But now I understood the reality behind the words. With luck I would never quite lose my understanding.

The prisoner was approaching high-stew mark in a hopeless sector. I canted the pot over and put my finger directly in his path. Without pausing, he crawled up onto it. I lifted him onto the table and shook him free. He went on crawling across the shining brown tabletop.

I put the pot back on the table, picked up my clipboard, and jotted down half a dozen lines about the sausage fly and the cooking pot. Then I added: "Yet, in end, maybe statistically valid for the species. So why is ours better?"

I put down the clipboard. After all, which system had proved more successful—pure instinct or instinct tempered by logic and learning power? Were insects or mammals doing better? If you scored in numbers of individuals or different species in the world, or in niches or habitats occupied, the insects came out on top. Mammals probably ran up a higher total biomass (weight of living matter). But who dominated the earth? Who dominated whom? If you looked only at the passing frame labeled "today" you probably had to give the nod to the mammals, spearheaded by man. But what about tomorrow? What about such cracks as DDT backfires that had begun to appear in the mechanism of our dominion? Were they passing discomforts or preliminary death throes?

The sausage fly came to an edge of the table, began to crawl over it, teetered, fell. It fell out of the light and down into the blackness that was the shadow of the table.

I walked a few paces from the table and urinated. Out there, away from the hissing of the lamp, I could hear the full tumult of the night. The frogs had stopped now, but the rest of the orchestra was still hard at it. I went back to the center of my white dome and put the food box in the car and shut all doors and windows. Then I carried the lamp to the tent and put it down just outside the door. I unzippered the mosquito netting of the door, crawled inside, reached out and turned off the lamp, and quickly rezippered the mosquito netting. For a moment I sat just inside the tent, looking out at the suddenly starlit night. The mosquito netting seemed very flimsy. I unzippered it, zippered the nylon doorflap up to about a foot above the ground, and rezippered the mosquito netting. Then I sat back and looked again. That foot of thin nylon might not even be noticeable to a lion or hyena standing outside, but from the inside it made all the difference.

I eased backward onto my mummy bag. This was definitely an improvement on the car. The tent's nylon walls, bulging orange in my flashlight beam, did not really cut off the night. And the nightsounds drifted in, unmuted, through the mosquito netting. With them came a tendril of breeze. I undressed, slid down into the mummy bag, switched off the flashlight, put it in my moccasins, lay back.

The night moved even closer. Now I could hear every instrument in its orchestra. I tilted my head. Out through the mosquito netting of the tunnel entrance I could see a segment of black sky. It was rich with stars. Black leaves, blacker than the sky's blackness, half framed them. Yes, this was much better than the car.

I closed my eyes, began to slide down out of the day. No, the fiction idea would not work. Not for me. But for a while the excitement had been there, that was what mattered. I had to be careful, though: I must not go the litmus paper route again. I must busy my mind with the complexities, with specific interrelationships, such as the way mammal and insect interlocked in the larger Mara pattern, the way . . .

A mosquito whined, close. It zoomed in and landed on my forehead. I slapped at it. It circled overhead in a brief holding pattern, then zoomed in again. Another slap. Another whining, mocking hold-off.

I reached out, felt the moccasins, found the flashlight, switched it on, found the insecticide, located the mosquito on the bright orange tent wall, and raked it with spray. The insect fell, finished. I switched off the flashlight, returned it to the moccasins, and lay back. I began trying to pick up the threads again, failed, and sank down and away into the night.

After breakfast next morning I left Waterhole Camp and drove down to the Sanctuary gate.

Yes, said the ranger, Tipis had returned the evening before.

But he was not in his thatched, white-washed office at Keekorok.

"He will return today," said the clerk in the other hut. "But I cannot say at what time."

All day I kept returning to the offices, past the soccer field with a group of three zebras back in possession; and at last, late in the afternoon, there was a Land Rover standing outside.

"Mr. Tipis is expecting you," said the clerk, and led me toward the second hut. Before we reached it, the door opened.

"Ah, there he is," said the clerk.

Out into the sunlight stepped an arresting figure. The soiled white slacks and dark blue shirt were singularly undistinguished, even on such a well-built man. But the face was big and round and responsive. There was none of the nervous "one-eyed" business that T-B had warned about—though the eyes did seem to swivel on axes that were not quite parallel. The unaquiline, un-Masai face supported a great bulbous bush of a beard and was crowned—or, more accurately, "pimpled"—by a very small gray woolen sock cap. At first glance, Tipis looked less like a Masai game warden than Thelonius Monk masquerading as a bandit.

As soon as he saw me his face widened into a smile. *"Jambo sana!"* he said, holding out his hand. *"Habari ya leo?"*

I think I stopped dead in my tracks.

The Swahili greeting—"Hullo! How are you today?"—was utterly routine. But not once since I came back to Kenya had I heard an African whom I knew could speak English launch a conversation in Swahili. Officials in particular almost always built barriers of stilted, insecure English that made them virtually inaccessible as human beings. And now here was an official playing it cool like a hippie. For a moment I was too astonished to answer.

Tipis, naturally reading my reaction as a failure to understand Swahili, muttered something in an embarrassed tone, then went on, in a pleasant and only slightly disappointed voice, "Good morning. I am glad you have come. I met T-B on my way back from Nairobi and he said I must expect you." His English seemed entirely adequate.

We shook hands and exchanged small talk and I hunted frantically for a way to explain the Swahili business without giving either offense or proof of idiocy.

Before I had glimpsed even the chink of a solution Tipis was saying, "I'm afraid I have to leave straight away, but if you can come back tomorrow morning at eight o'clock we will have opportunity for a real discussion."

I made appropriate noises.

"Good," said Tipis. "But there is something I must give you." He went back into his office and came out with a sheet of paper. "I am sure you will obey all our rules, but here is a list of them." He held out his hand. "I look forward to seeing you tomorrow."

As I walked out to the car I checked the Sanctuary prohibitions: fires, litter, radio and gramophones, pets and domestic animals, sounding of horns, speeds above 30 m.p.h., all travel between 7 p.m. and 7 a.m., startling of wildlife, and getting out of cars within sight of a living animal. The rules also stated that wild animals had the right of way, but as I reached the car I saw that the lodge area was clearly an exception: the three zebras had been dispossessed again and a soccer game was in half swing.

I stood watching the game gain momentum. As men arrived they joined one side or the other. Rangers played alongside cooks, waiters with drivers, garage hands with porters; Masai teamed indiscriminately with Kipsigis and Kikuyu and Luo. I found myself wondering if a Welshman would prove acceptable. After a while I asked and discovered he would. My first soccer game in twenty years was not what you could call very scientific stuff but we all raced enthusiastically after the ball and sweated and enjoyed ourselves. Toward the end I even managed to achieve a hint of a passing game with a tall, rather good-looking Masai. When I camped just outside the Sanctuary's main gate my blood was still racing enthusiastically after the ball. "I must do it more often," I said to the night.

Next morning, Tipis received me in his office. It was a pleasant place, cool and airy under its thick thatched roof. The only big piece of furniture was Tipis's table. On the wall behind it hung a portrait of President Kenyatta.

Tipis shook hands cordially, then sat down and took off his woolen sock cap. A haystack of genuine bandit's hair erupted. "T-B told me in rough what you wanted," he said. "But perhaps you will tell me fully."

This time I had taken care not to overprepare my spiel, and it went much better. Because I remained unsure about Tipis's English I made it all as simple as I could. I think I managed to avoid making the simplicity sound condescending. Anyway, Tipis seemed to understand everything. He asked occasional questions, and at the end he said that it all sounded reasonable enough but that he would have to talk to T-B again. "He has no official jurisdiction over me but . . . well, he is not an old man but we think of him as our father. So I must discuss this matter with him."

I asked about presenting my case to Narok County Council.

"Oh, I don't think that will prove necessary."

"Good," I said. "It was just that T-B mentioned the possibility."

Tipis studied a paper on his desk. "Yes, perhaps it would be a good idea after all," he said. "But it may be a week or two before the next meeting. In the meantime, why don't you write the council a letter, setting down exactly what you want? Bring it to me and I will see that a copy goes to them at once."

I said I would make a spare carbon for him to keep.

"That would be good. There is no immediate hurry though. Any time within the next four or five days will do. In the meantime I will give you a temporary permit to move in and out of the Sanctuary without paying. And you can camp without paying too, anywhere the rules permit you. I must confirm all this with T-B and with the county council, of course, but it will be all right for now."

I thanked him.

"I'm sure you will obey our rules. I wish we did not have to write them down like that, but not everyone obeys them, you know." Tipis looked at me, quickly. "There was one such man here last night, trying to drive through the Sanctuary at half past ten. As you know, all gates close at seven o'clock. Even I do not come in after that. The rangers refused to let this man pass the barrier, so he tried to drive around it and ended up with his Land Rover in the ditch. When I talked to him he still did not seem to understand that he had done wrong. He was one of those scientist people from down in the Serengeti who think they can go anywhere and do anything. But we can get on all right without them. We can get along fine on our own."

Tipis was staring down at the table in front of him. "You know, Mr. Fletcher, there are still some Europeans who can't talk to us without thinking of the color of our skins." On the table, the fingers of one black hand brushed across the black skin of the other. "That's all they can see, the color. They don't understand that I can do what I want to here. If necessary I can send a man to prison."

But soon we began to talk about the otters and the banded mongooses and a big herd of buffalo I had passed as I drove in that morning. After a while, a little hesitantly, feeling my way, I contrasted the Mara's peacefulness with the discords of Nairobi.

Tipis nodded slowly. "I understand you," he said. "I also dislike politics. But of course, our president . . ." He swiveled around and faced the picture on the wall. When he turned back his face was solemn. "Our president is a great man. We owe everything to him. . . . I was in politics myself, you know. But I was driven to it by the treatment we got. And . . . Well, I don't like having to say it, but my appointment here was partly political. I was the first African game warden in Kenya, you know, and I am very proud of it. I feel that . . . Oh, I wish you could speak our language. It would sometimes be so much easier."

Just for a moment the opportunity was there. But I hesitated. I hesitated in part because I was not sure he meant Swahili: "our language" might be Masai. But I also balked in the face of the bleak knowledge that I had still not glimpsed even a halfway acceptable explanation.

"I will write that permit for you," said Tipis, and unclipped a pen from his shirt pocket. He began to write, and I knew the last chance had gone. It would be too embarrassing now to come out with any flat explanation. If he heard me speaking Swahili to someone else I would have to say with mock surprise and no explanation that there must have been a misunderstanding. It was a pity, though. Such things built barriers, on both sides.

As Tipis wrote, his haystack of hair bobbed above the table. Yes, definitely a bandit, I decided; but a bandit gone straight. And now, thank God, a man sure of himself, with no need to put on a show. After Nairobi, that was an immense relief.

Tipis finished writing and handed me the note. "That will see you through any gate, any time of any day," he said.

I mentioned that I would probably drive up that morning to visit the Dawsons, the zebra hunters I had met. They were due to pull out the following day and I did not want to miss the chance of seeing how they operated.

"Yes," said Tipis. "It might be good to see that side of it too."

"I'll come back down with the letter tomorrow or the day after," I said. "And then I'll make a quick trip down into the Sereng—" I stopped. Tipis was already looking away. On the table, his hands moved. "—down to the Serengeti Research Institute. T-B said I might be interested in some of their work."

Tipis slid a sheet of paper toward him, then slid it away again. "Yes," he said. "I suppose it wouldn't do any harm if you went down there."

I fumbled for a verbal bandage. T-B and he would both come into the book, I said, so could I accompany him once or twice on his normal work rounds? It would be a great help.

Tipis smiled cordially. "Of course. Any time you like. Just fix it up with me a few days in advance, that's all."

I thanked him for all his help and we got up and went outside into the morning sunlight.

As we shook hands Tipis said, "Well, I hope all your plans work out, Mr. Fletcher. And let me know if there is anything I am able to do to help. For one thing, you would probably like a ranger to show you around, and when you are ready for that let me know. There are usually one or two spare ones here and they only sit and do nothing. Do not forget, you have only to let me know."

Half an hour later I pulled under a thorn tree just outside the Sanctuary and drafted the letter to Narok County Council. Even with my yellow T-B script to follow as an outline I found the letter hard work. Back when I was the young farm manager who wrote occasionally for the *Kenya Weekly News* I could toss off a thousand words in the bath and send them in still damp. No more. Years of practice have honed me to a state in which I can hardly write an IOU without a rough draft, and two drastic revisions left the county council letter still rough as a rasp. But by ten o'clock I knew it was as good as it was going to get that day, and I put it aside to cool and drove on up the Narok road toward the Dawsons' camp.

It was only then, with the day thrown suddenly wide, that I grasped the measure of my new freedom. The Tipis meeting had been the last big barrier. I still had to see the Serengeti scientists; but their cooperation, though desirable, was hardly vital. There was the county council meeting too, but T-B and Tipis both seemed to regard it as little more than a formality. In any case, it was at least two weeks away. So for the first time I was free to wander. In a sense, I had been free the day I drove to Mara Bridge. But I had known, then, that the hours were only an interlude. Now the days stretched out ahead—days in which I could confirm at my leisure that in the Mara I had indeed found whatever I thought I had found.

I drove slowly northward, reveling in the new luxury.

All things considered, four o'clock seemed the time to reach the Dawsons' camp: just right for a sociable cup of tea, plenty of daylight left, and no awkward suggestion that I was inviting myself to dinner. The place Dawson had marked on my map as his campsite was barely forty miles north of the Sanctuary, so even with a full hour for lunch I needed to average only eight miles in each hour. Three weeks earlier, driving down that stretch of road on our way to Keekorok, we had seen very little game; it occurred to me that I might have trouble finding enough to occupy the hours.

I suppose I should have known better. I should have learned my lesson from that leisurely day's drive to Mara Bridge when, with eight hours in which to go little more than twenty miles, I had ended up racing the darkness to camp past nonexistent elephant shapes. It had been pure Parkinsonian principle: the day's doings, unwatched, had expanded to fill the available hours. But I had failed to learn my lesson. Failed completely. Driving toward the Dawsons' with time to burn, lingering luxuriously to savor its smoke, I let the morning get away from me. At lunchtime I discovered with astonishment that in three hours I had gone barely ten miles out of the forty.

I am still not altogether sure how it happened. The morning was hardly a game-viewing saga. The only "big" game turned up at the very start, and even then I saw little more than the extreme front ends of half a dozen animals and the rear end of one.

Thirty yards to the left and down a slight slope, in a clump of thorn trees, movement. I stopped and peered through tall grass flanking the road. Shapes, perhaps, among the trees. Or perhaps not. I was still wondering when a thin gray trunk snaked up. Then another. And then another. Soon, a line of six gray trunks, some large and some small, all periscoping above the thorn trees. I reached down, felt the binoculars, lifted them to my eyes. For perhaps thirty seconds the ends of the periscopes—double-suction-opening ends with two blunt but sensitive fingers at their tips—were all turned over toward me, and all of them waved to and fro, doubtfully, questingly, like fronds of kelp at slack tide. Then all six had submerged and the shapes among the trees—definite shapes now—began to move. They moved to the right, and away.

At first, down in the dark thorn trees, there were only these darker masses, retreating. Then one of them snapped into focus. For perhaps three seconds I had a clear view, framed between trees, of a huge, wrinkled, elephantine rear end. And then there were only branches in my field of view, and waving grass and sky.

I sat still, peering down the empty slope. Just what was it, I wondered, that gave an elephant's arse such presence? In most four-legged animals you generally do not—failing a distinctive patch, as in Grant and Tommy—pay much attention to the rear end. It is simply there—just a rounding off, a bland conclusion, or, at most, a mere architectural fact, a junction of rear legs and tail and alimentary exit with sexual undertones. But an elephant is different. I had first registered this fundamental fact at Treetops Hotel, near Mount Kenya, where from roof or veranda you look steeply down onto the animals that have come out of the forest to the lake and salt lick. There is something about looking down on things that always brings out the spectator in you, and at Treetops your plunging line of sight reveals every square inch of the huge, sloping expanse that is an elephant's rear end. You see the whole length of backbone, ridged and curving, all the way down to its termination in the odd triangle of skin that in turn gives way to the ridiculous tufted tail. The tail is ridiculous, I mean, until you recognize what an efficient fly whisk the tuft makes with its opposed combs of black hairs that stand stiffly out for six inches and more. Hanging below that huge, sloping rear, the hairs look almost gossamer; it requires effort to connect them with the thick black strands that look so strong and wiry when worn, the way some people choose to wear them, as bracelets.

Backbone and tail, then, are definitely a part of it. But they were not the most vivid images I carried away from Treetops. Stamped across a corner of my mind like a waving gray cancellation mark across the corner of an envelope was a huge, wrinkled expanse of gray skin. And now, looking down the slope through binoculars and catching that sudden clear view of the retreating elephant framed between trees, it had been the same. What I had seen was more than a mere junction of limbs and tail and tracts. Much more. Sheer size had something to do with it. And the wrinkles. The wrinkles, in fact, had a lot to do with it. And the way the back sloped. These above all were what made an elephant's rear a thing of such character—a ridiculous, digni-fied, hanging, propping up, incredibly wrinkled statement that its owner bore the woes and weight of the ages. Yes, that was it, carrying the ages. And hanging.

But perhaps no one can grasp this message until, close up and down a slope, he has come face to arse with a big African elephant.

I drove on, paddock by paddock, and for a time there were only brief and minor encounters.

Close beside the road, in short grass, half a dozen small-terrier-size animals. Side view, with mouthlines turning up in faint grins and outsize ears looping attractively forward, they looked as mischievous and irresistible as puppies. Head on, there was a hint of cunning; and the ears looked even bigger because the angling sunlight dug deep, dark shadow-pools in their caverns—and thereby floodlit the name "bat-eared foxes."

On the edge of the next paddock, a male ostrich ballet-dancing across a gap: neat black coat and clean white collar, but dirty white mop of a tail and ridiculous naked pink neck and legs. Enter, right, from donga-decorated wings, two dull brown fe-males. They legged it, *con anima*, after the *premier danseur*. They caught up. One of the girls fell in behind him like a dutiful African wife; the other swept past, Carmen to the last flounce. Then all three had exited, left, and I drove on. In the ostrich world, who wooed whom?

In the middle of the road, a tortoise. I got out and introduced myself. The tortoise stayed put, neck craned around toward the car, legs just as exposed and vulnerable. The gently humped, four-by-six-inch house-on-his-back was so encrusted with mud that I could see the shell only at its edges, where it was a dark, incon-spicuous brown. When I lifted him from the perilous road his head went indoors. His feet remained partly exposed but at each leg opening he ejected a little thick yellow liquid. It did not seem to smell. The underside of his shell was dark brown, streaked with yellow. When I put him down on a patch of bare earth, ten feet

from the road, he promptly retreated with all tortoise haste into
the shadowy cloisters of a very small bush. Inside, he sat motionless, meditative. His mud-encrusted shell blended with the soil and
its dark edges with the shadows. You could have walked past a
hundred times, your foot within inches of him, and never sus-
pected his presence.

I was still admiring this summary camouflage act when I heard
a curious clapper-rattle sound directly overhead. I looked up. At
first, nothing but blue sky. Then I located a small bird hovering
about forty feet up. Its wings fluttered almost clumsily, like a
bat's. From it, at intervals, came a distinctive three-phrased clap-
per rattle, the final phrase a shade longer and louder than the
first two. I walked to the car. Through binoculars the bird was
still only a silhouette vibrating against the brightness of the sky:
no tinge of color offered a clue to its identity. Then it stopped
fluttering and began to glide. It planed steeply down with wings
held high and rigid, like a miniature high-winged monoplane.
Barely two feet above the ground it flattened out; and in the
instant before it landed in tall grass I thought I glimpsed a pale
brown back. The dive had suggested "bird of prey," but it hardly
seemed possible that such a tiny creature could prey on anything
bigger than insects. I walked to its landing place. Nothing. I
went back to the car. Before driving on I riffled vaguely through
the bird book. It was frustrating, not even knowing which
section to look in.

Soon, a paddock apparently set aside for hartebeest.

Strictly speaking, there is only one true hartebeest in the
Mara—Coke's hartebeest or kongoni. Topi are classified as "bastard
hartebeest." But you do not need a biologist to tell you the two
are close cousins: they are clearly built on the same chassis. Both
have high front ends, humped shoulders, tapering body lines, and
long and rather stupid facial grills. Only the extras come different. Most striking is the horn trim, fitted to both sexes: in topi,
a subdued and tasteful curve; in kongoni, a bizarre, bracket-
shaped double flair, very ostentatious, very Detroit. Yet the
kongoni body-finish is a subdued tan that pales to cream at the
rear end, while topi come with pewter patches on face, forelegs

and thighs, and the rest of their bodywork a sleek purplish-bay that in sunlight can glow rich and ruby, like claret held between eye and candle. Side by side, the cousins look as basically similar and superficially different as a Buick and an Olds.

The relationship carries over into road characteristics—a fact confirmed that morning by a mild, delayed-action confusion. You most often see both kongoni and topi moving either at a walk or at their galumphing, porpoise-roll canter, so you tend to think of them as clumsy creatures; but that morning as I drove into what turned out to be the "hartebeest paddock," a kongoni half hidden behind a bush failed to notice me until I was twenty yards away—and then, startled, took off. Within half a dozen strides his awkward hartebeest canter had smoothed out into an elegant and effective gallop. He raced away across the open grass, pouring it on—neck extended and back half hunched yet his whole body poised and under perfect control. For the first time I understood, beyond books, that speed was the prime hartebeest defense.

But note that I say "hartebeest defense," not just "kongoni defense." For clarity's sake I wrote "kongoni" in the preceding paragraph; but I was simply taking myself off a hook. For when I jotted down a few notes about the incident a little later on I found that because I had been concentrating on the canter and gallop—movements common to all models built on the hartebeest chassis—I could not remember whether the animal had been a kongoni or a topi.

Near the far end of the paddock stood a male topi with a broken right horn. He stood alone, forelegs planted on an ant-hill in the popular hartebeest on-guard pose. I stopped. The topi eyed me back.

The sun streamed in through the car window, and without the breeze that driving created it was surprisingly hot for mid-morning; almost sultry, as if rain was lurking. I drove slowly forward into the shade of a roadside thorn tree. The topi continued to eye me, but he stood his ground. In spite of his long and rather stupid hartebeest face he had about him an air of experience that bordered on wisdom.

It was cooler in the shade, but outside the tree's dappled shadow the sun beat down. I switched off the engine and leaned back in my seat. The topi did not move a muscle. Were topi on their own like this always males? Always elderly males? It seemed a fairly common arrangement among mammals. Old buffalo and wildebeest bulls certainly tended to live alone: people said they couldn't seem to stand the noise and fuss of the women and children. Old bull elephants often did the same. Old men too.

Out in the sunlight, the topi still stood motionless. In the small of my back, the shirt was damp and cool.

It was astonishing, now, to look back and remember that the young farm manager from Nakuru had not been interested in the wildlife of his new country. There had been occasional encounters, of course, even on the farm—even apart from the orphan dikdik that died and the baboons that left blood on the boulders as they escaped up the cliff. There was the afternoon in that same little meadow—the sloping meadow with the granite boulders strewn around it—when a leopard had come out from the forest at the foot of the cliff. The leopard had appeared on the very edge of the milking herd and I had watched, horrified and then astonished, as one of my quiet old Guernseys put her head down and shook her horns and the advancing leopard stopped, stood for a moment—and then turned and faded back into the forest. Away from the farm, I had often seen giraffes and zebras and Tommy and ostriches, and there had been a couple of memorable encounters at night—notably my floodlit confrontation with the eland on the slopes of Mount Kenya, and a swerving, seventy-mile-an-hour near-miss of a huge ant bear lumbering across the main Nakuru-Nairobi road. There had been other near-misses too, when I was equally thankful they were misses: fresh elephant droppings beside a trout stream; and the time that two of us, slogging unarmed through bush country along the lower reaches of another trout river, came on a native cow with its entrails ripped open and still warm, and the soil wet from spilled stomach liquids, and in this soft soil the huge and undeniable imprint of a lion's paw.

But I had only once gone deliberately looking for game. It

was during my last year in Kenya. Finding myself with a couple of free hours in Nairobi, I decided to drive out to the new game park on the edge of the city. Almost at once I saw a big herd of wildebeest and was astonished at their inane grasshopper faces and flowing white beards and their air of being so hopelessly out of date that you felt they belonged not to the streamlined present but to an earlier and less efficient age. It was not until I left Africa that I realized what opportunities I had missed. Later, in a kind of shamefaced bravado, I would sometimes boast, with accuracy, that I had lived in Africa for six years and seen neither a lion nor an elephant.

During my Kenya years I had certainly been unaware that the country's wildlife might represent its real riches. And I knew now that there were many other things I had been unaware of in those days. Unaware of, I mean, along the busy freeways of my mind, where I could see them steadily, as signposts to every action. It is often like that, I find, when you look back on one of your former selves: the knowledge was there, or at least the germ of it, but you do not seem to have used it; you went on acting as if the old, established truths were necessarily true.

Out in the sunlight, the topi shifted position, then settled back into immobility. He was still keeping an eye on me.

The established truths were often valid, of course. But by no means always. And it looked like being a lifelong business—the shucking of things you had been taught were true (because of your time and place) but which did not stand up to experience. For unless you are one of those people born with their eyes open—people I never really know whether to envy or pity—you have to learn down the years, scene by scene. You see some-thing—or hear it or smell it or feel it, or perhaps all of these things at once—and the scene burns deep. And from then on, though you do not know it yet, the moment is there, imprinted. Much later—ten years later, perhaps, or twenty—you understand. And you find that all the vital detail is still there, sharp, waiting.

I can remember now, almost as if I were still sitting in that cold and dark and silent bus, a night in Bournemouth, in southern England. The bus was standing at its terminus and I had been to see somebody I did not know very well (I no longer know whom), and now I was waiting for the driver and conductor of the bus to come out of their retreat (I seem to remember a small hut nearby). But they took a long time to come and I sat on, alone, in the silent bus. All around me, outside the dirty windows, pools of light shone bleak and white on a wide, gray, open asphalt space. I think it must have been wartime because the street lamps cast no more than dim, detached pools of light. Or perhaps it was peacetime and a foggy night. Anyway, there was nothing between the pools of light or beyond them except the blank, black night. And the bleak, white pools of light revealed nothing all around the dark and silent bus except gray, empty, meaningless asphalt. And the asphalt, at that moment, covered everything, so that there was no room outside it for any other kind of world—for any kind of world with warmth and un-certainty and the possibility of error and growth.

Now Bournemouth is a seaside resort and a not unpleasant place. It is certainly not Cleveland, Ohio, seen from the air in February, or one of my Welsh coal towns seen almost any time, or that garish roadhead halfway up Mount Fuji, where the litter is. But that night in Bournemouth, sitting in the dark bus, I knew, deep like a dagger, the wrongness of what I saw. At that time I can hardly have been more than twenty. So at least fifteen years passed, and probably more, before the scene was up there, crystal-lized at last and translated and posted along the freeways of my mind; before I understood—steadily, before every action—not merely the grayness and bleakness and dead hopelessness of the strictly utilitarian man-world but also the wrongness of it; before I understood, I mean, that the earth was not meant to be covered over and buried by a pall of dead gray asphalt, and that when-ever such a thing happens there must be some nonhuman god, somewhere, who cries out in anger.

There is another scene.

After I left Kenya I spent six months in what was then South-ern Rhodesia. Part of that time I helped build a road into a new tea estate on the slopes of the country's highest mountain, and among other things I drove the only bulldozer on the job. One day as I made the first cut down a new grade I came to a little fold in the open, grassy hillside. The crease of this fold held moisture, and in it grew a single tree fern, about the height of a man. Now tree ferns have a rare and fragile beauty that is touched with fantasy: their bare but vaguely fuzzy trunks look very solid, even when you know they are soft and vulnerable; and from the head of each trunk there sprouts, like an aspidistra from a Victorian parlor pot, an umbrella of oversize ferns. That morning, as I bore down on the lone tree fern, the sun slanted in from the right, so that the plant was part silhouette against rain-washed blue sky and part a painting in warm but vivid browns and greens. I saw the tree fern like this—saw its startling beauty, I mean—only in the last instant before I eased the bulldozer blade down into the fold. I like to think I hesitated; but I know that I drove on and that the tree fern quivered and then shuddered and then began to lean. And then it lurched and began to topple. And then it was falling, already finished, like a man cut down by machine-gun fire. For one brief but wrenching moment I knew that I had done wrong; then I was driving on again, slicing my swathe across the virgin hillside.

A hundred yards beyond the wise old topi who seemed to live alone, a mixed herd of topi and kongoni drifted into view. I checked through binoculars. There were several calves, all of them too young to have horns. Some moved along close to adult kongoni, others close to adult topi; yet all their coats were a dull, uniform, kongoni-brown. Then, almost at the same moment, two calves began to suckle, one from a kongoni, one from a topi. Their actions answered one question all right; but it raised others. At what age did the coats of young topi change color? And what was the reason for this confusing arrangement? The herd drifted on. Soon, it was out of sight again. The old male continued to watch me from his anthill. A cloud shadow slid across him. It engulfed my patch of shade. I leaned back in the seat.

And a few days after that moment with the tree fern I stood beside a stretch of the new road and looked down a thousand feet into a steep valley. Sunlight was already streaming in behind a storm, glinting on the creek that cascaded down that valley after each heavy rain. It rained copiously on that mountain—in my last ninety-three days there it rained ninety-three inches—but between storms the sun shone vivid on the open slopes. That morning, the line of the creek showed white and clean all the way down the valley until it met the brown, freshly bulldozed line of my road—the road I had reconnoitered on horseback, the road I had surveyed with a level and marked with sticks, the road I had bulldozed myself, the road I was already damned proud of. And at its junction with my road—my brand-new, rain-washed road— the creek changed. It changed from white and clean and pure and beautiful to brown and turbid and soiled and unlovely. The change was abrupt and absolute, another death. And in that moment too I knew I had done wrong. Like the moment the tree fern fell, it did not last. Not on the surface. But it too burned deep. And a decade or so later it surfaced, steady and signposting at last, and I became aware in all my actions—aware in most of them, anyway—that we men have simply got no goddam right to tear the place apart.

I still suffered, no doubt, a certain residual guilt about the tree fern and the raped creek, just as I probably did about the little dikdik that died and the baboons I had wounded as they escaped over the granite boulders at the foot of the cliff. I certainly did not approve, now, of these deeds done by the young and unaware manager of the farm near Nakuru or by the young and unaware road builder on Inyangani. But I still could not label him "bad," let alone "evil." It was the old difficulty: evil deeds were not as a rule done by evil men. If they were, the world would be a much simpler place to set straight.

It was hard, though, to remember about unaware men—to hold the knowledge available all the time, steady and signposting. It was even more difficult than trying to remember, here in the Mara, all these years and metamorphoses later, that the young farm manager had simply not been interested in the wildlife of his new country. That he had in a sense hardly been aware of it.

A breeze curled in through the car window. I stirred. The shirt shifted on my back, damp and cool again.

Two hundred yards away, a quartet of black shapes was

moving across open, sunlit grass. I lifted my binoculars. The big, turkey-size birds were walking in line abreast, etched against the grass like sculptures hewn from gleaming coal. I focused on the nearest. Legs black and sturdy, made for a lifetime of walking. Body black and sturdy too, the folded wings giving it that solid, almost armor-plated look we learn to accept as normal in birds, especially black birds, but which is, when you stop to consider the matter, an unlikely impression for feathers to convey. Bill black and massive, long and tapered, with a bulbous swelling just in front of the eyes. The eyes set in a bright red face mask. And a pendulous neck wattle matching the mask's startling hue. On the game-viewing safari we had seen several ground hornbills, but there had never been a chance to find out what they did for a living; so when the birds began to move out of range I started the car and moved after them, out of my pool of shade. The topi watched me go.

The four hornbills continued to advance in line abreast, spaced at roughly ten-yard intervals. Soon I was tagging along the same distance from their left-wing member. We moved on across the paddock, a quintet. Each bird scanned the ground immediately ahead of it, and from time to time one of them would jab down, come up with some morsel in the tip of its bill, flip back its head like a man about to gargle, and open the bill. The captured object fell down its throat.

I studied my left-wing hornbill. Mostly, when it reached down into the grass for a morsel, it moved deliberately. But once, without warning, it darted to its right and in the same sudden movement began to make a reaching jab. A large, grasshopperlike insect flew up and away from the target zone. The hornbill stopped in mid-jab, watched the fleeing insect with obvious and comic chagrin, then flounced forward again. Apart from that failure, the hunt was a controlled and highly efficient operation with a sedate, regular rhythm: unhurried promenade; deliberate downward reach; backward flip of head; a moment when the bird stood there in gargling pose, bill agape, while the morsel of food fell; then the slow promenade resumed.

It occurred to me that such large birds as hornbills must, in order to make a living, need a very large number of the morsels on which they seemed to subsist. And after a while, watching the way "my" hornbill worked, I began to appreciate the efficiency of its massive, tapering bill. It was not really the clumsy tool it seemed to be. Only the tips of the closed bill came fully together: there was always a gap in the midsection. But the tips met neatly—and they functioned with the precision of surgical forceps. In fact, the bill's strong base and open middle section and precisely meeting tips made it essentially the same instrument as man, facing similar tasks, had devised in the form of forceps—or pincers or tongs. The bill might look somewhat overengineered; but it had to perform hour after hour, day after day, and if it suffered serious damage its owner would inevitably die of starvation. So it needed plenty of reserve strength. Its apparently excessive length made sense too: the bird could walk comfortably upright and still carry its bill poised for a short, economical thrust; and the upright stance held its eyes high and so afforded them a wide field of view not only down onto the ground where the food normally lay but also forward and out to each flank, where enemies might lurk. Whichever way you looked at it, the bill was a precision instrument, perfectly adapted to its task.

After a while I also began to appreciate the efficiency of the hornbill's eyes.

From each side of the rather thin head protruded an eyeball. The bright red face mask—which I could now see was bare red skin—covered two-thirds of each eyeball's dome, but a porthole revealed the part we normally think of as the eye. The hornbill kept swiveling this porthole around the surface of the eyeball-dome. It moved like the nozzle of one of those hot-air drying machines you find in public washrooms and can adjust so as to direct the blast onto hands or face. Mostly, the bird directed its eyes downward, into the grass, but from time to time it would flick the porthole up and survey the surrounding plain. At such moments I found myself staring through the binoculars into a warm golden iris with a round black pupil at its center. This eye, set in its bulging red dome, had a character of its own: slightly sinful but decidedly wise.

Surrounding the porthole and swiveling with it—and thereby shielding the pupil—was what looked like a circular black tube projecting about three-quarters of an inch from the dome's surface. I studied this tube closely, and after a while I scribbled in my notebook: "And we think we invented camera lens hoods!" For that, it seemed clear, was how this eye hood worked. When its owner was scanning the ground it masked the sky's glare and allowed the pupil of the eye to open up and make full use of the dim light down among the grass stems. When the porthole flicked forward or sideways the hood still screened out the sky and so allowed the pupil to remain at least partly enlarged and therefore in a more efficient state for surveying the plain and also in greater readiness for the return to grass-roots work. It would be difficult, I decided, to devise an instrument more perfectly suited to its task. It would be difficult even if you could start from scratch, as the maker of the first camera lens hood had done, and did not have to begin, as the evolutionary process almost always had to begin, with something designed for a totally different task.

It seemed reasonable to assume that the hornbill's eye hood had evolved from eyelashes. But I found that I could detect no hint of individual hairs, no sign of flickering movement. The little black tube projecting from the dome might have been made of rigid black metal. I eased in toward "my" hornbill. Eight yards. Seven. Still not close enough to be sure about the eyelashes. I edged even closer. The bird flicked up its porthole and fixed Rohosinante's hood with a piercing stare. Then it ran forward, opened its wings, and took off. Its companions followed suit. The quartet vanished over a tree-lined donga.

I drove back onto the road and crossed the donga into the next paddock. There was no sign of the hornbills. But on the far side of the paddock I saw a large, loose assembly that included impala, topi and kongoni, a waterbuck herd, and several groups of zebras; and I noticed at once that the animals on the assembly's left flank—the impala and several zebra groups—stood on guard, alert, facing a patch of bush. I picked up the binoculars. Just for an instant I glimpsed, on the fringe of the bush, two low, dark shapes; then they had vanished.

I turned off the road and drove across the open paddock. The two shapes broke from the patch of bush and began loping away. Even without the sloping backs and gray, black-spotted flanks, there was no mistaking that lope: it was a sort of fore-and-aft sea roll that never quite got completed without a hint of impending tragedy because the rear legs were always being left just a quiver behind, as if forgotten until the very last moment, and then hurried stiffly forward, not quite under control, to catch up with everything else. As I watched the shapes go I remembered reading that one of their Masai names means "the limpers" or "lame ones." *

* *Africana*, the magazine of the East African Wildlife Society (Vol. 3, No. 1 [March 1967]), carries this translation by the late Lord Claude Hamilton of a Kiplingesque Masai folk tale that explains how the name arose:

"Once upon a time a crow met a hyena and said to him: 'You hyenas are always hungry, but you never complain. Why don't you climb up into the trees where the Masai store their meat and eat that?'

"The hyena answered: 'Have we wings that we can fly up into the trees?'

"Then the bird said: 'Go through the country and collect all the hyenas here and I will tell you how to get the meat.'

"So the hyena went off and journeyed far and wide collecting all the hyenas, and eventually they all arrived at the crow's home.

"Then the crow told them: 'First one of you goes and sits under the tree where the meat is. Then another one climbs on that one's head, and a third one on the second one's head and a fourth on the third and so on, and then I with my wings will fly up and guide the topmost one to the meat.'

"So the first hyena went and sat under the tree where the meat was and, one after the other, all the others piled themselves on each other's heads and then the crow flew up beside them, but none of them got the meat because the bird was tricking them and guiding them to the moon.

"At last the hyena on the ground found that the weight of all the others was more than he could bear, so he wriggled out from underneath them to see what had happened to the meat.

"Then all the other hyenas came crashing down and as they hit the

The hyenas disappeared into a donga. The zebras and impala relaxed. I drove closer.

There were, as usual, two impala herds: a harem controlled by one ram; and a bachelor herd, from which would come in due course a ram to defeat in combat and so replace a lord grown weary from the exercise of his demanding marital duties. At least, so I had been told. It was one of those fragments of animal lore you picked up very quickly, the kind of thing even I had been able to pass on to my party of game viewers and so help camouflage the ignorance I was always and painfully aware of. Frankly, the impala's conjugal arrangements are pretty obvious. Males carry impressive lyre-shaped horns, females none; so the harems and bachelor gatherings stand as distinct and divided as hippies and hard hats. But the two herds are rarely far apart. The bachelors may even wander into the harem and mingle with the women, though if you watch closely you will see that from time to time the lord and master makes small assertive movements, and that the bachelors always defer. Sometimes the bachelors drift so far away that you cannot see them, but normally they hang around within good girl-watching range.

That morning, the two impala herds were grazing less than fifty yards apart. The lord had positioned himself squarely between harem and bachelors, and the bachelors showed no sign of minding anyone's business but their own. It was curious, I thought, that although everyone talked about the impala's social setup no one said much about the other antelopes' arrangements. Did Tommy, for example, behave the same way? I would have to avoid getting bogged down in such matters—the facts would only be my stepping-stones—but I would have to ferret out the answers to such questions. There were communal matters too. Why, for example, these sudden convocations of many species? You often drove for miles and saw only a few scattered animals. Then you crossed a donga into a small paddock that looked just

ground they broke their back legs and ever since that day all hyenas limp."

Just so.

like all the rest and found an assembly that might run to two or three hundred animals of six or seven species. Could it simply be that by feeding close together the animals pooled their keenest senses—sight in one species, hearing in another, smell in a third—and so tightened their defenses against predators? That seemed likely enough. But such a bond would hardly be very strong.

And then it occurred to me that the bond holding this particular assembly together had indeed not been very strong. All the time I was watching the impala I had been moving closer to them. I had done so by such small increments and so slowly that neither they nor the other animals had become alarmed; but in driving forward I had thrust directly into the center of the assembly. I had been vaguely aware that the waterbuck and the topi and kongoni had tended to drift away from me. Now I saw that the assembly was dispersing. The groups had all along preserved their autonomy; but now they had separated out, almost as if centrifuged. The waterbuck had circled to the right and halted. The impala harem had moved directly away from me and the bachelor herd was tagging along, still within girl-watching range. The topi and kongoni were drifting off to the left. The five or six original zebra groups had formed into two larger units, and each of these was now trekking slowly in scattered single file toward a gap in the tree-lined donga into which the hyenas had vanished.

Yet there was still no sign of alarm. The whole dispersion, in fact, had been a casual and languid affair. I could detect no firm intent behind it—nothing remotely like the clear purpose that had lain behind the movement of the zebras that first morning we game-viewed in the Mara, when the whole herd had bunched together, suddenly alert, and then had edged away before the advancing lions. Instead, each species-group had responded almost idly, apparently against no very great resistance, to the stimulus of my incursion. A weak centrifugal force, in other words, had caused total dispersal. So the force holding the constituents together must also have been weak. And that was certainly consistent with my idea that the only thing holding such assemblies together was a vague, instinctive awareness that by grazing close together they gained a measure of collective security against such predators as the hyenas. My simple "theory" would need a lot more evidence than that. But for the moment it would have to do.*

I swung my glasses around onto the waterbuck. One big and superbly dignified bull stood watching me, very much alert. The

---

* I think this was the occasion (though it may have come a lesson or two later in my education) on which it occurred to me that once you begin to understand the subtle and delicately balanced harmony that infuses the life of a largely nonhuman community such as the Mara—a harmony in which no group rules but each contributes to the whole by constantly interacting with others (though not one of them is aware of this fundamental fact)— then the understanding might just possibly generate an antidote to the Personalized Conspiracy Theory of History.

The Personalized Conspiracy Theory of History is a world view, impervious to logic, that is held like a vice by a very large number of humans. It is particularly popular among those who feel that in some way or other they have not succeeded quite as they deserved. If you are a true believer (an unwitting one, of course: adhesion to the theory is by reflex) then you attribute all the woes of the world—all *your* woes, that is—to "them." Without "them" the world would be a huge, delectable dish of peaches and cream from which everyone could eat his fill in peace and brotherhood and perpetual sunshine. For "they" are a ruthlessly efficient group bent on exploiting the virtuous for their own selfish and invariably nefarious ends. Depending on where you stand as you watch the Passing Show, "they" are the Communists or the Capitalists or the Establishment or the Hippies or the Liberals or the Conservatives or the Blacks or the Whites or the Browns or the Yellows or the Christians or the Jews or the Arabs or the Hindus or the Muslims or the Protestants or the Catholics or Big Business or Government or the Texans or the New Yorkers or the Members of The Country Club or Those Who Are Not Members of The Club or the Giants or the Dodgers or the Montagues or the Capulets or the Hatfields or the McCoys or—if your case has progressed to the ultimate and hopeless stage—the Rest of the World, Outside You.

I suggest, as I say, that even a partial understanding of a community such as the one that thrives on the Mara might generate an antidote to this fantastically popular view of How Things Are. For it is blazing clear that this is simply not How Things Are on the savanna, where no group rules but each contributes to the whole by constantly interacting with others. And it seems to me that even a subcutaneous injection of this truth might just possibly provoke, in all but hopeless cases, at least a suspicion that this is not How Things Really Are in the human world either, outside blinkered human imaginations.

rest of the little herd looked almost comatose. The heat of the day was clearly having its effect . . . the heat of the day. . . . I glanced at my watch.

It was then, at a few minutes past one, that I felt the Parkinsonian presence. I could almost hear the man chuckling to himself in the back of the car. For the morning had gotten away from me. In three hours I had come barely ten miles.

Almost at once I saw that it did not really matter. There was still plenty of time to get to the Dawsons' camp by four. Even with a full hour for lunch I had only to drive fifteen miles an hour for two hours. And now, forewarned, I would be forearmed against Parkinson.

For the present, though, I was hungry. It is astonishing what looking at a watch can do to your stomach.

Off to the left, the last of the zebras were disappearing through the gap in the donga. On the spur of the moment I began to drive after them. It would be more private in the next paddock, screened by the donga's vegetation from any vehicles that might pass along the road.

I came to the gap in the donga. What lay beyond was not so much a paddock as an orchard gone to seed. An octopus's orchard, perhaps, just off Abbey Road.

Two hundred yards away, parallel to the donga, ran a low, stony ridge, its crest no more than twenty feet high. The corridor between ridge and donga was grassland of a sort. But the grass was thronged—and thereby shaded, and so kept greener than the paddock behind me—by an anarchy of vegetation. Bush had claimed whole side bays of this wildness. It had even established colonies out in the main: reefs of scrub, barely surfacing above the grass; round clumps of shrubbery, solid as islands; and tall but straggly superstructures like wrecked oil rigs. Trees, singly or in clusters, studded the whole enclosure: tall trees, short trees, fat trees, slim trees and trees whose shapes were shapeless. There were thorn trees drawn up into umbrellaed tracery and others that stood hunched and daunted. There were broad-leaved trees that squatted or swelled or mushroomed or bubukled or even tried to do all these things at the same time and sometimes almost made it. There were live trees bursting with vitality, moribund trees leaning gauntly toward the grave, and dead trees whose skeletons had already crumpled into chaos. Here and there, dark candelabrum euphorbia thrust up stark, surrealistic arms. And across this bizarre diorama, like Picasso horses drifting through a Dali orchard, moved a concourse of zebras.

The leaders had already passed me. Their followers reached back to the right—small straggling group after small straggling group—until the vegetation shut off my view. The farthest animals were perhaps five hundred yards away, and I had no means of telling whether there were more crowding in behind.

The zebras seemed to fill the orchard. Some animals moved in pairs, others in threes; some groups were a dozen or even twenty strong. Thirty yards might separate group from group; or a mass of black and white bodies might drift together, intermingle, separate, and then blend again. The concourse moved, unmistakably, from right to left, but you could hardly call its progress a trek: the slow forward drift—untidy, fitful and capricious—was too desultory an affair for that. Some groups plodded along in single file with only brief and infrequent halts. Others grazed erratically, in loose clusters. A few stood still. Such a kaleidoscope makes any estimate of numbers suspect; but when I first came to the gap in the donga there could hardly have been fewer than two hundred zebras in sight.

For perhaps five minutes I sat and watched them. Then I drove slowly out toward the center of the orchard.

I did so only after a brief skirmish with my conscience. By lunching directly in the zebras' path I would undoubtedly interrupt their forward drift. But the distress would be no greater, I told myself, than that inflicted by any pride of well-fed lions, innocent of aggressive intent, that happened to rest up for the day in the same place. Provided I behaved like a decent animal, in other words, I would create no real anomaly.

It did not take me long, I admit, to reach this welcome conclusion. It would have been hard to resist the prospect of lunch in the middle of a zebra cavalcade.

When I drove out into the orchard I caused very little commotion. A few of the nearer animals broke into an uneasy trot. One or two galloped briefly. But in general they made no more than a quiet, controlled adjustment. The zebras to my left continued to drift forward without check. Those immediately ahead of me veered away: by the time I parked in the shade of a tall thorn tree, midway between donga and ridge, all of them had either moved well to the left or had detoured onto the ridge. The animals to my right, whose path I now blocked—and which were also downwind of me—reacted more sharply. Groups within about two hundred yards swung off at right angles, toward the ridge. These were the ones that broke into a trot or galloped briefly. But even among them there was no panic. Most of them paused on the low, stony crest of the ridge and turned to face me. They stood for a time, watching. Then they began to drift on again, away to my left.

The groups that had been following them through the orchard stood their ground. Animals from further back moved up among them. Soon a solid line had formed, stretching almost completely across the orchard and curving slightly at its extremities so that every animal was about two hundred yards from the car. Almost all of them stood watching me, alert. They gave no impression of real alarm: they just seemed determined to wait out this contretemps, whatever it might be. But they set up a barrage of protests that ranged from asinine honk to peevish whinny.

As the minutes passed the zebras' lament diminished. Their alertness slackened. Some of them began to graze. A few turned and stood facing back the way they had come. But the crescent held firm.

Moving very slowly, I got out of the car. The zebras watched. Still in slow motion, I opened the rear door of the car and set up table and chair. Down the orchard, a minor ripple animated the shallow black and white crescent. The protests mounted to a brief crescendo. I opened a can of soup and lit the stove. The zebras watched intently. I might have been Julia Child.

All through lunch the zebras watched me. A few drifted off and vanished over the ridge, but by and large the line across the orchard held. As time passed, more and more animals began to graze. But the majority continued to stand and watch.

Between mouthfuls, I watched back. Through binoculars I could see alert black eyes fixed on the car, could pick out screens of white hair lining cocked ears, could watch twitching, velvety muzzles. The muzzles were the only all-black parts of the skins, and even they were short, like mini-nosebags. Thin black stripes flowed upward from them, diverged over the faces, then reconverged and, tapering almost to vanishing point, reunited in midforehead in pleasing near-asterisks. With a little mildly sick imagination you could picture each muzzle as having been dipped in black paint and then held high so that rivulets of paint ran down a previously white face.

The coats offered no other foolish answers to the old question of whether a zebra is a white animal with black stripes or a black animal with white stripes: black and white alternated with almost geometric equality—except for small areas of total whiteness on each bulging belly, on the insides of the legs and at the crease of each pair of amply padded buttocks. The markings varied from animal to animal, but an overall design persisted: on neck and mane and forepart of the body, roughly vertical stripes; on legs and haunches, a pattern that flowed horizontally.

It is a fact, I think, that zebras tend to arrest your attention rather than engage your sympathy. They have none of an impala's fragile grace or an elephant's wrinkled wisdom and they do not impress you with the kind of sensitivity you feel quivering through domestic horses. In fact, they do not convey an immediate impression of any particular characteristic. The fault probably lies with their striking camouflage (assuming for a moment that camouflage is the "purpose" of the stripes). What usually happens, I think, is that your eye gets flagged down by this bizarre costume and looks no further. But that lunchtime in the orchard I found myself looking behind the stripes.

I found no single label like "grace" or "wisdom" or "sensitivity" that I could file neatly away for future pigeonholing of the species. But as I swung my glasses slowly along the crescent, lingering over velvety muzzles and alert black eyes, I began for the first time to see the animals as something more than ciphers in a herd. It was impossible, I found, to distinguish between the sexes but very simple to distinguish individuals. One animal near the center of the crescent stood stock-still, impassive as a riderless equestrian statue. Another faced resolutely back down the orchard so that I never saw anything but its fat slab of a butt. A third kept glancing toward the car, grazing nervously and then rechecking me before walking a few yards to graze again. Two foals lay on their sides, spread-eagled, the way foals often seemed to lie. An adult couple rested heads across each other's backs in what I was beginning to recognize as a typical zebra pose; from time to time they nibbled at each other's coats caressingly, affectionately. Nearby, a tall animal kept wrangling with neighbors, head tossing, upper lip bared. Slowly I swung the binoculars around to the right wing of the crescent. Near its tip, four adults stood together in head-resting reciprocity. They looked almost as interlocked as those infuriating little metal puzzles that relatives used to give you when you were young, no doubt hoping to keep you quiet for a few minutes. I lowered the binoculars. Once again the crescent became a line of assembled animals, of ciphers that did no more than compose the whole. But now it was different. I knew that each animal was an individual. Each had its own life, centered somewhere inside its own skin, the way each of us has a life mysteriously centered somewhere inside our skin. And each animal had its fears and foibles, its loyalties and enmities, its quirks and moods.

Now I am by no means sure that in saying "I saw individuals" I have said anything at all. Each of us knows perfectly well that every organism is an individual. We tend, though, to know it only with our intellects. So most of the time we can conveniently forget the knowledge. But during that quiet lunch in the orchard, with the black and white crescent furnishing one end of my dining room, I learned about the individuality of zebras with a certainty that seemed to hold at least some promise that I would never forget it. Not for too long at a time, anyway.

When I drove out into the middle of the orchard I had hoped that as I lunched zebras would flow past on either side of my table, close and natural and beautiful. But, except for the waiting crescent, the orchard remained empty. The few animals that drifted away from the crescent disappeared over the ridge. Not one passed between car and donga.

At first I felt disappointed, almost cheated. But it was quiet in the orchard. The road beyond the donga did not really exist. My curiously vivid first impression of the orchard's vegetation had worn off: my eyes no longer saw it as bizarre. And as I sat on in the shade of the big thorn tree and watched the zebras standing patiently in their shallow crescent I began to realize that I had had another lesson in the way things work on the savanna.

It seemed reasonable to suppose that the zebras' initial detour and persisting crescent were the standard response of a moving concourse when it came up against a barrier that posed no active threat but demanded an evasive maneuver and the kind of eternal vigilance that is the price of all freedom. Zebras were no doubt used to meeting such checks—even if they more often took the form of dozing lions than lunching Welshmen. And their response fitted in with what I was beginning to learn about the fabric of savanna life: most of the time, no dramatics; just quiet readjustment to a series of natural and often recurring situations. I was getting used to that now. Most animals, most of the time, gave the impression that they were doing whatever happened to occupy them at the moment in an aimless, almost automatic sort of way, with no real awareness of what their bodies were about— much as a man kicks the tire of a car he is thinking of buying. That was why the ebb and flow of the herds that lived on the plains—their continual drift and eddy—seemed to the casual human eye to be lacking in purpose: the movements were *not* purpose-ful—not in the sense of reflecting conscious purpose. And so, to the casual human eye, they were often incomprehensible. It was all utterly different from the straight-line way the human animal operated. Or thought he operated. Yet in the long run perhaps the results were not so different. Here on the free and open savanna, for example, we humans spent much of our time racing down confining roads toward paltry deadlines, trailing clouds of nothing more glorious than dust.

I looked at my watch: already past two-thirty. I washed up. By the time I slid into the driver's seat it was quarter to three. Only thirty miles to the Dawsons' camp—and four o'clock was hardly a rigid deadline; still, even forearmed, it seemed better not to waste too much time.

I took a last look at the zebras. As soon as I began to break camp they had become more alert, but they still stood in their long, shallow crescent. It did not make much sense, really, waiting like that instead of outflanking me. But I could not help admiring their patience, and there was something sad, now, about having to leave them.

I started the car, swung it around, and drove back through the gap in the donga. When I glanced over my shoulder for a final look at the orchard, the black and white crescent had already begun to disintegrate. I crossed the paddock and came to the road and turned north.

The road skirted the apron of a bush-clothed hill, then cut across unpaddocked parkland. The parkland was flat and open, but scattered trees grew tall and stately, eliminating all risk of monotony. Soon the road swung east, toward a shoulder of the Loita Hills. Overhead, a smattering of clouds eased westward, smudging slow shadows across the golden grass. A herd of Tommy watched me rush by. A dozen zebras trekked southward. I looked away and held the speedometer at a steady thirty.

Five miles, and the Loita Hills looming close: dark forest clothing folds and curves. The road cut through an outpost of bush, reemerged into grassland, and then, almost at the foothills, curved left. At the curve, a track angled off to the right. Beside it stood a large, white, wooden sign. I slowed down. WORLD GOSPEL MISSION, NAIKARRA, 20 MILES, said the sign. Beyond it, the track cut across grassland in a gentle curve. I stopped. Beyond the grassland stretched a belt of green trees. And beyond the trees—ten miles away, or fifteen, or perhaps even the full gospel twenty—swelled a body of low blue hills, all bosoms and cleavages. I checked my watch: ten past three. Less than fifteen miles now to the Dawsons' camp. Provided I could resist the entice-ments of this curiously intriguing sidetrack I would be there comfortably by four. Besides, I would have plenty of time to explore the track some other day.

I drove on.

Off to the left, strung black and caveman-friezelike across a paddock, a half-mile-long column of wildebeest. The animals moved slowly, almost horn to butt, in orderly single file, as if confined within an invisible channel. And suddenly I remembered a story a game warden had told me. He had taken a decidedly rural Masai into Nairobi in his Land Rover. They happened to arrive during the afternoon commuter hour, and as they passed the lines of traffic doing their bumper-to-bumper crawl back out of town, the Masai gazed wide-eyed. "*Eh, sawa sawa nyumbu tu!*" he said at last. "Why, they're just like wildebeest!"

Five more miles, and twin signs announced a boundary of Block 61. Then the road broke free of the last bush skirting the Loita Hills and I drove out onto the Loita Plains. They stretched flat and open all the way to the Dawsons' camp, and I felt myself relax. The openness somehow made it surer.

The dusty road cut northwest across the plain, arrowlike and apparently empty. But I had driven barely half a mile when I saw —though only in the instant my front wheels ran over it—a thin black line that stretched across the road from bank to low bound-ing bank. I am no longer sure whether I actually began pressing the brake pedal before or after I realized that the line was a col-umn of ants.

As soon as the car came to a stop I opened the door and looked back. The black line was no longer visible. I began to back up. It had looked like a very dense column, and with it out in the open like that I would be able to see everything that went on. I could certainly spare five or ten minutes.

My rear wheels crossed the black line before I saw it, and before I could stop, the front wheels had passed over it too. I pulled in to the side of the road and got out and walked forward.

At both places the wheels had crossed, the line had broken. I went down on one knee. Only two or three ants had been killed in each disaster area, but within the track marks and for several inches on each side of them the orderly column had disintegrated into a chaos of rampaging mobs. Individuals rushed about on erratic, unpredictable courses. There was no pattern, only seething confusion. I could almost smell the panic that prevailed down among the particles of dust, the particles that must look like boulders.

Between the track marks, order still reigned: the column flowed smoothly forward across the crown of the road—a motile black band an inch and a half wide, teeming yet disciplined. I bent closer. The ants were advancing across the dust within a shallow trench, barely visible to my coarse-grained eye, that had been pounded out by the feet of those who had already passed. Each individual marched an independent course, weaving and wavering, but not one deviated from the trench. I could almost hear the hoarse commands of the master sergeants, up and down the line. Or perhaps it was the crack of flailing whips. I bent even closer and waited until a puff of breeze had died away. Then I held my breath. I *could* hear something! Up from the column came a low rustle, a sort of subclinical buzzing, so faint that it took me a moment or two to penetrate my own picket line of disbelief.

I sat back on my heels. Somehow I had never thought of ants as making any kind of noise. But now that I came to think of it there was no reason at all why they should not. In fact, there seemed every reason to assume that, like many insects, they might make sounds that were audible even to coarse-tuned human ears. I leaned forward again and moved my head along the column until it arrived above the left-hand disaster area. There, among the mobs, was where the noise seemed loudest. So perhaps the buzzing meant confusion or fear or anger or all three. There was no doubt about the confusion, down there among the dust-boulders. Fear certainly seemed a reasonable enough reaction to expect if you had just been run over four times in succession by roaring, crunching, incomprehensible juggernauts. And before long I found evidence of anger.

Near my feet, where the advancing column hit the left-hand disaster area, it lost its cohesion: as the leading ants met the mob they fanned out on both sides of the line of advance, much as the point platoon of a column of human soldiers will deploy when it comes under enemy fire. And soon I sighted a patrol advancing on my feet.

Although the patrol's members appeared to act independently, they had all zeroed in on my moccasins. And they advanced without check, looking recklessly determined as they veered and tacked around stones twice their size, three times their size, twenty times their size. Flailing legs flicked aside dust-boulders. Thrusting bodies rocked towering pebble-crags.

One of the ants reached the toe of my left moccasin and began to climb it. From his head projected vicious-looking pincers. He closed on the row of lacing holes that ringed the top of the moccasin. The moccasins were old, going on ancient, and at most of the lacing holes there was plenty of room for you to pass between lace and leather if you were a determined ant out on a fighting patrol. I tapped my toe on the ground, sharply. The climbing ant fell off. But the movement galvanized the patrol into even greater effort. And I thought, though I could not be sure, that I detected an increase in the number of individuals questing about in open country where column met disaster area. Some of these reinforcements were already moving toward my foot.

I retreated a full thirty inches. The patrol's ardor seemed to slacken. One or two members even showed signs of weaving back the way they had come.

A distant pounding began to beat against the edges of my consciousness. For an instant, with my mind still down beside the boulder-strewn trench, I was eerily aware that the sound had a huge, sky-filling, otherworldly quality. I felt a first half-prickle of fear. Then I looked up. And there in my regular world, two hundred yards away, pounding down the road toward me and sucking along its dust cloud, came a zebra-painted minibus.

I went far enough back into the regular world to move off

the road. The minibus pounded closer. It slowed, as if to offer help. I waved it on. It picked up speed again. It passed. Faces peered from windows. Hands waved.

I waved back. It was, I am sure, a half-hearted kind of wave. Memory suggested, faintly, that the humans in the minibus were having a wonderful time. But a sizable sector of me was still down there on the road among the dust-boulders and pebble-crags, cowering beneath the roar and pound and crunch of two more incomprehensible juggernauts.

The minibus receded. The din subsided. The dust cloud drifted slowly westward across the plain, thinning toward extinction. I glanced at my watch: still only three twenty-five. I could spare a few more minutes.

I hurried back to the trench.

This time there was remarkably little disturbance at the places the wheels had pounded over: weak patrols probing the flanks, nothing more. Beyond, on the long slope down to the bank that bounded the road, the army continued to advance. I followed the black line of the column down the slope and up the bank and on through a forest of grass. The head of the column was disappearing, like a stream of black water, into a small hole in the baked brown soil. I walked back along the column, pacing. From hole to rearguard it measured twenty feet.

I went back to the head of the column. Just short of the hole, the line of march crossed a patch of bare soil. I squatted down, bent close, and held my breath. There was no breeze now. But I could detect no sound rising from the column. I peered down into the throng of black, glossy, jostling bodies. There were at least two distinct kinds of ant. The bigger and more robust individuals, about a quarter of an inch long, were the pincer-equipped kind that had patrolled out toward my moccasins. With some confidence I labeled them "soldiers." The small and rather frail-looking ones had brown heads. I peered closer. Either they had brown heads or every one of them was carrying a large, round, brown object in its mouth. Could they be transporting eggs? To a new nest, perhaps? I peered even closer. But still I could not decide whether what I saw was head or burden. There was too much bustle, down there in the trench. What I needed was a close, unobstructed inspection of one individual. I broke off a blade of grass and held its base down in the seething black stream in front of a scurrying brown-head. Neatly and without hesitation, the brown-head sidestepped my spar from the sky and went determinedly on its way. I probed again. And again. And again. Each time it was the same. But at each attempt I captured a whole troop of soldiers: the moment I lowered the grass blade they converged on it and, as far as I could see, attacked it savagely with their pincers. Two or three always began to climb up toward my hand. Face to face like that, finger to pincer, they once again looked appallingly fierce and determined.

I had just shaken one of them off the grass blade when I noticed, three or four inches from the column, among tall grass at the edge of the clearing, two ants locked in fierce combat.

One of the ants was a soldier. The other looked twice as big as any I had seen in the column, and it had a mat-finish armor altogether different from that of the glossy-bodied ants in the main army. I moved over for a ringside view. But the fight's ferocity hid all fine detail. Locked head to head, the antagonists writhed and lurched and rocked and rolled and floundered and pitched and staggered and stumbled and tumbled and twitched and jerked. And their frenzied flailings never let up. So furious was the action that I could not even see who gripped whose head. On the whole, the somber giant seemed to be dragging the glossy soldier along in spite of the way his frantic legs kept hooking around blades of grass; but if the plan was to carry him captive to some secret stronghold, it was not going well. The fight raged in erratic, inconclusive circles, never looking as if it would spill outside the jungle patch of towering grass, four or five inches across, in which I had first seen it.

After a while a second soldier, apparently passing through that corner of the jungle by accident, came to his comrade's assistance. He closed on the giant, grabbed hold of a leg with his pincers, and hung on. The trio thrashed about in the under-

growth, a confused, palpitating structure of black blobs and con-
necting black lines, like a working model of an organic molecule
in extreme Brownian motion. Then the contortions of this loosely
linked structure levered it up more than an inch into some thick
grass on the edge of the jungle patch; and at apogee the second
soldier lost his grip. He fell. For a moment he was tumbling
headlong, a lonely atom seeking new linkage. He landed in open
country. Briefly, he ran in confused circles. Then he scurried off
toward the column.

The original combatants fought on, apparently oblivious of
where their convulsions carried them. Down into a sun-filled
clearing of the jungle they fell, then levered themselves back up
into a tangle of dark vegetation. And all the time, no matter
where the battle raged, there was no letup in its ferocity, no sign
of weariness, no hint of a slackening in fatal purpose.

I watched in growing awe.

At last I became vaguely conscious that the light had bright-
ened and the sun was beating down on my unprotected head—and
that my hat was in the car. I fumbled in my shorts pocket and
found a piece of string and bundled it into a loose mat and pushed
it under the ants. They battled on. To and fro across the string
they struggled, then deep into its meshes. I carried them to the
car, laid out their mat in the middle of the hood, found my hat
on the front seat, jammed it on my head, and hurried back to the
hood.

The ants had fallen off their string mat. And now there was a
change. The soldier's flailing legs could find no purchase on the
car's smooth paintwork and the giant was backing steadily and
dragging the soldier more or less as he pleased. But he seemed to
derive little profit from the achievement: the contest still moved
in erratic, inconsequential circles around the huge, white, glaring
desert of the hood. I suffered a twinge of guilt. If you are going
to observe free nonhuman nature you should strive to do so without interfering: you should neither rescue the weak from the
strong nor knowingly tilt the scales of any battle. (Removing a
tortoise from the man-created perils of a road is perhaps a differ-

ent matter. Perhaps.) The reason we should try not to interfere is that the natural forces that select the fittest individuals from a population are almost always too complex and also too blind for us to understand or even to detect when we see them at work in any isolated event—and our parochial, though necessary, human concepts of justice and cruelty are almost guaranteed to lead us astray. But by moving the ants' titanic struggle onto my car hood I had undoubtedly tilted a scale: the solder no longer had blades of grass to hook his legs around; and the smooth paintwork obviously impaired the gripping power of both combatants' legs. Still, there was no denying the difference in spectator comfort between my ringside stand at the car hood and a ringside squat at the grassy jungle patch. So I compromised. I slipped a sheet of yellow typing paper under the ants and sprinkled a handful of roadside dust onto it. Then I picked a few blades of grass and scattered them on the dust and finger-nailed the grappling ants onto the dust. The soldier's flailing legs began to find occasional purchase. The giant's backpedaling lost momentum. My conscience recomposed itself.

The gladiators had met each change in their arena with magnificent disdain. Locked head to head in the same grip as when I first saw them, they had battled on without letup. But at last I began to detect some slight slackening of tempo. Once, just for a moment, both bodies paused long enough for me to see the giant's pincers locked like a vise around the isthmus joining the soldier's head and thorax. Then the struggle resumed. But now the soldier was failing. At times he did little more than writhe feebly in the giant's grip. It had to happen in the end, of course. It always happened in the end, even in those old-time marathon prize fights in which bare-fisted professionals hammered it out, round after savage round, apparently for hour after hour. And even assuming that I had come in near the start of this fight, these two had been at it for a long time. A very long time. I began to glance at my watch.

Raising my wrist was enough. The movement established connections. Even before I saw the watch I had moved back to the fringe of my regular world. Then the watch came up white and solid in front of my eyes and its hands were proclaiming half past four.

I stood staring at it. More than an hour since I drove over the black line of the road. Almost ten miles to the Dawsons' camp. All the same, I could still make it before five. The only question was whether five o'clock was a bit too late in the day.

Still debating, I carried the sheet of yellow paper back onto the grass, located the original jungle patch, and decanted the ants into it. They battled on. Come to think of it, the Dawsons had seemed to invite me carte blanche. So perhaps it would be all right. But I lingered a little longer, squatting above the fight, still half mesmerized. The soldier had almost reached the end of his tether. Soon the giant pulled him clear of the jungle patch and began to drag him, still writhing, across open dust country.

Something made me look up. Fifty yards away, on the far side of a patch of long grass, a male Tommy was bounding away with the peculiar stiff-legged gait called "stotting" that is said to indicate alarm. I glanced at the patch of long grass. It looked more than thick enough to hide a crouching lion. A prickly sensation skimmed down my spine. The Tommy stopped. I checked him through glasses. His eyes were fixed on me rather than on the long grass. I stood up and rechecked the grass. It looked very thin now. Far too thin, certainly, to hide a lurking lion.

I looked down at my feet. Nothing, from that height, except scraggly grass and baked red earth.

I turned and began to walk back toward the car. Disaster areas up and down the road, desperately real. Mortal battles, titanic on every scale except physical size. Sudden death, or the sudden fear of it, always lurking in the golden grass, no matter what you were doing. Even within the Mara's beauty and harmony, life could be grim.

I came to the road and stood looking down at the faint trench the army of ants had pounded out with their passing feet. Empty, it looked very forlorn. And then I began to smile. Life on the Mara, even in miniature detail, was by no means unrelievedly grim. Like life in most places, it was good and bad, soft and savage, frightful and ecstatic. In the middle of the road, close beside the ants' trench, clearly convinced that no one would be watching them, were two black beetles, copulating.*

I got into the car and began to drive down the road. Provided I did not stop again I could still be there by five. The question remained, though, whether it might not be better to camp nearby and go in the morning. After all, the Dawsons had expected to leave some time next day, and on this last evening they might have some kind of family party. Perhaps I ought not to risk intruding. . . .

And then, still in the midstream of my indecision, I saw a pair of ground hornbills.

Like the morning quartet, they were advancing slowly across open ground, hunting as they went. And I saw at once that, because they were moving down a long, gentle slope, I would be able to taxi along beside them with the engine switched off and would with luck be able to get close enough to make sure about the eyelashes.

My indecision evaporated. The civil time to visit the Dawsons was obviously the morning.

I took my time working in close. But at last I was almost as near to the leftmost bird as I had been to the left-wing member of the morning's quartet. Except for occasional glances, it ignored me. I switched off the engine. The world was suddenly very quiet. Outside my open window, tires crunched over dry grass. We went on down the slope. Light touches on the brake pedal were enough to hold me in station and now, with the engine silent, the bird seemed totally tolerant of my presence. I edged closer. Ten yards. Eight. Seven. Finally, no more than four or five. And then there was no point in trying to edge closer: even with my binoculars screwed fully out, the red face mask of the nearest hornbill kept blurring in too close to focus.

We went on down the slope. The grass complained quietly at

---

* For remarkably parallel behavior in two-legged coleoptera, see—or rather hear—the quartet's exhortation in their generically titled white album (side 2, band 7). See also—photographically and explicitly and twice—the jacket of the post-Dissolution McCartney *Ram*.

the tires' oppression. The bird walked, annexed morsels, flip-gargled them down, walked again. I watched its one visible eye. The sun sank lower.

And at last, at a moment when my binoculars had the black tube surrounding the eye-porthole gripped in precise, knife-edge focus, the bird stopped. It stood motionless, porthole swiveled forward. I held my breath, screwed my eyes to the sticking point. The tube stood out against the face mask like an ebony carving displayed on red velvet. Sunlight glinted on its surface. And in that sharp and gleaming moment I was very nearly sure—though not sure beyond all shadow of error—that the tube was made of eyelashes that spiraled up and away from the eye's margin in a dense, meshing helix. The degree of twist was not very great; but it seemed enough, with each hair pressed flush against its neighbor, to lock the structure rigid.

For perhaps three seconds the bird held its pose. Then it moved, and the fine edge of focus blunted. But the picture was still there, sharp in my memory. And it made sense. For the tube's helical construction no doubt meant that the hairs could fold down flat and so perform what was probably one of the more orthodox functions of eyelashes: blocking out light that might intrude between lids closed for sleep.

The hornbill resumed its promenade. I let it go. There was no way I could get a closer look, here on the savanna. Confirmation would have to come from some other source. I glanced westward, toward the Triangle. Another ten minutes and the black line of the Isuria Escarpment would snuff out the sun. I started the car, drove back to the road, and turned north.

Far ahead, out on the evenness of the rolling plain, something gleamed white. I stopped, picked up the binoculars. It was an isolated rocky outcrop—the kind of feature always known in East Africa by the Afrikaans name, *kopje* (pronounced "copy"). This kopje looked the sort of interesting place that something would surely call home; and beyond it ran the line of trees that I knew must hide the Dawsons' camp. I drove on down the road toward it.

Beyond the plain, high above the bush country north of Narok, sunlight still gilded a huge dome of black and threatening clouds, but all around me the rays struck thin and almost level. Before I had driven two miles the Isuria Escarpment had cut them off. Evening washed across the plain. Its pastels began their slow slide toward monochrome. I put on a sweater.

Soon the kopje stood pale against the darkening sky, half a mile to my right. I found a place to turn off the road and began to drive up a smooth, grassy slope. Now the kopje was little more than a jagged blackness against the almost black sky. Northward, beyond Narok, the towering cloud dome had melded with the night.

I drove without lights. Rohosinante responded and we floated up through the pale half-darkness. But soon the slope steepened and the grass grew coarse. Small flotsam obstacles surfaced. A wheel hit something hard. I switched on the headlights.

The beams cut a brilliant, efficient swathe. Each passing tussock, for its moment on stage, stood stark and vivid. Each stone was sculpture. But outside the moving beams the night had dropped like a set of black velvet curtains and cut me off from the plain.

I swung right to skirt one of the gaping holes that ant bears dig in their quests for termites. And suddenly, on the margin between light and night, less than ten yards away, there were shapes. I spun the steering wheel. My swathe transfixed the shapes. I stopped. All four of them were peering at me: gray, black-spotted bodies; big, rounded ears; big, wistful eyes set in powerful faces with curiously ambivalent expressions, half tragic, half comic.

For perhaps four seconds we held our tableau. Then one of the hyenas turned its head. From behind it emerged two much smaller animals. For a moment I took them to be bat-eared foxes, but almost at once I realized that the ears were too small. The black bodies and brown heads were wrong too. Besides, hyenas probably ate foxes. I reexamined the two small faces. And this time, looking for it, I found beneath the rounded blandness of youth the first hints of both tragedy and comedy. The mark came earlier in hyenas, then, than in the other tragicomic species.

The young hyenas retreated behind the adults and almost at once the whole party turned and moved out of the light. I backed a yard or two, swinging the headlight beams after them. The young had already vanished. The four adults were loping away across grassland so thickly pitted with the shadowed black saucers of ant bear holes that it looked like a heavily shelled battlefield. I sat and watched the gray shapes lope away with their curious almost-forgot-my-hind-legs-again limp.

I watched until the night had ingested them. Then I swung the car left and drove on up the slope. Outside, there was once more only the swathe, white and brilliant, probing the blackness. Inside, I had the simple dials of Rohosinante's dash.

Twenty minutes later, on the far side of the kopje—cut off by its bulk from the pinpoint lights of the Dawsons' camp, my own territory solidly established with table and chair and hissing white lamplight, my tent already squatting blue and orange and comforting on the lamplight's fringe—I sat down and opened a bottle of beer. A sausage fly came barreling out of the night and thudded against the lamp glass and fell, stunned, onto the shining, brown-grained tabletop. I took another sip of beer and let it wash, alive, around the flanks of my tongue.

A big black beetle thumped against the lamp and fell to the table. It was a solid, hump-shouldered creature, about an inch long, encased in shining black armor. I sat staring at it. Squatting there—encased, saturnine, gleaming, impenetrable—it would, but for one feature, have given about as much promise of information as a defensive tackle with his helmet on. The exception was the creature's horn. This huge black erection—a perfect miniature rhino horn—curved up and back from the little shrunken pea of a head, dwarfing it. I barely had time to decide that the creature would unquestionably be known as a "rhino beetle" before my mind was reporting an echo.

A week earlier I had interviewed in a Nairobi garden a chameleon from whose head protruded just such a "rhino horn." And now, sitting there content in my dome of lamplight, sipping cool beer and looking at the horn protruding from the beetle's head, I found myself struggling to formulate a question.

The structures that life forms had evolved to meet the demands of the earth's environment tended to follow repeated patterns: ears, eyes, bendable limbs in pairs. Even less common responses such as scaly protective armor or swim bladders or pairs of horns arranged side by side on top of the head tended to be widespread among certain groups: paired horns, as far as I knew, were restricted to mammals—but a considerable number of mammal species carried them. And oddities often turned out to be mere variations on established themes: the hornbills' eye hoods, for example, looked like being modified eyelashes. But here were three comprehensively unrelated creatures—one insect, one reptile, one mammal—all bearing on their heads, centrally mounted, horns of almost identical form: thick at the base, tapering fairly uniformly, and curving backward without convolution. I could think of no other animals, even close relatives, that sported similar structures.

I opened another bottle of beer and started to cook dinner. The rhino beetle began to crawl across the tabletop. As I watched its laborious progress I tried to speculate on the horn's function, but my mind kept coming back to chameleons and rhinos. The coincidence of form in their horns did not seem to be a case of "convergent evolution"—the name given to evolution's habit of coming up with remarkably similar structures (sharks and dolphins, for example) when totally dissimilar life forms (in that case, a fish and a mammal) faced similar ways of life. After all, it was difficult to conceive of any common process that might have helped mold these three horns. And each horn was made of different material: rhino "horn" was not horn at all but closely packed, hairlike fiber that grew from the skin; the chameleon's horn had looked like genuine horn and would, in any case, hardly be hair; this beetle's horn seemed to be made of the same shining black substance as its armor. For some reason, this diversity of materials worried me, and during dinner I tried, rather vaguely, to formulate my worry into a coherent question. But by the end of the meal I do not think I had done any better than, "What the hell goes on here?" *

I pushed aside my empty dinner plate. The beetle took off with a whirr and shouldered his way out into the night. I leaned back. All day the questions had kept turning up—some straightforward, some nonsense, some barely half framed. Another emerged: "Why are many young animals a different color from their parents?" The day had shown me topi and hyenas, and there were no doubt plenty more: spotted lion cubs and dappled American fawns for a start. In birds, come to think of it, the arrangement was almost standard. Was it simply ontogeny echoing phylogeny—the growth of the individual, from conception, echoing the evolution of the species? Or did the young gain some advantage from their disguise? For example, did the color difference ensure that adults did not react to defenseless young in the hostile way they would react to strange adults that invaded the herd or family circle? That might be it. Anyway, the idea was worth following up sometime: it was the sort of thing that could help in making the connections that I would soon have to start making. There was no hurry though. Most of the answers would come in the end—not necessarily during these brief weeks of reconnaissance, of course; more likely in the months of real research, when I came back. Then, there would be plenty of days as free as this one had been.

I drank the last of the beer. It had been a good day, this first

---

* Later, when untrammeled by two large bottles of beer, I produced: "What combination of factors presently known to us can account for the evolution of this precise structural form on three unrelated animals, in roughly the same position on their bodies but in materials of disparate nature and apparently in response to totally different demands?"

I am by no means convinced that this mound of verbiage really poses a meaningful question. But I know a question is still there all right, quirking around inside me.

It turns out, by the way, that I was wrong about there being no other animal with a "rhino horn." Similar structures appear on several other East African chameleons and also—though paired side by side—on two African snakes, the gaboon and rhinoceros vipers. But I do not think these minor extensions invalidate my question. If it is a question.

"free" one. A very good day. Less than forty miles in nine hours, that was how good. Parkinson and beyond. As usual, nothing much had happened, but the savanna's routine events had held me tight. Looking back, I could measure just how tight their grip had been: I had not even remembered to stop for afternoon tea.

Lightning flashed, off to the north. So it was still there, that towering dome, still billowing up, layer on black layer, somewhere above the high country beyond Narok.

A cool breeze brushed my bare legs. It too came from the north. I could not remember a north wind before, here on the Mara. It almost always blew from the east. I drew air deep into my lungs. Again the lightning flashed. It seemed closer now, but I could still hear no thunder. The breeze came again: stronger, cooler, sharper. Once more I inhaled, trying to make sure. This time there was no doubt: rain, quite close.

I began to stow the food back into Rohosinante. But I did not really hurry. It had been a good, clean smell. And it too had brought, along with its warning, more than a hint of a promise.

I eased up on one elbow and peered out through the mosquito netting: grayness and slanting drizzle and little blobs of water sliding sullenly down nylon guy lines. I went back to sleep. When I levered myself out of the tent at last it was eight o'clock and still drizzling.

Through binoculars I found a cluster of tents in among the line of trees, a mile across the plain, exactly where Dawson had marked his camp on my map. I found a Land Rover too, and a lorry. But I could see no sign of movement, no hint of smoke.

After breakfast there was still no sign of life in the Dawsons' camp, and for almost two hours I sat in the car and rewrote and re-revised the letter to Narok County Council and then retyped it with a spare copy for Tipis. By the time it was done the last tiptoe patterings on the car roof had stopped, though clouds still hung low over the gray plain. I rechecked the Dawsons' camp: a slow spiral of smoke; and then moving figures. Even at that range I seemed to detect in the way the figures moved a hint of the heavy, yawn-infested, mind-still-halfway-lurching-through-dreams, yes-guilty-dammit-though-I don't-know-why kind of oppression that always burdens you when you have lain in bed too long, no matter how unsoiled your reasons. Fortunately it is a load that can be floated free if flooded with tea or coffee.

Half an hour later I turned off the road into the *vlei* that supported the line of trees in which I had seen the camp. (A vlei—an Afrikaans word rooted in the same origins as "valley" but pronounced "flay"—is a piece of flat, low-lying ground, normally long and narrow, into which water drains. After heavy rain it may become a swamp but once it dries out the grass grows lush. Sometimes big trees prosper by tapping all year long the moisture locked up in the rich, deep soil that the centuries have spread.)

I followed a track through the trees. Even wrapped in grayness, the vlei was a beautiful place. Pale grass stretched flat and even, cropped short like a lawn. From it, at wide-spaced intervals, rose the yellow trunks of fever trees. Sixty feet above, their huge umbrella canopies halfway hid the lowering clouds.

About a quarter of a mile into this English-country-seat parkland I came to the Dawsons' camp. There were half a dozen tents and two vehicles. The family stood grouped, cups in hand, under the green canvas awning that was their dining room. This time there were only four of them: Jock Dawson, his wife, and two of the children.

"Took the two older ones back to school last Monday," said Dawson.

Soon I found myself sitting down to a second breakfast.

"Hell of a time for it, I know," said Dawson cheerfully. "But if you're striking camp on a day like this what else can you do except lie in and wait? Thank God it doesn't happen often in the Mara this time of year."

Over eggs and bacon I found myself launching for some reason into a story about a wedding in a Dawson family that I had known in my farming days—the family to whom Jock Dawson had said he was distantly related.

Fergus Dawson's bachelor party had been a wow, even by Kenya standards. Next morning I had for medicinal purposes inspected on foot and in detail many fields that did not absolutely demand inspection. The earth had palpitated before my eyes and trembled beneath my feet, but by noon the fresh air and exercise had injected me with a fair degree of stability and after lunch I had felt fit enough to sample the wedding. Over the first glass of champagne somebody had said, "That was quite an earthquake we had this morning, wasn't it?" "Earthquake?" I had said. "What earthquake?"

As I finished my story, Mrs. Dawson smiled. "Yes, it was quite a wedding too, wasn't it?" she said. "I'd almost forgotten."

And our eyes met across the table.

Now I do not mean that we flirted briefly and innocently, the way it sometimes happens at such moments. And we drew blanks on further common memories: her maiden name meant nothing to me, and she clearly did not remember me at all. It had been a big wedding, anyway, and we probably never met. But for me, at least, the conversation was a little different after that moment our eyes met across the table, across almost twenty years. From then on, sitting there under the big green canvas awning, sharing breakfast with that very typical settler family, I came closer than at any time since I had landed in Mombasa to remembering how it had been to be the young farm manager who lived near Nakuru. I do not mean I achieved anything that even bordered on total recall. But for a while that far-off young man was no longer a total stranger.

During breakfast the clouds began to thin, and by the time we had finished snippets of blue sky were sailing past above the treetops. Soon the sun had pinned strings of glistening beads on grass and trees and tents and awnings and even on the sullen, no-nonsense vehicles.

The Dawsons began packing. Jock supervised two Africans striking tents and we went on talking.

I mentioned the hyenas near the kopje.

"Yes, there's a surprising lot of them around, and they don't miss much. The other day I was all lined up on a zebra I wanted when a male wildebeest moved into my line of sight just as I squeezed the trigger. The bullet hit him low in the neck and he dashed off on his own, swerving and staggering all over the place. But he'd hardly gone fifty yards when a hyena came racing out of a patch of scrub and began to close in from behind. There was something awfully deliberate about the way it happened, as if the whole thing had been planned, almost as if it had been rehearsed. And when the hyena caught up with the wildebeest it lunged forward, just once, and bit his balls off. You've never seen anything so neat and clean. The wildebeest went straight down. I drove over and put the poor thing out of its misery, and by the time we'd driven a hundred yards away there were three hyenas feeding on the carcass."

For a while it was all hunting talk.

"No, it didn't take the zebras long to cotton on. When we started we could drive to within fifty yards of them and they'd just stand there and look at us until I shot one. But for weeks now I haven't been able to get closer than about three hundred yards, and of course that makes the job a lot harder. For one thing, we've got to be careful we only shoot stallions. One of T-B's rangers is with us all the time, anyway. And the skins have got to be perfect. No cuts or marks of any kind, or we'll never be able to sell 'em. And we've got a license for exactly eight hundred skins, not one more, so you can bet your life we scout out every animal we shoot pretty bloody carefully."

The two Africans finished striking the tents and began stowing them in the Land Rover. Dawson and I strolled a few yards from camp, toward the edge of the trees.

I asked if the skins turned a good profit.

Dawson smiled. "Oh, with luck we'll about break even. Might even make a few quid. But I don't really do it for the money, you know. I'd make a hell of a lot more sticking on the farm. But doing this gives us a free holiday. Eight weeks of it we've had, with a couple of weeks back on the farm in the middle. Wonderful. For the whole family, I mean. In fact, I think I do it for the kids more than anything else. To them, this is the only life—camping, and then going out every morning after the game. I told you we took the two older ones back to school the other day? Well, you've no idea the job we had, getting them off." He smiled. "Almost a revolt!"

We came to the edge of the trees. Dawson stopped and stood looking out over the plain. He was still smiling. The last cloud shadows were scurrying westward across the golden grass. All around us, sunlight streamed through the thorn-tree canopy and the bead-strings still glistened.

Dawson sighed. His smile tilted at one edge. "This morning," he said, "I could stage a sizable revolt myself."

From somewhere out beyond the trees came a familiar, staccato clapper-rattle. I tried to locate the bird that I knew must be hovering, a tiny silhouette, somewhere against the brightness of the sky.

"That *brrr* noise?" said Dawson. "Oh yes, that's a flappet lark. No mistaking its mating display."

We stood a while at the edge of the trees, looking out across the rolling savanna, then strolled back to camp.

The two Africans had finished stowing the tents. "*Tapanga ngozi sasa, Bwana?*" asked one of them. "Shall we load the skins now?"

"*Ndio*," said Dawson, and walked toward the lorry.

I watched him go. He walked well. Balanced and controlled. Confident but without airs. A man at reasonable peace with himself. And as I watched him go I found myself wondering why it was that as the years passed so it became more and more difficult to find things that would stay pinned neatly down so that you could love them or hate them without doubts and reservations and glimpses of the other damned side of the coin. When you were young you saw right and wrong in everything, clear and shining. But it didn't last. Once you had accomplished the change it was very satisfying, of course, knowing you were so Christly tolerant. Sometimes, though, there was the suspicion that it had left you halfway castrated. And it was still far from easy to accept every time, click, that you could like somebody very much but detest what he was doing. The proposition was only a notch less unpalatable than its equally self-evident obverse: you could heartily dislike somebody but thoroughly approve of what he was doing. Anyway, it was hopeless, trying to dislike Dawson. He was certainly not an evil man; by most standards, he was not even a doer of evil deeds. As I watched him stop and unlatch the tail-gate of his lorry I found myself wondering, more than a little hopefully, if he was the kind of man the young farm manager from Nakuru would have grown into if he had never left Kenya.

He moved out of sight on the far side of the lorry and I walked forward to join him. As I came around the tailgate he was bending down and pulling aside a big green tarpaulin protecting what I had assumed were stores of some kind. Underneath, stacked on another tarpaulin, dazzling in the dappled sunlight, lay two piles of zebra skins.

"These are the last of 'em," said Dawson. "The last twenty-five. At least, I hope there are twenty-five."

The two Africans began loading the skins onto the lorry. Dawson counted them as they went in and made sure that each one fitted neatly at the edges, without sharp bends or buckles. "You've got to be so damned careful with 'em," he said, pushing at a stiff black and white wafer that protruded between two of the lorry's stout wooden side-slats.

And afterward, when I had said good-bye—leaving Dawson and his wife smiling and the two children standing golden-haired and happy—when I had left them alone to say good-bye to their camp beneath the trees, when I had driven back to the road and turned south toward Keekorok and had come out of the trees onto the open plain, when I had done all these things and they had washed over my mind one after the other and had begun the slow, lifetime work that all events begin merely by happening—the work of eroding from your memory, molecule by molecule, the way wind and water erode a mountain, all preceding events except the most craggily vivid—when I had done all these small things and had begun to move southward across the sunlit plain, it was the zebra skins that, above all, stood vivid and craggy and unveilable in the proscenium of my memory.

The skins had been flat and stiff. Laid out on the dark tarpaulin in sunlight that streamed down through living trees, they were flat and lifeless, flat and two-dimensional, flat and pasteboard thin. And in their flatness and their stiffness they were closer to unyielding, zebra-painted minibuses than to the living animals they had once enclosed. The black and white stripes were still there, were still bizarrely beautiful. But that was all.

Each skin had been slit down the length of its belly and along the underside of the neck to the tip of the muzzle. The muzzle, no longer velvet and quivering, had been squashed flat. Even the nostrils were flat. They lay side by side, distorted, dessicated, flat as a pair of old, shrunken cowpats. The thin, flat legs stuck stiffly out. They were awkward, inert, gruesome.

In that whole lorry load of skins, stacked one on top of the other like so many Formica sheets, I had detected no hint that each skin once clothed a breathing, pulsing, unpredictable animal and held it intact and separate from the rest of the world, the way skins hold all of us intact and private. The stacked pasteboards had nothing whatever to do with individuals that wandered free on the sunlit plain or waited patiently in shallow crescents, living out lives of their own, each life mysteriously centered some-where inside a skin, each life colored by its own set of fears and foibles, loyalties and enmities, quirks and moods. The skins in the lorry were not even ciphers in a herd. They were chattels. Their owners had been liquidated, cancelled. The remains had been re-duced to their most superficial and least meaningful terms. And now—still bizarrely beautiful but nothing more, nothing more at all—they would be hawked around the surface of the earth for money and more money and more money, palm into itchy palm, until they were sold at last, one by one, as baubles and trappings for individuals of another species—individuals with minds so shabby and crippled that they had still not even glimpsed the nature of the terrible things their species was doing to the rest of the world.

And as I moved on southward across the sunlit Loita Plains, driving angrily fast, I knew that what I had seen at the Dawsons' camp was only a still, small start to something that hung thick in the East African air. It was a clean start too, out in the open, close to the soil, carried out by people about as uncorrupted by the profit motive as any of us is likely to remain.

It would not end there.

In high local places, game-cropping schemes were being hatched by the clutch. The newspapers—and also the wildlife management conference I had attended in Nairobi—were full of realistic, practical, hard-nosed projects that dealt in "surplus wild-life populations" and "protein deficiencies in human diets" and "elephant abattoirs" and "exploitable markets." The projects did not spare game parks and reserves. And they would be operated by the kind of realistic, practical, hard-nosed men who are essential for the efficient operation of such projects—the sort of eminently practical men who, undreaming and rudderless, have overseen the rape of our planet. An Englishman at the wildlife conference had shown slides of an elephant abattoir in Zambia. It was a gaunt, concrete slab of a building, erupting from green bush like a cancer. You could almost smell it, there in the lecture hall. The Englishman was very proud of his abattoir, and everyone had seemed hugely impressed.

The arguments behind such a project are always eminently sound, practical, realistic and humanitarian: the elephants have grown too numerous and are out of balance with their environment and are destroying it; the human population is starved of protein; an abattoir will solve both problems and will also provide employment and money-income.

When you oppose such a project because you know in your gut that it stinks you often run into difficulties: you find yourself raising mundane, practical, realistic, humanitarian objections. I had done exactly that after the wildlife conference, and I did it again that day as I drove south and fast across the Loita Plains. For one thing, I advised the unheeding savanna, cropping would reduce the animals' game-viewing value: hunted zebras, Dawson had said, soon learned to give vehicles a wide berth. It would also lower their general standard of health: left alone, a population that outgrows the resources of its environment is culled and kept up to date by processes that spare those individuals best suited to survive the ever-changing conditions; man cannot begin to match such subtle efficiency even when armed with the loftiest of criteria for killing, and he certainly will not do so when he shoots only those individuals whose skins seem most likely to fetch a high human price.

But even as I formulated these objections I knew they missed the real point. I had done better after the wildlife conference. Then, I had objected in private conversation that the elephant abattoir would become as self-perpetuating as most of man's works. When the elephant population had been culled to its "correct" level, would men really call a halt to the killing and thereby write off the capital invested in the abattoir and also dismiss the administrators and hunters and butchers and drivers and distributors whose livelihoods had come to depend on the project? And would they simply tell the people who had come to depend on the protein that there was no more?

That objection had at least seemed a sniff less Pecksniffian than the others; but I knew it would not do. What I wanted was something more fundamental. When asked on a Nairobi radio program, "But what use is an elephant?" I had volunteered to provide a satisfactory answer just as soon as someone produced a satisfactory answer to the question, "What use is a man?"

At the time I had felt rather pleased with myself. After all, everyone at the conference had seemed to assume without question, as most humans still assume in their hearts, that the earth was made for man. But now, driving away from the Dawsons' camp, I was not so sure about my cleverness. Many people I respected, such as T-B, had apparently come to the conclusion that the only way to save the animals was to make them economically profitable. And cropping was one of the big sticks. So as a practical matter I would probably have to accept it as an interim measure, until the local peoples became well enough fed and then enlightened enough to see matters differently. But the idea still stank.

I came to the edge of the plain and began to cut through thin bush skirting the Loita Hills. And all at once I saw that there was nothing wrong with cropping. It was poetically as well as scientifically valid. It had not been carried to its logical conclusion, that was all. I would hurl my support behind any such scheme provided the species that caused all the disharmony would count ourselves in, along with the rest.

And after that I found myself driving more slowly: there is something cathartic as well as triumphant about the conviction—justified or not—that you have forced logic into mesh with things as you know they are.

The road swung westward. And there on the left stood the big white sign: WORLD GOSPEL MISSION, NAIKARRA, 20 MILES. Beyond it the track curved toward green trees and beyond the trees lay the curvaceous body of blue hills. I stopped. The rain had washed the midday light into early-morning freshness, and the track and the trees and the hills beckoned even more insidiously than they had done the day before.

I consulted the map. Six or seven miles ahead, the track forked. One branch held southeasterly, skirting the Loita Hills. The other cut southwest, to Keekorok Lodge. Whichever route you took to the lodge—regular road or gospel track—it was still between thirty and forty miles. I glanced at my watch: one o'clock. I had already decided to camp just short of the Sanctuary that night and make an early morning start for the Serengeti Research Institute, so there was plenty of time to take what would no doubt be the slower route. I put the map away.

At the first trees the track plunged into and then careened up out of a deep, dry donga. It was the kind of obstacle only a tank driver could safely ignore and I paused on its brink before easing Rohosinante forward. Going down was like rowboating down a short, steep sea. And as soon as we had leveled off in the trough the exit slope was filling my windshield, its pale brown dust steep as an adobe wall. Rohosinante's head went up. I felt her take the bit between those ridiculous little front wheels. And then we were up and over and the track was only half as well used as before and grass humped high in its center and twice within fifty yards Rohosinante had scuffed bottom. The bush began to press in tight, very tight. The Loita Hills were rising steep and rough just off to the left and the track had grown even narrower—and all at once I was aware that we were in perfect rhino and buffalo country and perhaps elephant country too and that the bush was more than thick enough now to hide any of them, close and unpredictable, anyplace. We went on. The bush pressed tighter, taller, thicker.

And after less than a mile we came to the stream.

It was only a little bit of a stream, and when I got out and tested the rushing brown water with a stick the bottom was stony and solid and only two feet down. But when I got back into the car and drove forward, clutch slipping, it seemed a lot deeper than that. For a moment water was seeping in under the door and the little front wheels were spinning on the mud of the far bank. Then they had clawed their way up and we were out. Before I had caught my breath, momentum carried us up a low rise and began to take us down the far side.

And it was then, when I saw the track ahead, that my doubts thrust up into the open. For thirty yards the twin wheel ruts of the track were two long, narrow, miniature lakes divided by a steep-sided ridge.

By the time I had taken in this prospect our front wheels were down in the lakes and the only thing left to do was to avoid losing momentum. I gunned the motor. We bounced and shimmied our way forward. Twice in mid-lake Rohosinante thumped hard on the dividing ridge. But then we were out on dry land and I had pulled up and begun to breathe more normally and make up my mind.

I did not sit there for very long. With the bush still pressing close, still blotting out the distant hills, discretion rapidly emerged as the overwhelming component of valor. After all, there would be plenty of time some other day. Perhaps I should try it with somebody else along: having a push for a few yards when you got stuck could mean instant escape instead of a sweaty, dirty, frustrating, day-long jacking operation. I could bring the ranger that Tipis had promised. Or Steve Joyce from the lodge: he had said he would like to come out with me to see how Rohosinante coped. There was the suspension too: as soon as I had been down into the Serengeti I would have to make a quick trip to Nairobi to get various odd jobs done, and one of them would be having Roho-sinante's adjustable suspension raised to its limit, front and rear. That would make a difference on a track like this.

Ten minutes later I was back at the white signboard.

Before turning left I looked back and saw the track curving away across grassland into the green trees. Above the trees swelled the body of blue hills. I drove on down the Keekorok road. I drove slowly. Before long I felt able to admit to a sense of relief; but this time there was no sense of having come back into the Mara, the way there had been after my sidetrips to Ngulot and up the Isuria Escarpment—no sense of having established a new and incontestable boundary of my new domain. The mission track and the beckoning blue hills had, in spite of the way the bush pressed in, been very much a part of the Mara. I would try to take another shot at them. I would try within the next week or two. And if I failed to find time for it I would make a point of doing so when I came back for my six-month spell of solid research.

Two miles down the Keekorok road I came out into flat and open parkland. Almost at once I saw, lying in short grass no more than twenty feet from the road, a dead Tommy. I braked to a halt just beyond it and looked back.

The Tommy lay on its side, neck and legs outstretched, the way a child draws a sleeping animal, the way almost no animal sleeps. The body bore no obvious marks. And it looked clean and bright, as if only seconds before the little gazelle had been alive and minnow-flashing.

Then, as my hand began to ease the gearshift into reverse, I saw the cheetah.

It lay twenty paces beyond the Tommy, in the shade of a small thorn tree. It was panting heavily, the way an athlete pants, seconds after he has run his race. And the look on its face was the look of an athlete who, thinking he had won, now hears that he may be disqualified. The cheetah's golden eyes bored into me. Its ears lay folded back, small and flat.

And in that first moment I knew exactly what I had just missed. I saw the scene clear and complete, like an instant replay, for it was a scene I had been daydreaming since long before I came back to Africa.

Cheetah had for twenty years occupied a special niche in my mind, up alongside the eland. And as with eland, the reason was a chance meeting.

Not long after my wife and I arrived in Kenya in 1947 we stayed overnight at the simple little hotel called Mac's Inn, half-way between Nairobi and Mombasa on what was then a bone-shaking dirt road. Next to hot baths, the inn's richest reward was its tame cheetah. When this lithe and gentle creature stood beside you its shoulder came almost level with your hips. When you stroked it you could feel bands of muscle under the soft, loose coat. The coat was creamy yellow with big, jet-black spots.

Out in the inn's red-dust forecourt I had posed like a domesticated dimwit with the cheetah's forepaws held in my hands while my wife took a picture of us. The cheetah was entirely cooperative. It stood there quietly, "holding hands" with an air of vaguely embarrassed contentment. I have just exhumed the photograph from the album in which it has for years lain buried. It shows a side view of a young man standing in the African sunlight and looking uncertainly down at a glorious cat that, because its forepaws are being held, stretches up and out in unnatural extension so that its body looks awkwardly long and almost ugly. But I know that the long-embalmed photograph, for all the information it passes along, is indeed dead. It quite fails to convey the realities of that moment. For I remember a warm, breathing animal with forepaws limp in my hands and golden eyes barely two feet from mine. And yet, although I was not fully aware of it at the time, I think I knew that I had not come close to the animal. I had come only near enough to sense the mystery that held us apart. I wonder now if the cheetah did not understand something I had not understood: the falseness as well as the value of our posturing. Perhaps that was why it seemed embarrassed, why it would not look me in the eye.

Yet it had purred like a hearth cat fitted with a supercharger.

And down the years it was that ridiculous, wonderful purring sound that had echoed around the boxes of my memory. That sound, and one other thing. Come to think of it, the story the inn's owners told us may have been what generated the feeling I have called "mystery"—the hint that there were more things in that cheetah's philosophy than I had dreamed of. Not long before, the owners told us, this beautiful, gentle creature that purred so placidly had erupted toward a pet monkey that was frolicking in front of one of the cottages. Before anyone could move it had caught the monkey and killed it. That was why there was a big wire-mesh enclosure out in the forecourt. And why the cheetah was locked in the enclosure whenever small children came to the inn.

Almost fifteen years later, long after I had left Kenya, the cheetah's special niche in my mind received an unexpected furbishing. I went to see the Walt Disney movie *African Lion*. I went to see it mainly because the photographers were Al and Elma Milotte, whom I had met while they were in East Africa shooting the film and whose path I had also stumbled across years later, in a curiously remote and yet personal way, deep in Grand Canyon. But I sat on to see the movie around a second time because of the cheetah scene.

The scene opened with a cheetah loping easily across grassland after a herd of small antelope. The antelope—I think they were Tommy—did not seem unduly alarmed. It was an interesting but not enthralling scene.

Then the cheetah accelerated. And in the moment of acceleration it ceased to be merely a lithe and beautiful animal.

The long, low shape surged forward across the open grass. For two seconds, three seconds, the acceleration built, tension straining on tension. And then the velocity reached a limit beyond the credible limit—and held. Across the pale grass the golden creature streamed, no longer confined by such quanta as stride and gait but breaking out beyond them into a flow of forward motion that held constant and yet was every moment changing from a spring coiled above interlocking legs into an arrow that as it flew along above the grass was both tipped and feathered with slender, impossibly extended legs. The constant, rhythmically changing shape flowed on and on across the grass: coiled spring to flying arrow, arrow back to coiled and instantly releasing spring. And still through all the change there was no change, only motion. I waited. But the tension held and held and held, the way it does in one of those pure, time-suspended intervals when Beethoven tells you what he has just learned in another of his quiet talks with God.

Then the cheetah was in among the antelope. By now they had panicked into full and frantic flight; but compared with their pursuer they barely moved. The cheetah closed on one fleeing form. And then, almost without a check in the forward flow, there was dust and a tumbling antelope. And then the cheetah had turned and was arching through the air after the tumbling body —and the images on the screen had cut to a different scene that was no more than beautiful and interesting and I was left rigid in my seat, hands still clenched and moist but lungs functioning again and my mind rerunning what my eyes had seen. Already, I think, I was beginning to marvel that it had been all poetry and no violence.*

I saw the film to its end and sat through a second feature and then saw *African Lion* again. Second time through, the cheetah's motion was just as enthralling, just as time-suspending. When the scene was over I got up and went out into the night. I did not want to injure the memory with more images. And as I walked to my car along a dark, wet Berkeley-Bournemouth street, bleak and asphalt, I think I decided that if it were possible I would one day see a cheetah hunting in the flesh. Perhaps, come to think of it, that cheetah scene in *African Lion* was the seed, or at least was one of the seeds, that years later germinated into my decision to return to Africa.

And now here I was sitting in my car, less than thirty paces from a cheetah that lay panting under a tree, the way an athlete pants, seconds after he has run his race. And on the grass between us lay a dead Tommy.

---

* Facts: Cheetah have been clocked over short distances at seventy m.p.h. At full speed, a single stride may measure twenty-three feet. But facts, I am afraid, say almost nothing about what I witnessed on that movie screen.

Someone had told me that before cheetah can begin to eat their prey they must rest for a few minutes to recover from the colossal exertion of the chase. I looked out into the open park-land. Barely two hundred yards beyond the panting cheetah was a small, scattered group of Tommy. They had an unsettled, anxious air about them. And they all stood looking toward the cheetah.

I backed until I came level with the dead Tommy, then stopped. The cheetah rose to its feet and stood beside the thorn tree, ears flat, reaming me through with the kind of look a human animal achieves by narrowing its eyes. I do not think the cheetah narrowed its eyes, but only a moron would have failed to get the message. For a long, pungent moment the cheetah stood beside the thorn tree, hexing. Then it had turned and was walking directly away from me across the open grass.

It walked with a loose, athletic, hang-cat slouch, the way a professional basketball player removes himself from the court after a one-point, done-from-behind loss. It walked in a straight line for about a hundred yards. Then it turned and lay down. But it held its head above the long grass, watching me.

I backed off the road and parked twenty yards from the Tommy. My watch said two twenty-five. I ate some nuts and wrote some notes and kept an eye on the cheetah. By two forty-five it had made no move. I backed off another ten yards. By three-twenty my hunger was blunted and my notes up to date but the cheetah had still not moved. I drove forward and pulled up beside the Tommy.

It was a male. I could see two claw marks now, small but deep, one on the quarter and one near the eye. And on the neck a band of ruffled hair still glistened with partly dried saliva. Otherwise, apart from another small patch of disturbed hair on the haunches, I could see no sign of violence. It seemed likely that the cheetah had grabbed the Tommy's neck and broken it as the little antelope, knocked off its feet in full flight, went tumbling across the hard ground.

I photographed the Tommy, then drove in a wide circle that was meant to take me behind the cheetah and so leave it an open route to its rightful prey. But I lost sight of the golden animal lying in the golden grass and then misjudged the distance. All at once the cheetah stood up, barely fifty yards from the car, and began walking directly away from the Tommy. I swung sharp right. In my rear view mirror I saw the cheetah hesitate, stop. It slouched a few more paces, then sank out of sight into long grass in the shade of another small thorn tree. I drove until I was at least three hundred yards from the tree, stopped, and looked back through binoculars. I could not see the cheetah. I switched off. The time was three twenty-seven.

For the next two hours I waited. I waited in several places, each progressively further from the little thorn tree in whose shade the cheetah had lain down. I kept an eye on the tree, wrote more notes, had tea, realized with surprise that no vultures had yet found the Tommy, and kept reminding myself that cheetah were said to be rare in the Mara. Once, the cheetah sat up and gave me a long, peering look, head craned forward on supple neck. It turned the head at right angles, stared toward the Tommy, looked back at me, then sank down again into the long grass. I continued to watch the tree. From time to time I detected, or thought I detected, a small, pale something in the tall, pale grass. But that was all.

At five-twenty, with the sun close to the distant blue line of the Isuria Escarpment, I drove until I was more than a mile from the cheetah and hidden from it by a line of bush. For almost half an hour I did my best to keep my mind on looking for other game. At five forty-five I gave up the charade and drove back onto the cheetah's side of the bush. Through binoculars I found the distant Tommy. Beside it, richly gold and beautifully spotted in the warm and almost level sunlight, stood the cheetah.

By the time I had closed to within a hundred yards, a cloud-bank above the Isuria Escarpment had screened the sun. The rich colors had died and the cheetah was pale yellow against pale grass. It was lying down, chewing at the Tommy's haunches. But it kept glaring at me, ears pressed back against its head. I am not sure that this time its eyes did not actually narrow.

I edged closer, biting off the yards eight or ten at a time, mak-

ing each advance as slowly as the engine would take it, trying to
mask the change of position by heading directly toward the cheetah. When I used the binoculars between advances I took six or
seven seconds to lift them from their neck-slung position to my
eyes. Once, when about thirty yards still separated us, the cheetah rose to its feet, retreated a couple of paces, then stopped and
glared at me. Its ears pressed back even tighter, flat against the
head. I switched off the engine and sat still. For perhaps a minute
the cheetah stood its ground. Then it stepped forward, lay down
beside the Tommy and resumed its meal.

In the course of the next twenty minutes I eased forward,
notch by cautious notch, until no more than eight or nine paces
separated us. The cheetah kept glancing up. But it went on eating.

It ate delicately, from the Tommy's rear leg. Behind the
brown and black and white of the flank, the whole haunch had
been laid bare. It was red and wet, like a raw steak. I could see no
blood on the cheetah's face but occasionally its tongue came out
and curled like a pink table napkin around the black and shining
nose.

From time to time it looked up, directly at me. And now,
through binoculars, I had brought myself almost as close to the
cheetah's eyes as I had been twenty years before in the dusty red
forecourt of Mac's Inn. The eyes were just as I had half remembered them: rich and golden, with pupils round like a lion's, not
elliptical like a house cat's. But from the inner corner of each eye
a black line ran directly downward, then curved out around the
whiskered nose; and these lines, although they must have been
there on the face of the cheetah at Mac's Inn, injected something
I had not remembered: a hint of melancholy. Running downward from the eyes of this sleek and rakish creature that kept fix-
ing me with such a hostile glare, they conveyed the almost irresistible impression that it had been shedding dark and heavy tears.

As the minutes passed the cheetah became less and less disturbed by my presence. Once, when it moved to attack the meat
from another angle, it stood briefly with its body broadside to me
and I saw—and remembered down the years—the way the bulk
and strength of the beast lay in its shoulders. By comparison, head

and haunches were slight. A short, ill-defined mane accentuated the bulk of the shoulders—and the sense of imbalance.

The cheetah moved a pace forward and with one paw holding down the Tommy's body bit into the flesh from a fresh angle. Then it raised its head and glared at me again. At that moment the sun broke through the clouds. Color flooded the scene. And for a long, knife-edge moratorium of time my binoculars held the cheetah in vivid portrait, tense above its prey.

The head thrust forward, low. Behind humped shoulders the body stretched taut. Head on like that, poised high on those thin, curving legs, it looked astonishingly slim. It was the body of a spare and spidery sprinter, a specialist refined to the brink of overspecialization. And in that moment I understood why a cheetah in full cry could make even a herd of terrified Tommy look sluggish.

Clouds repossessed the sun. The cheetah returned to its meal.

It ate steadily forward from the rump. Soon one leg had gone, and most of the belly. The light paled toward dusk.

All at once the cheetah stood up. It stepped back, glared at me even more malevolently than before, directly over the Tommy's body—and hissed. It hissed like a threatened house cat, lips drawn back. Then it retreated a dozen paces and stopped. I sat very still. The cheetah stood irresolute. And then it sat down and then in one continuing, liquid motion it lay down and rolled languidly over on its side. For the first time, I could see for sure that it was a female.

The cheetah lay on her side for perhaps a minute, making the small, satisfied movements of a contented diner. Then she sat up, stared balefully at me, and growled. It was an aggrieved rather than an angry growl. But it was, in its subdued way, a dog's growl. Until that moment I had forgotten that a cheetah, although a cat by most standards, does not have a cat's sharp, curving claws that can be sheathed at will in the footpads. Its claws are blunt and only partially retractable: closer, that is, to a dog's claws.

The cheetah continued to sit on her haunches, facing me. The light drained away. I glanced at my watch: six forty-five. Before long it would be difficult to choose a campsite.

I started the car and backed slowly onto the road. As I drove away I looked back. The cheetah sat motionless, watching me go.

I camped half a mile down the road, off to the left. While I was cooking dinner it occurred to me that the cheetah eating her kill had evoked no more sense of savagery than would a well-mannered woman eating a steak.

Next morning I stopped briefly at Tipis's office and left two copies of my letter to Narok County Council. Then I drove south across the border, past a big black billboard that stood beside the track:

TANZANIA NATIONAL PARKS

HERE THE WORLD IS STILL

YOUNG AND FRAGILE

HELD IN TRUST

FOR YOUR SONS AND OURS

And eighty miles further on I came to the place known as Seronera, site of a tourist lodge and headquarters of Serengeti National Park. It was also the headquarters of the Serengeti Research Institute.

Until a few years ago, most of the worthwhile information about East Africa's big game was bottled up inside people like T-B, who had spent their lives in slow, painful, haphazard accumulation of disjointed facts and then in piecing the facts together into wisdom. Such reservoirs were hard to tap. And, rich as they were, they suffered serious deficiencies. Basic questions about the daily lives of common animals remained unanswered, even unasked. And no one had begun to tackle the huge and fundamental problem: just what are the interlocking relationships between all the different species, vegetable and animal, that make up the complex community of the plains? Each species clearly has a "job" to do. Each has to contribute to the life of the community, just as butcher, baker and candlestick maker must contribute efficiently and accurately to a human community—or be supermarketed out of existence.

Questions like this are now being tackled all over the world with sudden, heart-warming energy—often with so much self-righteous energy, in fact, that our new shibboleth, "Ecology!" has already earned itself a perfectly understandable backlash. But fifteen years ago, in the world's richest reservoir of wildlife, the fundamental question had hardly been formulated. Then, in 1958, Dr. Bernhard Grzimek and his twenty-four-year-old son, Michael, made an aerial census of the huge herds of the Serengeti. At the very end of the project Michael crashed in their plane and was killed. But their efforts, popularized in the book *Serengeti Shall Not Die,* triggered an avalanche of research. A second generation of researchers, gathering in East Africa from universities all over the world, is using the latest tools of science to answer some of the more basic questions and so create blocks of knowledge that may in time build answers to that huge and fundamental question of how the many life forms of the plains community interlock.

The Serengeti Research Institute, the direct descendant of the Grzimeks' pioneering effort, is one of the biggest and best known organizations coordinating the work of such researchers.

I arrived at Seronera in midafternoon, and next morning I saw Dr. Hugh Lamprey, director of the institute. He could not, he said, speak for individual researchers—they worked independently and each would have to answer for himself—but he would certainly do all he could to help. He gave me a list of useful scientific papers, especially those on animal behavior, and told me at which libraries in Nairobi I could find them. And then, for almost two hours, we talked about predators—including poachers—and about other human threats. We also discussed grass management by deliberate burning. The value of burning, said Lamprey, was still an open question. New grass, which on the savanna sprouted within twenty-four or thirty-six hours of a rain shower, came up far stronger on burned land. Burning also kept gall acacia and other bush under control. But if done too often it impoverished the soil. Most people seemed to accept that. They did not agree on much else.

Lamprey smiled. "We held a grass management conference here just the other day. Experts from all over the world. But we couldn't get even two of them to agree on the best burning practices. The trouble is, nobody really knows." Burning, said Lamprey, was the kind of question the institute had to tackle: its job was to pin down at least some of the basic facts.

That afternoon, on my way back north, I stopped at Banagi, the original Grzimek camp and still a subcenter of the institute. There I met Tony Sinclair, an Englishman just starting buffalo research; George Schaller, the American author of *Year of the Gorilla*, now working on lions; and Hubert Braun, a Dutch grass expert. From each of them I received, in varying degrees of warmth, assurance of cooperation. Braun was particularly cordial. When he took me into his garden and pointed out some of the more important species of savanna grass I began to see that the subject was horrifyingly more complicated than I had imagined.

"I understand what you mean," said Braun, smiling. "And this is but a beginning. You will understand how I felt when I arrived here and found that my research area was bigger than my whole country."

George Schaller, who had already been working for a year on his lion project, expressed something of the same sense of daunting scale.

By five o'clock I had crossed back into Kenya.

There was no real difference, of course, between the country on either side of the border. But it was good, I found, to be back in the Mara. Half an hour later I pulled up outside the lodge. I went inside and had a late tea and looked up at the heavy wooden beams and then out beyond the swimming pool at the familiar contours of the view. This time, even the newspapers on the table had their moments: KENYA WARNS CHINA: WE WILL HIT BACK screamed the headline over a story of diplomatic hassles about treatment of embassy staff in Peking; and a photograph taken outside the Chinese embassy in Nairobi showed African demonstrators holding up a poster that proclaimed KENYANS IS MORE CIVILIZED THAN CHINESE.

After tea I overheard an experienced game-viewing guide ask Steve Joyce why there was so much game around Keekorok when down at Seronera you had to drive miles to see anything worthwhile. Steve allowed himself a lean, parochial smile and said, "Oh, probably because up here we don't chase them around and shoot darts into them and then measure God knows what and clip plastic tags on their ears before we let them go. Or perhaps because our rangers don't go around with matches in their pockets, burning every blade of grass in sight." And that was good too, as well as not so good.

Before I left Keekorok, I saw Tipis for a few moments. He had not yet had a chance to talk to T-B but he felt sure that by the time I got back from Nairobi he would have some more news, perhaps even a date for the county council meeting. I studiously avoided mentioning the Serengeti, for in the course of my evening at Seronera I had harvested a grain of enlightenment. "Simeon Tipis?" someone had said. "Oh, yes, he came down here once and was arrested for trespassing or something. Not much love lost now, I'm afraid."

And as I drove away from the lodge, racing the dusk to the main gate, I found myself considering the arbitrary way animal territories were established by chance juxtapositions of strength and weakness without regard for the natural divisions of the land. It certainly happened that way with some species. The story goes, for example, that when Britain and Germany were busy subdividing East Africa into bearable loads of the white man's burden, their politicians drew across the map a straight and tidy boundary line that chanced to cut directly through Mount Kilimanjaro. Kaiser Wilhelm, who had a thing about mountains, protested. Cousin Victoria, whose spirit was hardly the kind to soar toward peaks, graciously acceded. The line was redrawn, suitably kinked. Kilimanjaro became German.

But the new line still cut arbitrarily across many other natural divisions, topographical and animal. It divided the Mara, for example, from its ecological partner, the Serengeti. It also bisected Masailand. Naturally, the nonhuman animals ignored the line. But *Homo sapiens* continued, through sundry changes of territorial "ownership" and title, to use the line as a basis for building new unities and enmities. As usual, the big successes were the enmities. When far-flung supporters of Kaiser Wilhelm and of

Cousin Victoria's executors found themselves opposed in the first of their species' more or less global wars, the Kilimanjaro-kinked line duly served as their local starting battlefront. Now, with Chinese influence in Tanzania strong and growing, the line promised to become a fulcrum in the local struggle between two of the species' current political ideologies—those convenient hypotheses that so often provide us with license to do the things we want to do. But boundary contagions can flourish independently of ideologies: it now looked as if, saddest of all, one had infected the men charged with protecting the other, innocent species.*

* I hasten to add that this view of how certain specific events have turned out is naturally colored by my own territorial background. I have suggested, for example, that the local unpleasantness that occupied and often ended men's lives in East Africa from 1914 through 1918 was a peripheral skirmish of a disagreement that centered in Europe. But I was born in Europe. And it is entirely possible to see the matter quite differently. The Somervell abridgment of Arnold Toynbee's *Study of History* carries (in Volume II, Chapter 39) this footnote to a passage on egocentric illusion:

"When the Editor of the Abridgement was staying on the slope of Mount Kilimanjaro in A.D. 1935, he was told the Cause of the First World War as understood by the Chagga tribe, who live on the southern side of that mountain. Mount Kilimanjaro was first ascended by a German, Dr. Hans Meyer, in A.D. 1889. When he reached the top he found there the god of the mountain, who, gratified by an attention that he had never before received, made over to the worthy German mountaineer and his fellow countrymen all the Chagga country, but on one condition, namely that one of the climber's fellow countrymen should ascend the mountain every year (or was it once every five years?) to do homage to him. All went well. The Germans occupied German East Africa, and an industrious party of German mountaineers ascended the mountain at the proper intervals, until, in A.D. 1914, there was a most unfortunate omission of this duty. Justly incensed, the god of the mountain revoked his gift and made the country over to the enemies of the Germans, who declared war upon them and drove them out. This Anglo-German war in the East African heart of the World brought with it incidentally, as is the way with wars, some 'side-show' bouts of fighting in relatively unimportant outlying areas.

"The Chagga account of the First World War seems to be as good as many other accounts of it, and indeed better than some, in that it recognizes the importance of the part played by religion in history."

By the time I reached the main gate of the Sanctuary it was dark enough for me to decide without debate that I would not turn right up the little track, as I had intended, and drive through a mile of thick bush to Waterhole Camp. Instead, I drove on down the Narok road, meaning to stop almost at once in some convenient open place from which I would make an early start next morning for Nairobi. But an unheralded sense of exhilaration had boiled up in me and I kept driving on through the darkness, the way you sometimes find you want to do on such occasions. Rohosinante's headlights tunneled ahead, swinging and bouncing, unrolling the red-brown road, digging black pits in distant potholes and then filling them with a rush. A lone Tommy, blinded by their glare, stumbled and fell, then stood waiting for the horror to pass. Nightjars crouched brown and flat until the last moment, then fan-danced to safety. And all the time, inside, I had the friendly instruments along Rohosinante's dash and her smells and touches and movements—all of them friendly things now, because all of them had grown familiar.

I drove for almost an hour. Then I pulled off the road into a clearing in straggly bush. It was a dull place really, impoverished by overgrazing from a nearby manyatta. But the exhilaration was still simmering, and when I had built my private night world of white car and brown-grained table and green-backed chair, all held within the white and hissing dome of lamplight with the bulging blue lamp-base at its center, it became one of the best of camps. And as I sat down to dinner and paused for a moment to debate whether to put on long pants before I began to eat because now that I was sitting still the wind had begun to blow cool around my bare legs, and while another layer of my mind played with the thought that the Mara's prevailing east wind came from the direction of Nairobi, as I sat there halfway thinking about several things at once and not really thinking about very much at all, the wind rustled the leaves of the book that now looked so certain. I would, I saw, have to call the book *A Wind Blows on*

Mara. And I glimpsed, beyond this title, some of the things it would say.

I pushed my dinner plate aside and grabbed the clipboard and began to write. I wrote at white heat. The fiction idea had been dead for days, and now I buried it under facts. I think a corner of me knew, even as I wrote, that I was producing fleshless manifestos, mere sermons, fit only for true believers. But such bedrock outcrops always appear at some stage. They are part of the process. You need them, for from them you will quarry your book. Time will erode the sermons, of course. In the end it will annihilate them. Most of them, anyway. But at the start you need them as guidelines.

With the wind cooling my dinner as it sat untouched on the table, I opened my sermon with an attack on the crime of assuming that Kenya must follow us down the dreary road of industrialization to its inevitable Bournemouth bus terminus. As well assume that Wyoming or Idaho must be paved over, I wrote. The difference, after all, lay only in the nature of the boundaries. Must we pass along, unsolved, the problems of the overdeveloped nations? And from there I went on, page after pulpit age. But the pressure eased at last and the tiredness came, and once more I could feel the wind cold on my legs.

I put on long pants and reheated dinner. By the time I had finished eating, the tiredness had gone. I packed away inside the car all the things that might attract lions or hyenas and then shut the little roof of a door and took a couple of steps out from the center of my white and hissing world and urinated toward the darkness. And as I stood there, recycling and staring at the shadows of my legs but hardly seeing them, I did some idle arithmetic. I came up with the astonishing answer that it was still only ten days since I had driven out of Nairobi looking for T-B.

The answer was astonishing not only because it seemed a lot longer than that but also because in those ten days a pendulum had swung full arc. All through my first two months back in Kenya I had been bogged down. Now, everything had fallen into place. All the important people had promised to help. I was be-

ginning to see what I had to learn. And although, like Hubert
Braun and George Schaller, I might at times feel intimidated by
the enormity of my task, that would only sharpen the challenge;
for I felt even surer, now, that the Mara, for all its quiet surface,
would turn out to be no backwater. Above all, the excitement
was still there—and as long as it continued to burn, I had a book.

I finished and went back into the center of my white dome
and picked up the lamp and carried it to the tent. I put it down
on the pale dry grass outside the tent door. Then I crawled into
the tent and reached out and turned off the hissing lamp and
zipped down the mosquito netting and undressed in the sudden,
familiar, thunderous silence and lay down and pulled the open
sleeping bag over me and listened to the night's polyphony. A
dozen bars and I had sunk down and away.

Topi & Kongoni

Interlude

It began as soon as I passed the little red-roofed chapel and climbed the Rift Valley Escarpment.

It was always the same, now. First, the hawkers: young men, mostly, who clustered beside the road in groups of five or six and tried to flag you down by waving their woven baskets and place mats and other tourist trappings. Then the sheepskin peddlers: young men and boys who stood at intervals along the edge of the asphalt and moved out a step as you approached and held up whole, undyed sheepskins; and who, when it became clear that you were not going to stop, whistled shrilly and glared with barbed eyes; sad, impoverished, angry souls whom you had to brush past dangerously close if a car was coming the other way, and whom you could see long afterward in your mirror and then your mind, still standing amid the filthy sheepskin scrapings that lay littered like offal about the bare red roadside soil—the soil that had given the red to the black, red and green flag of the Republic of Kenya. And then a roadside market and a sea of sullen faces.

Soon, city streets. Some streets solid, held firm by well-proportioned buildings and still kept green and pleasing by palms and peppers and jacarandas. Most streets mere channels between money-grubbing rabbit hutches, overlaid with SHELL and COKE and FLY BOAC and the rest of the debased coinage that we Gresham around the world. But every street permeated, for me, with the Nairobi phoniness, old and new.

Four days of busying myself around the city. Getting Roho-sinante serviced, raising her suspension, and restoring the front passenger seat for the promised ranger. Running down the research papers Hugh Lamprey had recommended: buying a few, begging others, skimming through those that were bound to their libraries. Confirming in the National Museum's excellent bird display that ground hornbills' eyelashes indeed formed a helix. Buying a Masai grammar and topo maps of the Mara. And from time to time seeing such people as David Brown, about-to-be-Africanized Chief Game Warden of Kenya. (T-B had said, "You'd better let him know what you're up to. You'll have to get a long-term game department permit, anyway." "Okay by me," said Brown. "It would be civil, though, to call in on Mwangi, the D.C. at Narok.")

But underlying these chores, all through the four days, abrasion.

It is always there, of course, when you come back from the green world. You have been living by sunrise and sunset, by wind and rain, surrounded by the ebb and flow of lives that respond only to such simple, rhythmic elements. But now the tone and tempo of the days switch. Instead of harmony, jangle.

And in Nairobi, worse. There, more than the concrete and

car fumes and news and money compulsion and assorted thievery. There, everywhere, the hopeless, galloping inefficiency. And the West's cold wind whistling down once-sheltered streets.

On the door or window of every other store or office, the bleak little sign: HAKUNA KAZI—NO WORK HERE. On the wall of every office and store and hotel and even club that wanted to stay open, the photograph of President Kenyatta, his expression as benign as when I arrived two months earlier, yet somehow big-brothering it more now. Spewing out from radio and news-paper and permeating everything, politics. And so, lurking be-neath the surface, everywhere, division. An Indian tailor with the Kenya Asian's new fear in his eyes finding the courage to laugh as he said, "Oh, we'll have it ready for you all right, sir—if they haven't deported us by then." An old acquaintance, a European who had once supported African independence, sigh-ing as he said he would not teach his sons to run his farm because "it's no longer a place a white man can live." A revealing little item in one of the manacled newspapers: "It is well known that in certain rare instances soccer players refuse to pass the ball to teammates of different tribes."

Such puffs of reality kept slipping past the newspapers' shut-ters. Once, a letter from a man with a French name who de-scribed how, back in Kenya after forty years' absence, he was walking along a Nairobi street and feeling how good it all was when an African pretended to recognize him, maintained that he was assistant minister of something or other, and asked for a loan; the visitor went his way, saddened. And for me, reading his letter, an echo: the day before, in the men's room of the New Stanley Hotel, this same artist or a co-worker had fed me the identical pitch.

But life is an untidy affair. No background is ever a single color. All through those four days in Nairobi I kept stumbling on oases.

One morning I drove past a group of teen-age African girls, stiff and self-conscious in square-rigged, navy blue, English schoolgirl uniforms. They even wore boaters. "Ridiculous enough on English girls," I thought, "but on them at least they're not alien." And then, almost at once, I saw a line of much younger children in simple, bright blue uniforms. I was past before I could register details, but the simplicity and the color were enough: gaily and authentically African and undeniably right. And the children, though orderly, had gleamed and beamed and bounced.

Late one hot afternoon, on edge after many abrasive encounters, I went into the Avenue Hotel and asked at the reception desk for change for telephoning; and the African clerk, finding insufficient cash in the till, went out of his way to get some for me and did so with such apparent gladness that the abrasions ceased to sting and I felt a thrust of shame at having let the mood engulf me.

One evening when I had fought a grinding telephone war with incompetent and ill-mannered African officials on behalf of an elderly friend, just arrived, who thought he had lost his passport at the airport, an African girl came on the line and promised, very sweetly, to do all she could for me; and when, minutes later, my friend found the passport in his suitcase and I called back, the girl said with transparent sincerity, "Oh, I'm so glad you've found it. Now I needn't worry any more."

Some of the oases were extensive.

The day Rohosinante was being serviced I took a cab driven by a fat, amiable, relaxedly scruffy man of the Maragoli tribe. Like most Nairobi cab drivers, he failed to trip the meter. I remonstrated gently, in English. The driver answered in Swahili. We reached agreement about the fare, then drifted into conversation.

"*Nasikia America ni mahali mzuri sana,*" said the Maragoli. "I hear America is a very good place. Like a dream. Everybody who goes there says so. Lots of money."

"Yes," I said. "But you know, it is not a matter of money on its own. There is also the matter of men's hearts." In Swahili you can deliver such homilies without a pulpit.

For several blocks the Maragoli drove in silence. Then: "I hear that your tidings are clean. Here in Kenya these days, it is as if we want to hear only news of money."

We explored the satisfactions of money and beyond. Suddenly the driver lifted both hands from the wheel and in joyful discovery exclaimed, "*Eh, kumbe mungu* iko *tu!*"—a sentiment best translated as "So God lives after all!" It seemed to me that as a halfway true unbeliever I had done my bit for the day.

One evening I went for a walk in the city arboretum. By the time I had made a circuit of its lawns and shrubberies and was heading back toward the main gate, dusk had fallen. By chance I took a path that cut through a grove of trees. Almost at once their canopy snuffed out the last of the day's light. I stopped. Off to the right, where the evening sky showed beneath overhanging leaves, a band of paleness stretched long and low and restricted, like a western horizon when the clouds break clean at the end of a stormy day. Otherwise, wherever I looked, there was only velvet blackness. I peered down, feeling for the path with my feet, waiting for my eyes to adjust, beginning to wonder if I should turn back. And then I became aware that the blackness was no longer black. All around me, level with my knees, shimmered a ghostly carpet. The pinpoints of glowing light pulsated; and because each light moved—rising and falling, advancing and retreating, hovering, veering and circling—the carpet had depth, finite but definitely not definite. As I stood watching, more lights flicked on. The throbbing pile deepened.

Down at my feet, the path appeared, faint but sure. And as I stood there, quite still now, I felt myself slipping out of the rock-sure adult world and back into those youthful days when magic happened more often and more simply and more utterly. Then, the moments came when a blue iris grew tall and sudden on the edge of a wood, and in exciting, half-awake interludes under the bedclothes when it seemed possible to imagine being awake at midnight, and nearly always, and for many years longer, when a big fish swirled in a river, majestic and unattainable. But that was long ago. Now it happened very rarely. Even the image of a cheetah flowing across a screen, though wonderful in its way, was not the same thing. But one evening somewhere in the Deep South, past my fortieth birthday, I was clambering up a steep woodland bank when it, too, came alive with fireflies.

And that, while it lasted, had also been one of the magic moments.

In the arboretum, I do not know how long I stood knee-deep in the throbbing carpet, letting go and holding on. But at last some adult component of me registered that the pale band off to the right had darkened almost to extinction. I walked on down the faint path, feeling my way. The trees ended, and with them the fireflies. And then the sky was pale overhead and the world stretched soft and gray and ordinary. I walked across a lawn but my feet would not yet fully acknowledge the brutal truth of anything as solid and sensible as grass. I came to the main gate. And as I went out of it a well-dressed African came in. He carried a transistor radio. And as he walked he pushed back the soft gray silence with the attenuated but unmistakable voice of Elvis Presley.

Next evening I had dinner with the Harthoorns. Both Toni and Sue are veterinarians—and vegetarians. Toni is also detribalized Dutch, a physiologist, a pharmacologist, a university administrator, a pioneer in field techniques of tranquilizing wild animals, and one of the two men on whom TV's *Daktari* was based. Sue is British, an author, a yoga teacher and a dynamo. And the Harthoorns' house hums. It is a haven for orphaned animals and a concourse for humans who love or work with animals. That evening the house guests included a tree hyrax, two tiger tortoises, and a large and beautiful hawk, hooded and in training but still bodeful. Among the humans nesting overnight was a German zoologist, Hans Klingel, who had recently completed three years' field research on the social organization of zebras. I talked to Klingel earnestly and absorbently. By the time I left I was even more eager than before to get back to the Mara.

But the Harthoorns' house and the firefly carpet and the Maragoli cab driver and the other oases were only remissions in my Nairobi interlude. Mostly, it was a desert of jangle and abrasion.

It is difficult, I find, to focus the city's malaise. I cannot cite violence or confrontation. I cannot even paint telling little vignettes. I saw them, I am sure; but they must have been minor and muted as well as constant, and time quickly blurred their detail.

Now I do not mean that tension crackled along the city's streets. It was not like that at all. But you hardly needed fingertips to detect a quaking in the foundations. The background rumbled. And the portents were there in people's eyes. In European eyes, resignation and sorrow. In Asian eyes, fear. In African eyes, a growing awareness that the hope and promise that had flowered at independence were withering; and so, resentment and distrust and anger and often hate. I had not detected these undercurrents when I arrived, two months earlier; but I could feel them now, tugging, waiting.

And always, wherever you turned in public, the politics. The government line rolling out in daily radio editorials so unctuous and transparent that any free population would quickly have ridiculed them into reform. A yawning gulf between this government line and the obvious, everyday facts. And rift even within the line. Official pronouncements extolling the benefits of multiracial society; policy sharpening toward outright racism. Editorials denouncing alien Western ways; official acts, with pitifully few exceptions, surfacing as second-rate imitations of Western convention. One radio news story began: "His Excellency the President, Mzee Jomo Kenyatta, today signed into law an act establishing a College of Arms for Kenya. The chairman of the college—which will ensure that the designs of all coats of arms granted, whether to individuals or organizations, are in accord with the principles of heraldry—will be the Attorney General. . . ."

Beneath this froth, waiting for it to blow away, omens of the truly human syndrome. Outside the city limits but only a dozen miles down a ribbon of road, past lorries belching black into the still-clean air, down on the edge of the once game-rich Athi Plains, the source of the pall that you could always see smudging the horizon when you drove into Nairobi National Park: a gaunt gray cement factory defecating across sky and future.

I left Nairobi early on the fifth day.

It was raining, grayly. Lines of commuter traffic trekked inward along the wet boulevards, indeed like wildebeest. I penetrated the outer sprawl. It was no longer quite raining but from time to time the sky still dripped. I came to sheepskin country and the clouds began to lift and thin. The peddlers had not yet taken their stands. I drove between dark conifer plantations toward the Rift Valley. The clouds lifted higher. White fissures clove their grayness.

And then I came to the Rift Valley Escarpment.

It was as if a boundary had been drawn. Beyond the escarpment, the grayness ended. White clouds drifted across blue sky. And far below their shadows cruised serenely across the flat green-and-gold floor of the valley, westward toward the Mara.

I pulled off the road and stopped.

Fifty yards ahead, a group of Africans erupted from behind a roadside bush. Within seconds I could see nothing but gaudy tourist trappings thrust at windows and windshield.

I let the head of my anger subside. Then I said, firmly, that I was not going to buy anything. And I suggested as reasonably as I could that pestering tourists like a swarm of flies was not really an effective way of conducting their business. But our discussion soon outran the hawkers' schoolboy English. I switched to Swahili. The response ran the gamut that I was getting used to when Africans discovered I was not a tourist but a Swahili-speaking ex-colonial: momentary resentment; an almost immediate relaxation of prejudice and manner; then, provided I did not push, pleasure; soon, communication.

Their wares, the young hawkers said, were made of sisal. The womenfolk did the dyeing, but this roadside vending was a bad business. "Some days you sell nothing at all and just go back to your house."

One young man's nose wrinkled. "*Viashara hii ni kazi ya wanawake tu.* Peddling like this is mere women's work." He shrugged his shoulders. "But what can we do? There is no other work. And it is necessary to get food."

Our conversation continued down conventional channels.

"*Na siku hizi unakaa wapi?*" asked the young man.

I told him.

The young man—he was no more than a boy, really—tilted

back his head and looked up at the sky as if it were a blackboard. "Oh, yes," he said in excellent, meticulously programmed English. "San Francisco—principal port of the West Coast."

I bought a small basket.

By the time I drove on, sunshine had flooded in over the escarpment. I drove slowly, watching the rounded treetops and the green and shadow of rich forest and the way the flat floor of the Rift Valley came up to meet me.

When I reached the little red-roofed chapel with its miniature campanile, set like a jewel in its roadside niche, I pulled up in front of it and switched off. The silence rippled with birdsong. I got out. The sun, beating down on thick grass, was extracting the last nightscents. I walked to the foot of the stone steps and read again the inscription carved in the heavy stone door lintel by the Italian war prisoners who had built the chapel: CRUX DUM VOLVITUR. In a little alcove above the inscription, two bas-relief antelopes drank from what seemed to be a fountain.

I turned and looked out over the treetops, out across the floor of the Rift Valley, out across a quarter of a century.

In Nairobi I had found Noel Simon's book, *Between the Sunlight and the Thunder*, and in it I had read how, during World War II "teams of hunters were employed in shooting game to provide meat for the [prison] camps. . . . Day after day, month after month, for several years the slaughter went on. At night there was scarcely a pause and a constant fusillade went on with the aid of spotlights." By the end of the war "the game in many areas of Kenya had generally ceased to exist."

And now, looking out across the treetops, I could almost hear the fusillade echoing across the wide and golden plains that I remembered as almost empty when I first saw them, less than two years after the war. It fitted in, I thought, this slaughter that exterminated not only the antelopes but the lions and hyenas and other predators that depended on them. It had an obstinate, ingrown, crazy kind of human logic to it, this throwing of the lions to the Christians. For the British had offered up the sacrifice to sustain men who had set out from their homeland to kill or conquer them. And the Italians had ended up building roads for the British and while doing so had built the chapel as an offering to their common god—their man-centered god in whose Holy City, back in the Italians' homeland, you very rarely heard birdsong (although the god was reputed to endorse St. Francis of Assisi) because its noble citizens liked to see even the smallest birds lined up in neat, artistic rows on butchers' slabs. But still not evil men. Again, just unaware men. Humane men. All honorable men.

After a while I went back to the car and drove away from the little chapel and its carved inscription that meant: "The Cross, for as long as the Earth shall last."

The road leveled off. The rich and rounded trees of the escarpment gave way to flat-topped thorns and candelabrum euphorbia. I drove on across the plain. There was no game beside the road, only a double fence and a railroad track.

Soon I turned left onto the dirt road that led westward to the Mara. Rohosinante began to bucket and complain. The familiar dust cloud billowed out behind us. But now the plain rolled clean and golden. There was no fence, no railroad. And at last, off to the right, I saw a herd of Tommy. Then a herd of Masai cattle. And then, standing beside the road, waving and smiling, waving for the fun of it, waving and having a ball on the strength of it, a little group of half-naked, red-robed Masai children.

EXPLORATION

Narok is hardly what you would call a memorable place. If it strikes you as less grim than most small commercial centers in Kenya that is probably because its handful of *dukas*, or stores, cluster along one side of the main-and-almost-only street and your eye is therefore free to detour westward across an open meadow. But the dukas are the town, really, and they are money-trap rabbit hutches, all of them. And the men you find waiting around outside are rarely the moran who stride across the rolling Mara plains; they tend to be the sad, deprived kind of individuals who pass their days lounging outside the stores of Nairobi.

But when I drove in that morning, fresh from Nairobi, the place looked, by sheer contrast, like a suburb of Utopia. On the open side of the street the meadow sloped away wide and golden to a line of stately, green-decked fever trees. People smiled. I even caught myself detecting a hint of honesty about the dukas.

I filled Rohosinante's tank at the pump outside the main duka

and then went in for a drink for myself. After the sunlight, the interior was very dark. Drinking a Coke at one end of the counter was a short, moon-faced European. We chatted.

He was English and he worked, he told me, for the European contractors who were planting and harvesting wheat for Masai landowners.

"Out on the Lemek road?"

"That's right."

"Oh!" I said. And then, just in time—before the pause got too awkwardly long—I asked how the harvest had been.

"In places it came off fifteen or sixteen bags to the acre. Average ran almost nine."

"What's break-even point these days?"

" 'Bout five and a half."

"So the owners did well?"

"Damned well. We're really doing something for these people. Giving them a chance to pull themselves up."

I examined, very carefully, the inscription on my bottle. "Here it comes again," I thought. Not an evil man, not by a long chalk. This time, perhaps not even a particularly unaware one. And undoubtedly a man convinced he was doing nothing but good.

"What about rainfall?" I asked. The previous year's rains had been unusually heavy, I said, and we were probably in a wet cycle. When the dry years returned, what would happen to the wheat and to the men who had come to depend on the profit from it?

"Oh, you don't have to worry about that," said the man. He quoted figures to show that the crop would pay with no more than half the previous year's rainfall. He seemed to believe the figures, too.

"Had much trouble with game?"

"Not once we'd signed on our ten askaris." My eyes were getting used to the gloom now and I detected a smile rising toward the surface of the wheat man's moonlike face.

"Askaris?"

The smile surfaced, combusted into a laugh. "Yes, a pride of ten lions came and bedded down in one corner of our biggest field." The laugh snuffed out. "Before that, though, we'd had a hell of a time with the bloody buck."

I stood looking at the man, seeing his face all right now, hanging there in the gloom, but also seeing once more the open plain beyond Lemek and the little herd of Tommy taking flight when I was still a quarter of a mile away. I watched them racing together across the doomed gray grassland, racing for a moment in unison with a moving band of sunlight, racing as if they sought sanctuary in its illusory brightness.

I refocused the wheat man's face. Very gently—knowing it was useless, worse than useless, that I shouldn't really say anything of the sort—I suggested that the Mara was at best marginal wheatland. Kenya had a dozen far more suitable areas that were now producing precious little. And the Mara, after all, was one of the last reservoirs of big game left in the world. "Historically," I said, "wheat has always meant the end of the game."

I think I half expected the Englishman to pick up my cue and say with a touch of sadness, "You can't farm in a menagerie, you know."

But he muttered something that I think was "Can't help that," finished his drink with a flourish, paid and left.

After a while I drove on up the hill to the government compound.

Two weeks earlier, when I called in at the police station, I had been so intent on finding T-B that I had not really registered the rest of the compound. Not at the time, anyway. But later I realized that I had arrived after four o'clock and that the place was therefore at rest, and it occurred to me that except for the new Kenya flag on the flagpole everything had looked very much as it must have done after four o'clock in colonial times. Nothing stirred; yet you felt a kind of resigned confidence. No one would have accused the tin-roofed buildings of architecture but they managed to suggest that in the end what had to be done would be done—without flair, but with no nonsense and with no more than moderate bumbling.

Now, in midmorning, the present had taken over. I found a space in the almost full parking lot next to a Land Rover marked "KANU." (The Kenya African National Union is the ruling political party. It is Kikuyu-dominated.) When I walked into the main compound I found little groups of people clustered along shady verandas. A few crossed open, sunlit spaces. Through a window floated the stammerings of a typewriter being laboriously hunted and pecked. The sharp-featured clerk in the district commissioner's office made it abundantly clear that he resented being interrupted in the middle of his very difficult work, but in the end he deigned, with much fingering of his rather soiled tie, to instruct me where I might possibly be able to find the district commissioner. It was good to get out in the fresh air again.

Quarter of an hour later, on the outskirts of town, I saw a dozen men talking in the middle of a meadow, and the driver of a police Land Rover parked under a nearby tree confirmed that the D.C. was among them. He pointed him out. The group were discussing the construction of a playing field in the meadow, the driver said.

I parked in the shade of another tree. It was cool and pleasant there and I sat watching the little knot of men out in the sunlit meadow. The D.C. wore sports coat, slacks and open-necked shirt. For someone to whom the old colonial D.C.'s khaki drill was no doubt anathema, they seemed a sensible choice.

When the group broke up at last the D.C. headed for the waiting Land Rover. I walked toward him. He looked as Kikuyu as his name, and very young. I was still twenty or thirty yards away when he glanced in my direction. He promptly looked away again and changed course so that he was angling away from me.

I hurried forward. "Mr. Mwangi?"

"Yes."

"Can you spare a minute?"

The D.C. stopped. I caught up with him. He looked at me the way some Kenya Europeans used to look at Africans, the way I had sometimes looked at Kikuyu.

"My name is Fletcher. I'm hoping to do a book about Mara wildlife. I've got a game department pass into the district but David Brown said it would be civil to call on you."

"It is more than a matter of civility, I assure you."

"Oh, but . . ."

"Do you have the pass?"

I produced it.

Mwangi studied the slip of paper. He must have checked each item at least three times.

"Are you only concerned with game? Or will you also be having contacts with people?"

"Well . . . naturally I can't look at the animals in a vacuum." I smiled. "After all, every time I play soccer at Keekorok I make contact with people."

Mwangi squeezed out what I had to assume was a responding smile. "That is hardly what I mean. But if your book is in any way concerned with people you will have to go to the Office of the President and get a letter of clearance."

"But I've spoken to T-B and Tipis and they've both promised

their support, and I'm probably going to state my case at a Narok County Council meeting. I assumed that was enough."

"It is not enough. I told you, you must get a letter of clearance from the Office of the President."

I took out my notebook. "And who should I see there?"

"Mr. Arik. . . ."

I began to write, spelling out the name. "A-R-"

"No, no," said Mwangi testily. "Erik. Erik. E-R-I-K."

I gripped my pencil and took down all the details. Then, probing to test the thickness of the ice and not really to extract information, I asked a few questions about the Mara. It was a waste of time. But I think I succeeded in keeping my voice calm.

In the end I held out my hand, inches from Mwangi's. He hesitated, then accepted the inevitable. He even managed another thin smile. But the moment our hands came apart he turned away and the mask slid from his face and revealed once more the stony, Kikuyu-English, smell-under-my-nose expression. He walked quickly to the police Land Rover and got in. It bounced away.

I went back to Rohosinante and swung her around. All the way to Ewaso Ngiro I drove fast. Fiercely, stupidly, dangerously fast. When I pulled up at the barrier I was still angry.

The tall, severe looking Masai ranger on duty studied my pass for a very long time. He studied it for even longer than Mwangi had done, and after a while it occurred to me that this was strange: the only entries on it, except for the print that he presumably saw pretty often, were my name, two dates and a signature. I looked carefully at his eyes. They were fixed, unmoving, on the center of the slip of paper.

The ranger looked up at last and found me looking directly at him. His mouth came open and his eyes hardened in self-defense. I smiled. For a moment his mask held. Then he began to smile back, sheepishly at first, but soon giving himself up to the relief of sharing the difficulty and the joke. He was still grinning, ear to ear, teeth like piano keys, when he lifted the barrier and stood in rigid salute as I drove through into the Mara.

But before long I was driving too fast again. A pair of giraffes periscoped over thick bush. Tommy rubbernecked me by, black tails metronoming the hours away. A huddle of wildebeest caucused under a gardenia tree. But neither animals nor wide, golden grass could calm me. When I stopped for a late lunch I scribbled in my notebook: "A Nairobi s.o.b. Any more men of that sort and I drop the project." I think I knew, even as I wrote the words, that it was a ridiculous attitude. But I also knew that that was the way I felt.

When I reached the main gate of the Sanctuary I was still angry—and angry with myself for being angry.

The ranger on duty greeted me like an old friend, and that helped a little. No, he said, Tipis was not at Keekorok. Tomorrow, perhaps.

I swung the car around and drove back a hundred yards and turned up the track that led to Waterhole Camp.

The grassy clearing among the trees was just as I had left it. The trunk of its one big tree still twisted up like a melding of many columns. The donga cut deep and dark and mysterious and definitely not mine. And out in every direction stuttered the avenues that led nowhere, that never quite stated anything but were always hinting and suggesting. I felt my shoulders relax. It was the place I had remembered, all right: a retreat, a kind of personal sanctuary.

But when I had set up camp and begun to browse through the literature I had collected in Nairobi I found that my mind kept drifting back to the mask on Mwangi's face. When I gave up trying to read and did some laundry and a few other chores I operated in a half-hearted and inefficient way. Even afternoon tea failed to console me.

I did my best. It was all utterly unreasonable, I told myself. Stupid. Infantile. I simply could not let one arrogant young man cast such a cloud. But my strictures did no good. The minutes with Mwangi had struck at the roots of whatever I thought I had found in the Mara. When you fall in love with a place or a person because of something you see as pure and almost perfect, one harsh blast can bring the whole edifice tumbling. It shouldn't, of course. But it can.

About five o'clock it began to rain. For an hour I sat under the awning and re-grappled with printed words. It was still no good. And around me the bush lay gray and dank.

But just before dark the rain stopped. And before long the moon was rising over silvered cloudbanks and I was standing at the center of my hissing circle of lamplight with the grained brown tabletop in front of me and the green chair back behind me and Rohosinante's ridiculous little roof tilting up against the stars and the orange end walls of the tent peering out from under the blue fly sheet, bright against the blackness. And all at once, there in the white lamplight, everything was good and clean again, the way it had been before.

During dinner a hyena kept yowling in the distance. Once a lion proclaimed his neighboring land rights. Just before I went to bed, when I leaned into the car for something and by mistake touched the horn, I heard what I thought was a mild elephantine protest. When I crawled into the tent at last and zippered the mosquito netting across the entrance and then lay back and listened to soft nightsounds that the dousing of the lamp had unveiled, I found myself thinking, happily, I am not alone tonight.

Next morning I talked to Tipis in his office.

He had spoken, he said, to T-B and to the clerk of the county council. It would be two or three weeks before the next council meeting, the one at which I would have to present my case. No exact date was fixed yet, but until the meeting I could camp free anywhere outside the Sanctuary; and the temporary pass that he, Tipis, had given me for entry into the Sanctuary was valid until confirmed by the council. "And I do not think, Mr. Fletcher," he concluded, "that you need worry too much about the meeting."

I thanked him.

He asked how things had been going.

A little hesitantly, I told him of my meeting with Mwangi. And as soon as I began to talk it was all there again, welling up hot and ugly. "Frankly," I said, "I was very angry. In fact, I still am." I put one hand on the desk, face down, and brushed the other across it. "I felt," I said, "that he was only looking at the color of my skin."

I am not absolutely sure that Tipis caught the echo; but he took off his gray woolen skull cap, ran a hand through his bushy bandit's hair and pulled at his bushy bandit's beard. "I'm afraid Mr. Mwangi has had trouble with writers lately. Especially with one woman. She even photographed some meat that had been hung near a manyatta, and that meant it had to be destroyed. You see, Mr. Fletcher, it is our custom that if a woman sees meat it cannot be eaten by men. Naturally, our people were very angry. So they went to this woman's camp when she was out and found the notes that she had made for her book. The title was *The Last Tribe in Africa*, and even I was angry at that."

As I left, Tipis repeated his offer of a ranger for game-viewing. "Any time there's one free. And if I am not here you have only to ask my sergeant."

I said that I was planning to spend several days, perhaps as much as a week, over in the Triangle. Would it be possible to take a ranger for as long as that?

"By all means," said Tipis. "Just fix it up with me a few days in advance, that is all."

As I drove away I found myself wondering if I had not jumped to conclusions about Mwangi. After all, the writer business might well explain his behavior—even though it would hardly excuse it. But then I remembered the way he had taken evasive action as soon as he saw me, before he knew I was a writer.

Still, now that I had loosened my prejudices, there were other ways of looking at it. I could see Mwangi, for all the absence of khaki drill, as a carbon copy of a young British district officer from colonial times. Within their jurisdictions these young men had wielded great power. But they were naturally inexperienced and unsure of themselves in contacts with the wider world and therefore inclined to be defensively rude. But all of them, or nearly all, had been dedicated, upright, incorruptible men; and they generally became more human once they had gained experience and confidence and in the course of time become district commissioners. So I ought to allow Mwangi at least as much charity as I could now offer them. In any case, once I began looking back twenty years I ought to compare him not only with young D.O.s but also with a certain young farm manager who had been known—dammit, who had often been known—to wear a smell-under-the-nose English mask when he met strange Kikuyu. Not only Kikuyu, either. And could I really be sure I had outgrown such things, as I liked to imagine?

I came to the main gate of the Sanctuary. While I waited for the ranger to come out of his hut and lift the barrier I scribbled in my notebook, "Maybe I should try to talk to D.C. again." But I think I was aware, even as I wrote, that behind these intellectual exercises rumbled the remnants of my anger, still black, still ugly, still threatening the future.

A mile beyond the gate I turned left up the slope of a large, gently inclined paddock. That morning, as I drove down from Waterhole Camp, I had sighted buffalo on the far edge of the paddock and I was hoping to find them and discover that they were part of the huge herd, said to be a thousand strong and to stay mostly in that vicinity, which I had twice glimpsed in the distance as they flowed black and powerful through scattered bush.

I reached the far side of the sloping paddock. A line of uneven bush crowned the crest of the rise. I reconnoitered along the barrier, found a channel that suggested a clear passage, and swung the car toward it. Then, just for a moment, I hesitated. The channel was very narrow. On either side the bush pressed thick and concealing. It did not look at all a kindly place in which to disturb buffalo—or rhino or elephant, for that matter. Then the intellectual, percentage-playing sector of me had promised, a little thinly, that nothing would happen, and I was driving forward.

I passed through the neck of the channel. It began to broaden. And then, unexpectedly, I was out in the open again. I stopped dead, all thought of buffalo gone.

In that first moment there were, I think, no animals in sight. But off to the right a narrow paddock angled down the slope like a mile-long golf fairway. Beyond the rough bush that marked its left limit, along the entire flank of a long, rolling ridge, stretched another and even more Olympian fairway. And all around, pressing in on the openness of these two paddocks, thrust blocks and wedges and splinters of bush and scattered trees, green against the golden grass and rich in shade and resting places. Now you can find just such components, or reasonable facsimiles, in a hundred views near Keekorok, in a thousand views around the Mara. But this set of components meshed. Line dovetailed with line, color with color, texture with texture, line with color and texture. There was something else too—something that amplified, for me, this quiet concordance that is the essential element in any authentic "view." Westward, far beyond the second fairway, beyond thirty miles of rolling savanna, there stretched, long and low and blue, the wall of the Isuria Escarpment. And at its foot, flat and foreshortened but as mysterious and beckoning as ever, lay the pale grasslands and black wooded wedges of the Triangle. Even through binoculars I could make out few details. But the presence was enough.

Now it is possible that in trying to record this view I have injected elements that did not really impinge on my mind in that first moment I emerged from the bush. Or perhaps I have excluded elements that did. Come to think of it, I have not mentioned open sky or cloud patterns or the angle of the light—and in the Mara they are always a part of it. But the important thing is that the moment I came out into the open I understood the rightness of the place and knew that I was going to stay.

I camped at the head of the fairway, on a flat and almost level little plateau that was ridiculously like a huge natural golf tee. I camped close under the lee of the tall bush that lined the crest. The bush would protect me from the easterly wind that the hours would surely bring. It would also help reduce the danger of my being disturbed by game-viewers investigating animals that they had chanced to see as they drove along the road. The road passed only half a mile away; but because of the crest and the tall bush it was already cut off, safely back in another world.

Out on my open golf-tee of a camp, the sun beat down hot and glaring. Rohosinante's raised rear door provided only a very limited patch of shade and I extended it with a big plastic awning, held high and taut and stable by two seven-foot poles guyed out with nylon cord. Soon I was sitting at my ease, unencumbered by clothes, looking out over the brown-grained tabletop, across the sloping fairway and the very heart of the Mara to the Isuria Escarpment and the Triangle.

I had time, now, to look more carefully at the components of my view. At the way they fitted together. At the convergence or balance or other fit juxtaposition of fold and ridge, hill and donga, black distance and blue sky, golden grass and green bush. But "golden grass" and "green bush" do no more than hint at the contrast I am trying to record. For color is only a part of it; texture is the thing, really. It is the same all over the Mara in the dry season, just as it is in the coastal hills of California when summer has browned out their grasslands. It is the same, I suppose, in any savanna. But that morning as I sat looking out from beneath my awning I saw, more clearly than I had ever done before, in the Mara or back home in California, the contrast in texture between grass and bush. The bush, especially at a distance, was dark and mat, almost lusterless. The grass gleamed.

Close up, the grass had an almost burnished quality. It was long and dry and heavy with seed and its stalks curved up and over and partway down again in gentle arches, so sunlight was always reflecting back to my eye from some shiny, strawlike surface of stalk or seedhead. The grass gleamed even when it stood still—and when the breeze set stalks and seedheads nodding, my whole garden sparkled. Out in the miles of savanna that rolled and dipped and sloped and sometimes stretched flat and even, clear across to the foot of the blue Isuria Escarpment, distance dulled this luster. But the grass never lay dark and mat, the way the bush did. Its grain and glint might be muted, but they were still there, sharp and lively, far out across the miles.

I stayed at View Camp for forty-eight hours.

It was a quiet time. Mostly, there was only the savanna, rolling wide and empty. That, and the smell of hot grass surrender-

ing its moisture to the sun, and the whisper of wind flirting with
the grass or fretting as it bustled through the bush behind me.
Only these, mostly; these and the changing light.

Such animal acts as did appear on stage tended to be subdued
family affairs. It was like that at the beginning, anyway.

While I was eating lunch a big male baboon emerged from
the bush, fifty yards to my right, and began to cross the fairway.
Straggling along behind him in two and threes and singles, like
a happy human hiking party meandering across a mountain
meadow, came the rest of the troop—thirty or so animals in all,
about half of them young ones. Most of the younger generation
scampered and cavorted along independently of the grown-ups
but one infant rode its mother's back, jockey style, and another
traveled slung beneath its mother's belly, hands and feet gripping
her fur. A second large male brought up the rear.

The two males kept glancing in my direction. The rest, after
some initial curiosity, ignored me. The leader was halfway across
the fairway when two ram impala emerged from the bush on its
far side and began to walk across the mouth of a grassy bay. The
baboons ignored the antelope. But the impala, although they held
their original course, kept stopping to glance back over their
shoulders toward the baboons, who had now moved almost
directly in front of me. The impala were clearly uneasy. But after
they and the whole troop of baboons had vanished into the bush,
everybody still on course, I was left wondering—with no hope
of an answer—whether the impala had in fact felt uneasy about
the baboons or about me or about both species of primate.

In midafternoon six topi drifted onto the fairway. They
grazed slowly forward, then stopped. One put its legs up on a
convenient anthill and stood there motionless, on guard but
looking singularly unalert. Three of the group stood quietly
chewing the cud. From time to time one of them would lower
its head and take a mouthful or two of grass in an absent-minded,
well-I-suppose-I-might-as-well-have-another-bite sort of way, like
a sad, surfeited schoolboy nearing the end of an all-you-can-eat-
for-three-dollars dinner. Two of the topi lay down. They lay

with bodies upright, the way horses often lie. And, as far as I could see, they slept. At least, their eyes closed and their heads drooped. The heads hung so far forward that because of the long grass I could not see for sure, even through binoculars, if the tips of their noses really rested on the ground, the way they seemed to. But their pose put the finishing touch to the group's almost overpowering air of postprandial somnolence.*

The stars of that first day at View Camp were the bare-faced go-away birds.

They arrived when afternoon had already begun its slide into evening. They arrived unannounced, erupting over the bush behind me in a wildly chattering six-bird riot, and began to tree-hop down the line of bush. They were substantial, gray-coated, parrotlike birds with brown crests and black-masked faces and white shirt fronts. But the dignity of each shirt front had been wrecked by a large, round, green stain, dead center. It was as if six diners on the far side of a banquet table had taken careful and simultaneous aim and then hurled six plates of pea soup with Cy Young accuracy.

Through binoculars I could see that the birds' "masked" faces were indeed bare of feathers; but no matter how diligently I listened I could not honestly say that I detected in their confused choruses any hint of the "go away!" exhortation that they are reputed to make. Still, I remained grateful for their name.

The barefaced go-away birds did very little, really. Occasionally, when the troupe had occupied a new redoubt in the course of their tree-hopping advance, they would indulge in a sort of undirected internal mobbing, as if each of them still harbored a whole campaign of unexpended aggressions. But often they just sat, doing nothing. They did not seem to look for food,

---

* And provoked:

> *Does doze.*
> *Dopey topi*
> *Do too.*
> *Dodos*
> *Do ditto—*
> *Or diddo.*

and the only productive activity I saw was a little desultory self-preening. One way and another, in fact, they seemed singularly innocent of any clue to what they wanted out of life. But they were a great act to watch.

They borrowed from every branch of show business. The soup-stained shirt fronts and pale crests—like a man's hair standing up in hyperbolized surprise—were pure Laurel and Hardy. The black masks had obviously been requisitioned from Pierrot shows. The long-tailed gray coats—neat and Ruritania-military—suggested Sigmund Romberg. And the baggy white bloomers, tucked in at the knee, could only have come from a Cossack dancing troupe.

The birds were all born actors. But they overdid it. They never just perched; they posed. Whenever they looked at something they pointed like hunting dogs. And each time one of them took to the air it was a fly-past—head up, tail down, back arched, wings squeezing out every last flap of pageantry. They had clearly learned their trade in the silent movies. But they never stayed silent for long. One of the sextet would strike up a kind of hybrid squawk-cluck-chatter, and soon the whole ensemble would be belting it out, *fortissimo*. I could hear their raucous barnyard refrain long after they had tree-hopped past my camp and vanished into the wings down the right side of the fairway.

No one in his senses would try to follow such an animal act. And no one tried. Before long, a curtain of darkness fell across the stage and I lit my houselights.

Soon after dawn next morning I disconnected the awning from Rohosinante's uplifted rear door and drove down the fairway, looking. It was, I realized with some surprise, the first time since I came back to the Mara that I had gone out to game-view and nothing else.

The morning, like most of my hours at View Camp, turned out to be a quiet affair, absorbing but hardly dramatic.

Sunrise was still only a promise when I found a cluster of zebra and topi. Four of the nearest zebra were grazing slowly forward in line abreast, and I sat watching their velvety muzzles probe and test before they engulfed a tuft of grass or rejected it and passed on. The arch of radiance above the eastern horizon expanded and gained strength. At the moment the sun rose I had the line of four black muzzles held sharp and immediate in my binoculars' field. The first level sunbeams shone directly into the zebra's faces. I watched carefully, wondering how the animals would react to the sudden, blinding glare. Their response was unequivocally and absolutely zero.

Sunlight flooded across the grass, silting it with gold. The zebra's stripes jumped into dazzle-focus. The topi's coats flushed into their purple and pewter sheen.

A male topi broke free from the group and began to race across open grass. At first it moved in the clumsy, rolling, hartebeest canter; for a brief and beautiful interval the canter smoothed out into the low, liquid, greyhound gallop; then the animal slowed, stopped, began to graze. But now surges of random restlessness were sweeping through the topi herd, like gusts of wind through forest treetops. Another animal bolted, then two more. Then, as if a starter's gun had fired, the whole herd was in motion: at first, the rolling, porpoise canter; then the smooth, greyhound gallop. For another glorious interval—for a far longer span this time, so that I had time to share the thundering joy of it all—the topi flowed purple and pewter across the golden grass. And then, still racing at full tilt, they began tossing heads at each other in mock jousting bouts, as if even their wild and wonderfully unnecessary romp had not fully absorbed the surge of sunstruck energy. But the madness passed. The racing forms slowed, stopped. Soon the whole herd was grazing, spent, in a new and placid cluster, a quarter of a mile from the place the sun had struck them.

I drove on down the fairway.

A large warthog emerged from the rough and began to rootle near an anthill. He looked very black, very intent, very porcine. When I drove slowly toward him he raised his head and glowered at me like a serious writer (or do I mean a solemn writer?) who has been disturbed in mid-paragraph. Then he had pivoted and hightailed it back into the rough bush. I drove on.

As far as I remember, the warthog was the last mammal I

saw before breakfast; but I rambled around the fairway for two more hours without a minute's boredom. In the end my watch had to remind my stomach that it was time to eat.

Mostly, that morning, it was the birds. It often happened that way now, because I was looking at birds as I had never thought to look at them before.

For the first forty-four years of my life I had thought of bird-watchers, when I thought of them at all, as a frustrated and in-effectual bunch of fuddy-duddies, almost certainly sex starved, who funneled their energies into an amiable but pointless pursuit. My competence in their field was naturally close to zero. ("Natu-rally," because the firmest and most comfortable base from which to make sweeping judgments about any group of people is total ignorance.) But as soon as I bought my East African bird book I began to understand. It was not merely that birds, really looked at, turn out to be startlingly beautiful, nor even that individual birds, like individual humans, engage in funny, solemn, bitchy, pompous, brave, ludicrous, sexy, revolting and tender acts; after my first real attempt to identify individuals from the book I wrote, excitedly: "Fascinating. Not just collecting species. This business makes you see." Long before I reached the Mara I was a full-fledged convert, always eager to try out the new plumage by reaching for my bird book.

That morning I sighted no big, obvious, dramatic birds—no crested cranes, no saddle-bill storks, not one of the various bustards, no troupe of barefaced go-away hams. But just beyond the warthog I drove in on a grass-roots meeting of a dozen neat, almost toylike little bundles of feathers, pale brown but with bills and face masks and breastplates all painted vivid red. I con-sulted the bird book, reconsulted: waxbills. Soon afterward I found myself impaled on the gaze of a slim, nattily dressed little bird that stood upright and pugnacious in short grass, sizing me up with all the peevish intolerance of a true believer. The bird had long red legs. It wore a white miniskirt, a neat gray-brown topcoat, and an incongruous black cap with a white ring around its crown. And this time I did not need the book. I remembered that cap. The young farm manager sometimes played cricket in Nakuru, and one of these slim birds with the distinctive caps often patrolled the outfield with him, might even flutter distractingly when the ball was hit his way. The black cap with the white ring around its crown always reminded him of the monstrosities foisted on the uninnocent heads of English schoolboys, and it was so distinctive that I think even he, every inch an un-birdwatcher, knew that its wearer was called a crowned plover.

I reached the foot of the fairway. A small sunken meadow, roughly circular, lay cradled among arms of bush, masquerading most convincingly as a golf green gone to seed. And on the lip of a donga that guarded the green's left-handed approach I found, wedged in the fork of a dead tree, a hammerkop's nest.

A hammerkop is a sturdy chocolate-brown bird with a backward-pointing crest and a heavy, counterpointed bill that together produce a passable imitation of the head of a blacksmith's hammer (*Hammerkop* is Afrikaans for "hammerhead"). Hammerkops are about two feet tall and they build monumental, stick-woven nests that average five or six feet, base to roof. When I first saw the nest on the lip of the donga a hammerkop was sitting motionless just above its roof, on a branch of the dead tree. Soon a second hammerkop appeared, flying down the line of the donga, low. In its bill it carried a small stick. It planed in toward the nest and landed a dozen feet from the first bird. For perhaps four or five seconds it stood looking toward its partner, the stick still clasped in its bill. Then it opened the bill and dropped the stick. As far as I could see, the action was deliberate. The bird certainly made no move to recover the stick. It continued to stand, motionless, on the bare gray branch. But now I was sitting upright in my seat: the simple little scene had created for me a new and vivid reality.

I had long known that males of certain bird species often bring home to their mates some small object, such as a stick, apparently as a symbolic gift or offering. The act is one form of what behaviorists call "pair bond reinforcement." During courtship and nesting, it appears, the males of a number of bird species will sporadically arrive home bearing such gifts. (What may be similar behavior occurs, far beyond courtship, in at least one species of a totally different class: mated human males of the more attentive breed often bring flowers home to their wives.) But among some birds the male rarely returns without his gift. At least, so I had read—and had believed implicitly. But I had never seen it happen. Now, as I watched the stick fall from the hammerkop's bill, my belief made a quantum leap. For I felt almost sure that what had just happened was a regular occurrence in a well-established household. My near-certainty was preposterous, of course. It lacked any really solid evidence. But I knew that from then on I would believe in gift bearing among birds with a certitude that had, at the drop of a stick, leaped a huge gap.

Almost everybody, I feel sure, has experienced such mental quantum leaps when they first saw for themselves the reality of something they thought they already believed. I am not of course talking about seeing for yourself what you previously doubted. That is straightforward enough. I mean coming face to face with something that descriptions or photographs had deluded you into thinking you were familiar with. The impact may be readily explicable. Some unsuspected element has surprised you: the flimsiness of an unmanned space satellite, perhaps, or the sheer size of an elephant. Or you were unprepared for the harsh specifics of what had until that moment been an intangible: poverty, say, or death. But the impact can be just as real and jolting when what you see is exactly what you had expected to see; when the only change, in other words, is from not having seen to having seen. Such moments tend, for all their apparent uninformativeness, to generate a sharp and lasting pleasure—or pain. That morning at the foot of the fairway, as I watched the stick tumble slowly from the hammerkop's bill, there was no doubt about my pleasure.

Although that single act of stick-dropping satisfied my intuition, it naturally failed to convince my cynical, intellectual, add-one-and-one-if-you-want-two sector. So I waited. As things turned out I had to wait well over an hour. I do not mean that I waited impatiently, or even idly. The waxbills arrived and held a lively congress on the green. The light changed. Other birds flickered on- and off-stage and kept me busy at the bird book. The hammerkops made repeated local forays down into the donga. And at last, when the bird that I now assumed was the female sat perched on another dead tree, forty yards from the nest, the male once more came flying down the line of the donga with a small stick in his bill. He landed about twenty feet from his mate. By chance, his landing place was hidden from me by the branch of another tree. Quickly, I backed the car a couple of feet. The hammerkop was out of sight for only a few seconds; but when I could see him again there was no stick in his bill.

A few minutes later both birds took off. They gained height, contracted to pinpoints in the blue morning sky, and vanished. I glanced at my watch eight-thirty. And it was then, its memory jolted, that my stomach demanded breakfast.

Back at camp, in mid-bacon and eggs, a small antelope materialized on the far side of the fairway. I was looking through binoculars, trying to decide whether it was a dikdik or a blue duiker, when I heard a sound off to my left. I lowered the glasses.

A hundred yards away, emerging from the bush at the head of the fairway, ambling slowly and almost somnambulistically toward me, head hanging forward, low and relaxed, was a very large rhino. I sat extremely still. The rhino continued to advance along the edge of the bush—on a course that would bring it within a dozen paces of my table. When it was about eighty yards away I stood up without abrupt movement and walked, very slowly, to the open driver's door of the car. The rhino continued to amble forward. When less than seventy yards separated us, I slid down in the driver's seat and turned the ignition key.

Rohosinante's engine purred into life. The rhino's head jerked up. And next instant, with a dexterity astonishing in such a bulky beast, it had moved—half sideways, in a kind of twinkle-toes shimmy—behind a tall bush. One moment there was a rhino; the next, only the bush.

I put one foot outside the car and stood upright. The engine was still running.

A horned head reappeared beside the bush. The rhino eased forward until its shoulders and most of the gleaming black body were out in the open. Then it stopped and stood facing me.

I raised the binoculars.

The rhino gleamed because it had been wallowing. Wet, black mud coated its body. On the point of its bulging right shoulder a small leaf had stuck to the mudpack and it stood out bright green against the gleaming black. I swung the binoculars forward, past pricked ears, along the raised and vigilant head. There had been water as well as mud in the wallow: the front horn was washed clean. It thrust out at me, brown and massive. Below it, the pointed, prehensile upper lip quivered, like the lip of a nervous man fluttering with indecision. Uncertainty, in fact, seemed to infuse the rhino's whole body.

I am not sure just how I received this impression. I do not remember getting any message from the two small eyes set low and wide on the head. To my surprise, I am not sure I remember the eyes at all. But I know I was sure of the uncertainty. And I know that for long, suspended seconds the world had contracted to the world of my binoculars. At one terminal stood the rhino, facing me, uncertain. I stood at the other, facing back, waiting, even more uncertain, thinking how good it was that Rohosinante's engine had started first time and wondering if the nylon cord once more securing the awning to her raised rear door would snap quickly if we had to take off. I was also thinking, all in the same swirl, that it was a very different matter standing outside like this, unprotected. I had been closer to several rhinos; but always I had been inside a car, furnished with a sense of being protected as well as a reasonable confidence that I could escape if the beast charged. But also cut off. Now, nothing cut me off. There was just the rhino and me. A bright green leaf on a shiny, black, bulging shoulder. A nervous lip. And a massive brown horn, washed shiny clean and thrusting out at me. We stood like that, each of us motionless at our terminal of the world, for an interminable three or four seconds. Then, in a vastly relieving yet strangely disappointing anticlimax, the rhino backed up a few steps and turned and ambled off through the bush. It went quite slowly. But it moved with a firm tread, like a man who has made up his mind, and I knew our interview was at an end. Within seconds the huge black bulk had vanished.

Now I must make it clear that the rhino's shining blackness was entirely due to mud and had nothing to do with its common name of "black rhino." A black rhino's hide is gray—and so is the hide of the rare and larger "white rhino," Africa's only other species, which does not occur in the Mara. ("White" seems to be an errant anglicization of the Afrikaans word *weit*. And *weit* means "wide": the white rhino's mouth is a wide, squared-off instrument, admirably adapted for an animal that is predominantly a grazer. It can, almost as efficiently as a hippo's cavernous mouth, scythe off a huge helping of grass at every chomp. The black rhino, on the other hand, is predominantly a browser. Its more pointed mouth and prehensile upper lip equip it to grasp and break off twigs and small branches, rather as an elephant does with the tip of its trunk, though the rhino is far less deft.)

When the rhino had gone I went back to my bacon and eggs. They were almost cold, but they had acquired a new and sharper flavor.*

* Rhino horns seem to be essentially offensive weapons; but by a pathological twist of that inscrutable but pragmatic process we call evolution they may prove to be the rhinos' undoing. The twist is that another animal has got a wrong idea into its head.

In certain parts of the world, notably Asia, tradition has it that if a man consumes a little powdered rhinoceros horn then his sexual desire and performance will both rocket. Not unexpectedly, scientific tests expose the belief as hogwash. But men being men, it has brought death and dismemberment to countless rhinos. The three species of Asiatic rhino are tapering toward extinction: perhaps eight hundred individuals survive. And, because the Asian aphrodisiac market remains unsatisfied, African rhinos are now in danger. Other forces have contributed to the recent serious reduction in their numbers, among them the destruction or alteration or closing of its habitat for farming and other human purposes, and the urge of some ostensibly mature men to shoot any nonhuman animal, especially if it is big. But poaching is the main threat. A hideous amount goes on. Two

Only one other big-name animal appeared on stage at View Camp. It made its entrance in the middle distance, and it came no closer. Yet it impressed me, in its different way, just as much as had the rhino who almost came to breakfast.

A little before noon I noticed two kongoni cantering down the next low ridge, half a mile away. Twice the kongoni stopped and looked back up the hill. Then they vanished into thick bush.

I swung my glasses left, up and along the ridge, looking for whatever had disturbed them. Moving unhurriedly down the crest—steadily and inexorably, like a huge black tank across a battlefield—came an old bull buffalo. He was the biggest buffalo I had ever seen, and he was magnificent. The marrow of his magnificence lay in something beyond his size, beyond even the breadth and bulk of the horns that crowned his huge, hanging head. Perhaps it was the way he moved. For there was an aura of colossal confidence about his progress—an eloquent certainty that the world would defer, and a juggernaut indifference to those who did. I watched, fascinated, as the huge beast lumbered down the crest, regal, ancient, superb.

I was playing with the absurd but pleasing thought that he would walk on and on, day and night until he died, because nothing was capable of getting in his way, when he stopped. His huge head lifted. His nose swung toward me, outstretched. In spite of the thousand yards that separated us, it was almost as if I could hear the air being drawn in through his nostrils. And all at once I realized that the Mara's east wind had begun to blow, very gently, and was carrying my scent directly toward the buffalo.

After a moment or two the buffalo lowered his head and

hundred and ten illegally taken rhino horns were recently found aboard a single Arab dhow sailing north from Kenya. So if, as seems entirely possible, rhinos shortly become extinct it will probably be fair to lay the blame on man's misapprehension of what their powdered horns will do for him in bed.

That morning at View Camp, remembering the way the washed horn had thrust out at me, I wondered if the horn's phallic aspect might account for the aphrodisiac legend. On its own, that hardly seemed enough. But at the time I could come up with nothing better.

moved forward. A few steps, and he stopped again. Once more the huge, embossed head lifted. Once more the black nose stretched out toward me. Then the head went down and the beast was lumbering on, juggernaut and indifferent again, along the open ridge. This time the slow, inexorable march continued unchecked until, holding his straight and imperious course to the end, he vanished at last into thick bush.

I sat back in my chair.

For the first time I half understood why buffalo, for all their docile bovine aspect, have the reputation of being the most unpleasant animals to be charge by. Once committed, it is said, they never give up.

Fortunately, buffalo rarely charge unless wounded. So there remains some doubt about the correct response to the breathless question often posed by visitors: "What is the most dangerous animal in Africa?" I once heard a professional hunter suggest that it depended on your experience: "If you've had a few pretty close calls with elephant, say, your answer is likely to be 'elephant.'" But that morning at View Camp, remembering the huge unstoppable buffalo and then remembering the gleaming black rhino and then remembering what was happening to the world's rhinos, I decided that the most dangerous animal in Africa is the same species that is the most dangerous, to everyone and everything, on all the other continents.

That evening I did not drive out game-viewing again, as I had intended. I was content, I found, to sit under my awning and watch the changing scene.

All day the view had modulated. By noon, grass that had gleamed golden stretched pale and strawlike. Hills that had humped gold and green lay flat and black. And as the hours transmuted color and texture and emphasis, so the mood shifted: gleaming and fresh and vivid to tarnished and tired and almost vapid. By midafternoon the sun ruled. The savanna sprawled in bondage. At the foot of the Isuria Escarpment, three wide and ugly columns of smoke began to spiral upward. They met and merged and spread until they had smudged away the last flat landmark along the blur that was the Triangle. At breakfast I had been able to examine the rocky black caps of several low hills in the Triangle, just beyond the river. Hour by hour the sun had compressed these hills. Now the smoke pall eliminated them.

But by five o'clock the first cool fingers of relief were reaching out to restore the savanna's gold and gleam. I sat on in my chair, watching the landscape emerge from its ennui, watching color and texture and emphasis mirror the morning's transmutation. From time to time I lifted my binoculars and tried yet again to penetrate the smoke pall that still hung along the foot of the Isuria Escarpment.

The sun wheeled down toward the escarpment, plunged through the smoke, and died its daily death. Dusk softened the savanna, then smothered it. Night fell. The moon rose yellow and mottled as Stilton.

But the show was not yet over.

Just after I had finished dinner I heard, out beyond my hissing white dome of lamplight, a faint tapping or clicking that sounded like someone quietly knocking two pieces of wood or ivory together. The sound came only intermittently; but when it came the rhythm was regular. I peered out into the blackness. In spite of the moonlight I could see nothing but vague bulks of bush and grass.

I picked up my flashlight, pointed it in the direction of the sounds, and switched on.

Sparkling back at me, white like diamonds, a pair of eyes. Then another pair. Then two more. And surrounding each pair of eyes, a vague shape, possibly brown.

I put down the flashlight and picked up the binoculars and cupped my hands around them to cut off the glare from the lamp. Through the glasses, the moonlit savanna jumped into existence. Less than forty yards from my table, ghostly in the moonlight yet sharp against their unfocused background, stood four eland. One was grazing; the others quietly chewed the cud. In that first moment I think it was the animals' casualness that astonished me most: they ignored me, utterly, as if no bizarre and inexplicable phenomenon glared and hissed at them, forty yards away, there in the middle of the otherwise dim and muted savanna.

My eyes adjusted to the pale moonlight and I began to pick out details: fluting that spiraled up thick, straight horns; heavy dewlaps that hung loose and floppy; even—something I had never noticed before—a small rectangular black patch on the back of each foreleg that made each animal look as if it had been inoculated a few inches above the knee and then had the puncture protected by a big black Band-Aid.

One of the eland began to wander away from the group. At once I heard the faint, knock-on-ivory clicking. The eland moved only a few yards. When it stopped, so did the clicking.

Before long I had confirmed that the sound came only when an animal moved. But the clicks did not seem to synchronize with the hooves' impact. Not exactly. And the eland, even though they happened to be in a place that had been cropped short and almost lawnlike, were walking on thick grass. Every time an animal moved I watched closely, trying to correlate sound and movement.

But I do not want to suggest that during the fifteen or twenty minutes the eland were there, just outside my dome of light, I did nothing but sleuth away at clicks. For the scene I was watching had another kind of mystery to it, a kind that demanded no sleuthing, only acceptance and appreciation. It always seems to be there, this aura, when you look through binoculars in moonlight. Whatever you focus stands out with eye-riveting sharpness, embossed against a dim and fuzzy background. It is an effect a camera lens produces routinely, the naked eye only rarely. And working with this vividness as well as against it, you have, washed over everything, the enticing uncertainty of a pallid blue ghostliness. That night I watched the eland standing so close and calm and casual out in the dim, moonlit savanna, there was something else, too. My field of view framed the little group to perfection. And sitting there at my lamplit table I seemed to look through a window, from one world into another. It was rather like one of those unexpected scenes that you sometimes glimpse through an uncurtained window when you are walking at night in a city. The man reading the paper and the woman standing before a cupboard surprise you. Their quiet tableau informs you of the life that is going on all over the city behind those dark, blank walls. You had known about that life, of course, had known about it all the time. But you had never come to grips with its reality.

At first, nothing much happened, out in my moonlit window-scene. The eland stood still, grazing or chewing the cud. One of them might wander off a few paces. The others would join it, or it would rejoin them. A pair of eyes would catch the lamp-light and glint back at me, diamond-white; then there were once again only the four pale brown animals embossed against the pale blue savanna. The eland showed no fear of me, even when I stood up and moved away from the lamp's glare and leaned against the car to steady the binoculars.

Once, a small black shape appeared at the right edge of my binocular window. Quickly, yet with no untidy haste, it moved across my front, cutting silently between the eland and me. The shape was low and squat and strong and purposeful. I swung the binoculars, following it. But the focus was wrong, and before I could adjust my glasses the shape had vanished into thick bush and left me wondering—once again without hope of an answer, ever—if it had really been a honey badger.

I swung my glasses back to the eland. They had ignored the intruder. But two of them now stood facing each other, broad-side on to me. And as I watched, both animals lowered their heads. They lowered them at the same instant. They lowered them almost to the ground. Then, still in unison, they turned their muzzles under so that they pointed back between their legs and their profiles ran parallel to the ground and very nearly touching it. The straight, powerful horns projected directly forward, also parallel to the ground and almost touching it. There was a brief, barely perceptible pause. Then, with a controlled, slow-motion deliberation, the two animals moved forward. Their horns met, slid into mesh, locked. And then the eland began to push. Their pushing, like everything else they did, was slow motion and deliberate and controlled. There was no dramatic staggering, no mighty swaying. The two animals seemed to measure out the pressure and balance it, as if what they wanted was not the glow of victory but the sheer fun of pushing. From time to time I could detect a slight, near-rhythmic variation in their positions; it was the only sign of the force being applied through those powerful, interlocked horns. The two animals were barely thirty yards from me, but I could hear nothing except an occasional faint rubbing sound, horn against horn.

The opposing bodies leaned slightly forward, tense and straining yet balanced, almost as if posed. The locked heads, bowed in their stylized obeisance, presented the huge, muscular shoulders as a pair of beautiful, confronted curves that flowed back without a break along the straining backs and down the line of the tense, forward-leaning hind legs. Had it not been for the small, near-rhythmic variations in their positions they might have been a pair of those blown-glass animals you see in the windows of expensive stores, opposed but matching, melting your heart with the grace of their long, stylized, curving necks and long, stylized, curving bodies.

The ending, too, was quiet and controlled.

The other two eland began to wander off to the left. The locked pair stopped pushing and moved apart. Their horns disengaged. They lifted their heads. Then they turned and walked casually after the others. Soon all four animals had vanished into shadowy bush and left me alone and bereft, just as the eland had left me twenty years before when they slid away out of my headlights, one by one, on the slopes of Mount Kenya.

I went to bed.

For a while I lay looking up through the orange tent wall at the diffused orange globe of the moon. Through the window of my binoculars I had caught a glimpse of the life that was going on all over the savanna behind the dark, blank walls of the night—the life that went on every night, in every corner of the Mara. I had known about that life, of course, had known about it all the time. At least, I had assumed that it existed. I had never come to grips with its reality, that was all.

But now I had penetrated the blackness. The two quiet days at View Camp had done their work. For the first time since meeting Mwangi, for the first time since leaving Nairobi, I had moved back into the world of the animals. And it had been like coming home: warm, embracing, placental.*

When I look back on the fortnight that followed I find a peaceful and protected interval, an undemanding anticusp. Yet in a sense those two weeks formed the core of my time in the Mara. Unchanneled by things to "do," I began to explore the Sanctuary. And now I explored more than just spatially. I do not mean that I succeeded at once in grasping the savanna's complexities; but as the days passed I drew more and more of its ingredients within the perimeter of my awareness. By the end of the fortnight's exploration I had begun, to think, to grok.†

* I doubt if I would have had the nerve to write "placental" here if I had not, long after I left the Mara, heard a lecture by René Dubos in which the eminent bacteriologist and conservationist propounded a theory: that built into the human species is a yearning for landscape in which grassland alternates with tall, shade-giving trees. And Dr. Dubos suggested that this yearning might be an unconscious desire by the species to return to its placenta. For the birthplace of man is currently held by many anthropologists to lie in the vicinity of Olduvai Gorge, at the southern edge of the Serengeti Plain. And it seems that at the time of our birth, as now, the Serengeti and the Mara were largely savanna.

I am not sure I feel totally at ease with this attractive theory. It seems almost too tidy to be true (though come to think of it there are always trees in the Garden of Eden). But I recently chanced on unexpected support for it in a poem, "Thoughts of Africa," by Jennifer Townson: "Please let me be . . . here in this placental warmth." And I am hoping that poem and theory will between them justify my use of "placental," even in prose. I am almost sure it is what I mean.

† "To grok" seems to mean something rather like "to comprehend the essence of a matter, by empathy rather than logic." See *Stranger in a Strange Land* (especially Chapter 31), by Robert A. Heinlein. See the same book for "cusp," used in the sense of "a pivotal moment at which events reach a climax that can be resolved by immediate and drastic action." Or something like that.

But all through that fortnight I also kept learning on the logical level. At the time, in fact—as nearly always happens—I saw the amassment of information as the thing that mattered most.

Some of the learning began to come more easily now because I had gained experience. For one thing, I had become better at seeing. Practice had taught my eye to zero in on those small anomalies that are often the only markers of an "event" on the face of the savanna: a darker blur in the dark shadow of a bush, three giraffes swiveling heads in unison, or a pair of golden points protruding above golden grass so slightly that you could easily miss them if you were not in some submerged sense always on the lookout for lions' ears.

There was also another and more pervasive way in which I saw better. When we humans go into new terrain along a road, most of us impose a human grid. The road is a base line of our grid and we tend to see everything with reference to that line and to familiar human units. The Mara's gently rolling savanna, seen strung out like rolls of film along alien and arbitrary roads, had at first established no meaningful patterns in my mind. But now I began to fit its components, almost at first glance, into the grid of meaning the animals knew: thick bush on hills and ridges, thinning where the slope slackened; grassland on the flat, broken by "orchards" and clumps of "lion bush"; dongas fencing the grassland into paddocks. The animals follow the dictates of this grid even more closely than a modern city dweller follows the cultural commands of his city's grid: freeway and boulevard, ghetto and suburb, shopping center and industrial zone. And once I could see this other grid clear and whole it became far easier to slip new information into relevant slots.

One of my sources of information during that quiet fortnight was a Masai.

Mostly I still watched the animals on my own; but some mornings and evenings I made use of Tipis's offer and went game-viewing with one of his rangers. The rangers, in fact, were one reason why, for the first ten days of that leisurely fortnight, I rarely went very far from the lodge.

Three different rangers acted as my guide and instructor. One of them was the tall Masai with whom I had achieved some hint of a passing game on the soccer field. He was a slender, good-looking man, though he suffered from eyes that sometimes seemed set too close together. His name, Joshua, suggested that he had been brought up in a mission, but as far as I could see it had done him no irreparable harm. He was thirty-five, he said, and came from the high country north of Narok. He had been a policeman, but while helping to clear out a Kikuyu village during the Mau Mau rebellion he had gone into a hut and a man hidden in the roof had slashed down at him with one of the big local knives called *pangas*. The stroke just missed his head and cut deep into his shoulder. For a while he was partially paralyzed and he had been invalided out with a pension; but now the shoulder was perfectly sound again.

Joshua seemed to understand better than the other two rangers the kind of information I was looking for.

Sometimes his contributions were odd snippets of animal lore. A small convocation of vultures on the ground did not necessarily mean a carcass: the birds might have found a kill in that place a long time before and have fallen into the habit of congregating there when business was slack. Topi were afraid of thick bush where predators might be lurking, but they often moved in company with zebras, who were less fearful, and when a mixed group approached a patch of bush the canny topi would hang back until the zebras had gone ahead and confirmed or confounded their suspicions.

Sometimes Joshua answered questions that I had until then asked only of myself. Yes, it did seem as if many animals let you come closer when it was raining. Young topi's coats changed from kongoni brown to their rightful purple and pewter at about six months. "Dopey topi," lying down with heads sagging forward, held their noses just above the ground, not actually touching it; but they seemed to sleep in that position, and probably when standing up too. The eland's cowlike dewlap was indeed the reason Masai tradition allowed that particular antelope to be eaten. And the clicking that eland made when they moved came from something inside their legs.*

At my suggestion, Joshua tried to teach me his native tongue. Masai is a Nilo-Hamitic language—and a fiend. From the grammar I bought in Nairobi I had learned that even if you mastered the "place" gender, open and closed vowels, some hopelessly undisciplined consonants, and verbs that convoluted ("the verb system is very elaborate and contains the real spirit of the language"), you found yourself face to face with the "tonal system." Stripped of refinements, this means that what you think you are saying can be utterly transformed according to whether you pronounce it in a squeaky, standard or sepulchral voice. At least, I think that's it. Anyway, I soon turned to Joshua for help. But by the end of ten days' desultory coaching I had mastered only one phrase. In simplied form it can be written, *i-inkati kumok oleng.* Literally, it means "very many wildebeest." In terms of progress in my lessons it meant *la plume de ma tante.*

We did rather better, Joshua and I, when it came to the language of the savanna.

We began with droppings. We stopped at every pile and discussed size, shape, color and consistency. I soon came to recognize such indices as the surprisingly small size of eland pellets and the flattened ends that spelled "giraffe." Dating the messages proved trickier. So we concentrated on the easiest: the big ele-

---

* Toni Harthoorn, who had done a lot of physiological research with captive eland, later told me that he had crouched down close to their legs in an effort to pinpoint the sound and he felt sure it was made by the halves of a cloven hoof coming together when the animal's weight was taken off it. He rather thought that some eland enjoyed the sound and at times would even stand still and make it deliberately and repeatedly by shifting their weight from leg to leg.

Then a district game warden in northern Kenya who had an eland so tame that it would put its head through his house windows said he agreed with Joshua: he was sure the sound came from something, probably a bone, that moved inside an eland's leg when it walked.

But later still I discovered that both the Kalahari bushmen and Laurens van der Post agree with Toni Harthoorn (see *The Heart of the Hunter*).

So I guess I have yet to solve the Great Eland Clicking Mystery.

phant igloos. The dung beetles and ants that do such a quick and thorough job of dispersing other animals' dung, thereby helping to fertilize the savanna, seem for some reason to avoid elephant droppings, and the igloos take weeks to dry out and crumble. So for six or seven days, under normal Mara conditions, you can note the color of the crust (it grows lighter with age) and can thereby judge, once you have mastered the idiom, roughly how long ago that igloo was laid down. After a couple of scatological sessions with Joshua I felt that I had at least made a start on the huge task of reading the savanna the way a Masai did: deciphering almost without effort the tracks and droppings and bent grass stalks and broken branches and no doubt a hundred other signs still invisible to my untutored eye.

Joshua entered into the spirit of such lessons. All this time I was thinking ahead to my safari into the Triangle, and at the end of my second session with him I jotted down in my notes, "He'll be good, I think." When I mentioned the possibility of the safari, Joshua seemed eager. He knew the Triangle well, he said.

But my prime sources of information during those ten quiet days in the Sanctuary were the research papers I had collected in Nairobi. They covered a spectrum that ranged from a proclamation by President Kenyatta ("No country has such wildlife as we have in Africa. . . . Our animals work for us—they are employees of Kenya") to "an ecological reconnaissance" of the Mara by the world-famous biologist, F. Fraser Darling.

Among the early papers I read was Talbot and Stewart's "First Wildlife Census of the Entire Serengeti-Mara Region, East Africa" (in visualizing animal densities, remember that the Serengeti is about eight times the size of the Mara—and that many species move freely across the man-drawn boundary):

Species	Probable accuracy of count	Serengeti	Mara	Total
Wildebeest	Within a few percent	221,699	17,817	239,516
Zebra	Within a few percent	151,006	20,867	171,873
Topi	Within 10% (probably low)	15,766	4,111	19,877
Buffalo	Within 10%	15,898	5,934	21,832

Species	Probable accuracy of count	Serengeti	Mara	Total
Elephant	Within 10% (only listed species that may move in and out of census area)	702	455	1,157
Eland	Estimate based on partial count	4,900–7,300	1,500–2,250	6,400–9,550
Kongoni	Minimal count (population possibly much higher)	1,379	721	2,100
Lion	Rough estimate (based on proportion of known Mara lions seen from air)	300–400	250–300	500–700
Rhinoceros	Minimal count (only small proportion of total)	29	54	83
Thomson's gazelle	Rough estimate	—	—	480,000–800,000

These figures naturally offer no more than guidelines. The census—conducted primarily from a light plane but confirmed by spot ground checks—was made in late May 1961, and applies only to that period: some animal populations fluctuate from year to year by 50 percent or more. But although the census barely begins to suggest the richness of savanna life—even among major mammals, such abundant species as giraffe, impala, and waterbuck had to be ignored—it supplied my first food for any kind of quantitative thought.*

Now please do not get the idea that during those quiet days in the Sanctuary I examined everything with a strait and solemn scientific eye. By and large I went on doing exactly what I had been doing all along: looking about me like a tolerably intelligent opportunist steeped in ignorance. Watching the animals remained what it had always been: bloody good fun. But as the days passed I found that the reading had injected a new element into

* This is no science book, but at its end you will find a bibliography of the main scientific sources, such as this census report, that I have consulted. The bibliography is there partly because I wish to acknowledge my debts but mainly so that, if you want to get your teeth into meat that I can display only briefly and at the back of the slab, you will know where to shop.

my game-watching. And in the end the reading and the watching melded.

I did not, as I suppose I should have done, organize the reading into a tidy curriculum that carried me logically up the tree of evolution, starting with the grass and shrubs that captured the sun's energy and so fueled all the rest of us organisms that peopled the Mara and the planet. I read precious little about the vegetation: I think I classified such material as heavy freight and shunted it aside to be handled during the six months I would return for serious research. I did not read much about insects either. And I neither read nor saw a great deal of the reptiles.

I saw no snakes at all: on the savanna, as in most places, they are retiring creatures (but the cobras and puff adders and much rarer mambas are, unlike North American rattlesnakes, highly efficient killers of human beings, and it was always reassuring to remember the anti-venin in my travel grip, just behind the driver's seat). I did meet several agama lizards basking on granite kopjes near the lodge. The eighteen-inch-long males had flashy, two-tone bodies—part brilliant cobalt blue, part a kind of synthetic salmon pink (like white flesh on color TV, tinted too purple)—and seen head on down the barrels of my binoculars, almost filling their field, they made daunting spectacles. With forelegs extended and rigid, powerful hind legs flexed and frog-like, and mouths stretching clear across flattened, no-brow faces, they looked like gymnast-wrestler-bouncers, all muscle and pugnacity, hardly able to wait until they found some mild trespasser they could quietly and legally dismember. Aside from the agama lizards, I saw few of the Mara's reptiles. They are inconspicuous members of the savanna community.

But the birds were always there, pecking away at my attention: tiny, brilliant, nectar-feeding sunbirds that fill the same niche as American hummingbirds and, like them, quiver and dart and gleam and are the birds that make you smile; loose flocks of those polychromatic bundles—all splash and stripe and startling iridescence—that peacock about eastern Africa under the soft-sell label, "superb starlings"; parrot-sized lilac-breasted rollers—delicate pas-

tel studies when perched but exploding in flight into electrifying
ultramarine torpedoes; the big, dramatic birds, three or four or
even five feet tall, that you often see stalking across the grasslands
—the saddle-bill storks, for example, that manage to look stately,
almost majestic, in spite of red kneecaps and red, black and yellow bills that suggest a hurried welding job by some modern
sculptor caught with an irresistible inspiration but no materials
except panels from three different cars; and finally the ostriches—
so big and unbirdlike and such surefire attractions for un-bird-
minded visitors that it is easy to understand why they have been
called "honorary mammals." With such a cast it hardly mattered
that among my research papers I found only fragments of a
script for the birds.

By and large, the mammals monopolized the literature. And
by and large it was still the mammals that I watched.

You do not see many small mammals on the East African savanna. Over most of its surface, temperature and humidity
run to such extremes that only some specialized style of life, such
as burrowing, makes existence tolerable. But the hyraxes thrive.

Several colonies of rock hyraxes lived in granite kopjes near
the lodge. Six or seven of them would assemble on a sheltered
ledge and squat there, feet tucked neatly under furry bodies,
watching me watch them. They were plump, tailless little creatures about a foot and a half long, and although I knew that
zoologists persisted in classifying them as the closest living relatives of elephants, they looked to me very like young-of-the-year
American marmots.

From a research paper on a Serengeti hyrax colony I discovered why the species has succeeded where so many small mammals
have failed. I also detected, it seemed to me, a microcosm of the
Mara's complexity.

From a hyrax's point of view, kopjes are lotus islands in the
harsh sea of the open savanna. The hyraxes sleep in the kopje's
crevices, and readings taken continuously for two months in a
dormitory crevice of the Serengeti kopje and also in grass only
ten yards away reflected climates that seemed continents apart. In

the crevice the temperature never rose above 76 degrees or fell below 64 degrees; out on the grass—in shade, not sunshine—the range was 93 degrees to 53 degrees. In the crevice the daily humidity range only once exceeded 40 percent; outside it ran as high as 100 percent. By living in kopjes, in other words, hyraxes manage to have a pretty easy time of it. In fact, they have become so used to a soft life that they no longer seem able to withstand extremes of temperature, and their daily routines are much like those of the reptiles—which lack the physiological heat-compensating mechanisms that we mammals enjoy, and must therefore run their lives accordingly.

Except on cloudy days, the rock hyraxes emerge from their crevices at sunrise and bask. Soon they move out a short way from the kopje and feed on grass. Around nine o'clock they retreat toward shady ledges and thickets around the kopje's edge. There they remain through the heat of the day. For two hours in the cool of evening they once more feed in the open. Then they withdraw to the kopje's crevices for the night. In cloudy weather they do not emerge until midmorning but often feed throughout the day. In other words, they do not operate unless the temperature is right. Such behavior may seem odd in furry little bundles of life that look as cozily insulated as bears. But from what little I have seen of American marmots, which also live in rock crevices, I suspect that at least in the high country of the Sierra Nevada they run their lives on similar temperature-sensitive schedules. Perhaps they too have "grown soft" in the lap of luxury.

Tolerable temperature and humidity by no means end the list of conveniences that make a kopje an almost Elysian hyrax home. The only predators able to penetrate the kopje's crevices are snakes. And when, as sometimes happens, tree hyraxes share the condominium with rock hyraxes, they provide an elevated early-warning system for all residents: they feed on nearby thorn trees, and if they spot a predator from the vantage point of their high-rise dining rooms they sound an alarm call and every hyrax within earshot races for home and safety. The kopje's built-in fire service is excellent too. Grass fires that periodically sweep the surrounding savanna never invade the vegetation-free crevices and rarely do more than singe the dense, fire-resisting thickets that surround the whole outcrop. The utilities are also good. Hyraxes seem able to go for at least limited periods without surface water, but a kopje is, by savanna standards, rather richly watered: its surface acts as a small rain catchment area and also promotes condensation of dew. And other benefits follow. Because of the dependable water supply, trees and shrubs and tall grass tend to thrive around the outcrop and so provide ground cover and shade that in turn help conserve the moisture. And the hyraxes, thriving on this bullish market, do their bit toward boosting the gross kopje product. Rather than foul their crevice-homes, they defecate and urinate in only one or two places in the kopje. (And so are easily house trained: one pet hyrax "refused to relieve nature except when sitting upright on the edge of the lavatory seat.") Their communal toilets are periodically flushed by rain, and this water recycles energy by fertilizing the thickets and trees and nearby grass on which the hyraxes depend. The kopje, in other words, becomes an almost closed fertility cycle. And the hyraxes, borne along on the well-ordered flow of kopje economics, thrive mightily. As happens in other societies, the successful citizens of the savanna, once out of the rut, tend, through no inherent iniquity, to go on getting richer.

After I had read the hyrax paper I could grasp, whenever I looked at a kopje, at least the major filaments that interlinked rock and hyrax, grass and hyrax, tree and bush and hyrax, rock hyrax and tree hyrax. There were, I knew, finer filaments—such as the microscopic protozoans that lived in hyrax stomachs and enabled them to digest the cellulose walls of their green food. I was still liable to forget such invisible worlds; but I could now comprehend, at least in a coarse sense, the texture of the kopje world.

I could comprehend that texture because the kopje was a relatively simple and self-contained little unit. Out in the wide savanna world the life web would be vastly bigger and more complicated, and discerning its patterns—let alone each quirk and dovetail of its filaments—would prove vastly more difficult. But the bigger web would be built on the same plan, and it seemed reasonable to hope that what I had learned about the kopje microcosm might help guide me toward at least some understanding of the savanna as a whole.

The most visible strands in that broad Mara web were the big mammals, and it was with them, naturally, that most of the research papers dealt. But at first I found that my reading could often supply no more than footnotes to a day's encounters.

One afternoon, hurrying back to the lodge to pick up Joshua for an evening's game-viewing, I drove around a corner at thirty miles an hour—too fast for that narrow and twisting section of track—and had just begun to charge down into a shallow dip when I saw, thirty yards ahead and barely ten yards to the left of the track, browsing peacefully beside a tree, a rhino. By that time it was too late to do anything except accelerate, so I accelerated. I had covered ten yards of the vital thirty before the rhino lifted his head, ten more before he had turned to face me. By the time he began to charge I was almost level with him. And then, before he had really gathered momentum, I was past and the track was climbing the far side of the dip and my foot was halfway through the floorboards and Rohosinante was bucking like a mustang. I glanced up into my rear-view mirror. Because of the bucking and because of the red-brown dust that coated the rear window, I could see only dimly. But he was there all right, dead astern, perhaps twenty yards back, head down and coming, as broad and squat as a battleship and just about as stoppable. But by the time I had glanced ahead at the track and then back into the mirror I knew we had made it: he was losing ground; and then, almost before threat had ever quite crystallized into danger, it was all over. His charge slackened. He swung left, off the track. I eased up on the gas pedal. Rohosinante regained her cool.

At the top of the rise I stopped and leaned out of the window and looked back. He was standing beside a small thorn tree, head uppish and alert, horns thick and thrusting and phallic. Even broadside and stationary, he still looked squat and battleship—and no more than halfway re-gruntled. After a few minutes I left him standing there and drove on.*

Next day, my first real inspection of the savanna's scavenger service taught me how little I knew about it.

In late afternoon I found, just outside the Sanctuary boundary, clustered thick around a dead zebra, in open grassland near a donga, about two hundred vultures and a dozen marabou storks. When I drove slowly to within forty yards, most of the birds flapped or walked a short distance to the left, away from the donga, and then stopped, strung out in loose clumps, like mourners after a funeral. But twenty or thirty stood their ground in two groups, one at the head of the carcass, the other at its tail. The five-foot-tall marabous, white and gunmetal gray, towered slim and upright above the brown, turkey-size vultures. The marabous' bills were long and straight and massive and yellow; the vultures', small and short and hooked and brown. But the heads and necks of both birds were naked except for skimpy coverings of gray down.

Before long, the birds around the zebra went back to work. Everyone who could find something to eat ate. Those unfavorably placed waited. There was remarkably little jostling, but one marabou, apparently convinced that a vulture had encroached on his preserves, shoved it testily aside with his huge bill. The vulture turned and grabbed the tip of the bill and hung Davidly on while Goliath tried to shake the annoyance free and at the same time retain his dignity. After a while he attained one goal, though hardly the other, and both birds resumed their meal. The rest of

---

* My reading provided only a tangential footnote to this incident. The day before, I had browsed through a research paper called *Mating and Courtship of Black Rhino* and in it had found the answer to my question about how men came to believe in the aphrodisiac qualities of rhino horn. It seems that the time animals take for coition does not depend on size. Elephant, for example, average only fifteen seconds. But observers of copulating rhino have recorded elapsed times of twenty-nine, thirty-two and thirty-six minutes. It is easy to understand how reports of such performances might blow the minds of failing men.

the crew had ignored them. The sun shone down and from all that scattered assembly of huge birds came no sound that I could hear.

Because the birds feeding on the zebra still clustered thick I could rarely see, even through binoculars, exactly what any individual was doing. I restarted the car and edged closer. At first the birds ignored me. Then, as I eased within ten yards of the carcass, they fell back and formed a rough crescent about the same distance on its far side. I stopped, switched off, and sat still, watching and waiting. The birds stood silent, reciprocating. Between us the zebra lay sprawled out in the sunlight. I could see now that its head had been picked almost clean, down to bare bone, and that its quarters had partially collapsed, as if hollowed out. Otherwise the body, although thin and emaciated, or perhaps just shriveled, seemed free of any wound such as a predator killer would have made. The poor beast had probably died of disease, I decided, or perhaps from snakebite. And after a while, as I sat looking at the striped, unbroken skin, it occurred to me why the vultures and marabous had clustered at the zebra's head and tail: in spite of their efficient-looking bills they could not puncture the skin and therefore could feed only at places such as eyes and mouth and anus that gave them an opening.

We sat and stood there in the waning sunlight for over an hour, those birds and I, with the zebra stretched out black and white between us. Apart from a few mockish fights and perfunctory squawks from the vultures, silence hung heavy in the air. And until the sun dropped at last behind a line of distant trees everyone present seemed, with one exception, perfectly prepared to wait this thing out.

The exception was a lone, bold vulture who soon began to move back toward the zebra. Eying me warily at each tentative step, he would advance slowly but without check to within a yard or so of the zebra's tail. Then, each time at about the same place, he would pivot away in panicky, shambling retreat. When he reached the crescent of passive waiters he often worked off his frustration by attacking one of them. These brief aggressions seemed to set him up, almost at once, for further attempts at overcoming his fear, and before long he had brought himself to within pecking distance of the zebra's anus. He stood there, poised to peck, eyes flicking from zebra to me and back again. And then, as far as I could see, he began to salivate. I checked through binoculars. No doubt about it: clear water was dripping from his bill. Then he had turned once more, panicked back to the crescent, and begun taking it all out on yet another of the innocent bystanders.

It was about then that the jackal arrived. He trotted in through a gap in the waiting vulture-crescent, ignoring the car and moving confidently toward the zebra. He was a silver-backed jackal, the common species of the plain—about the size of a fox terrier, though longer in the leg, and with a coat that looked as sleek and clean and strokable as a well-tended German shepherd's. Except for a saddle of grizzled hair across the back, his color was roughly German shepherd too. The foxlike face was perhaps a shade too sharp and cunning to evoke total human trust, but the golden eyes and cute pointed ears, alertly pricked, would have drawn choruses of clucks and orgies of patting from dear old ladies clear around the world.

The jackal trotted unconcernedly to within three or four paces of the zebra. Then he stopped. I got the distinct impression that he had suddenly sensed, perhaps because of the way the vultures were standing back from the prize, that something was wrong. And at that moment the bold vulture made his move. He stalked forward to within a foot of the jackal and halted. The pair stood facing each other, eyeball to eyeball. But I shall never know how the confrontation would have ended. For at that cuspish moment I took a photograph—and at the click of the shutter the jackal flicked his head toward me. For several seconds he stood his ground, taking stock of the car. Then he turned and strolled coolly, almost nonchalantly, back through the gap in the waiting crescent. He walked for perhaps fifty yards and then lay down in long grass, head raised and watching. Now there was the same air of resigned patience about him as there was about the waiting birds.

Soon after that, the bold vulture made it. First he jumped onto the zebra's back and struck a curiously self-conscious, I'm-the-king-of-the-castle pose. The waiters watched, visibly impressed. The bold one came down to earth and began to peck at the zebra's anus. Soon, after cocking his eye long and warily in my direction, he inserted his head. At first he kept pulling clear and checking on me. But before long he was confident enough to thrust in so deep that his head and long neck were enveloped clear down to the shoulders. When he foraged inside the zebra's quarters I could see his head moving its loose skin. When he withdrew, his head and neck glistened with moisture from the zebra's gut. And all at once I understood why the heads and necks of vultures and marabou storks were almost naked: in such carrion eaters, feathers would collect moisture and blood and so would soon mat thick and useless and reeking.

The sun set. As its last rays receded, the waiting crescent moved forward. Soon, half a dozen of the bravest birds were feeding at the zebra's half-eaten head. Down at its rear end, the bold one retained sole possession.

Five minutes after sunset, the jackal gave up. As he walked away he cast backward glances that spoke unprintable volumes about voyeurs in little white cars. Ten more minutes, and the vultures began to disperse. The birds that had been waiting patiently in their little mourners' clumps, strung out to the left, took off one by one and flapped heavily to the tops of the thorn trees that lined the nearby donga. There they roosted in new clumps. Within fifteen minutes not a bird was left on the ground.

I drove forward until I was close beside the zebra. I confirmed that there was no visible wound on the animal's far side, caught a whiff of the sickly smell of death, then drove two hundred yards and—grateful that I was just outside the Sanctuary and could therefore camp where I pleased—stopped in a patch of very short grass from which I had a clear view of the dead zebra. I got out of the car. Two jackals were already at the carcass. I could just make out in the fading light that they were standing still, ears up, watching me. Then I glimpsed, away to the right, a familiar loping movement. I lifted the binoculars. It was a hyena all right, moving in on the zebra. But almost at once the gray shape stopped, looked at me, backed off a dozen yards, and stood waiting.

For a while then, busy with setting up camp before the light failed, I could not really watch. But when I had lit the lamp and begun to pitch the tent I heard, out beyond the hissing of the lamp, a chorus of high-pitched, doglike yelps. Through binoculars I could just make out, a few yards to the zebra's left, three jackals circling each other warily. Two others had moved in on the carcass.

During dinner, undecipherable sounds kept drifting in from the direction of the dead zebra. Once, a lion *yangu yangu yangu*-ed, close. I went to bed. All night, the deep and varied calls of many lions kept brushing aside my dreams. And at least once, clear and unmistakable through a gap in my winding sheets of sleep, I heard the mournful-risible yowl of a hyena.

In the first pale light of morning I could see nothing at the zebra site. I drove over. Still nothing. Absolutely nothing. Not so much as a bone. But a hundred yards away, out in the open, I found the zebra's pelvis with both rear legs still attached. Everything had been chewed clean; only vestiges of red meat remained. But the bones were whole, undamaged. I decided that neither birds nor jackals could have dragged the heavy remnant so far. Anyway, the birds were still clumped high in their thorn-tree dormitories. And if it had been the hyenas they would, I felt sure, have crunched at least some of the bones. That left the lions.

I sat looking at the awkward bone sculpture. The sun came up. A jackal arrived. He gave the remains the once-over, apparently found nothing to interest him, and went his way. Several vultures flapped and glided down from the trees. They came in slowly, legs and heads low, tails fanned, wings black-umbrellaed— a fan of foot-long feathers protruding at each wingtip, feeling the air and responding with delicate deflections to its invisible vagaries. The birds pecked briefly at the bones; then they too gave up. When the last of them had flapped into the air, cleared the thorn trees, and vanished, I drove back to camp and cooked breakfast. While I ate—sitting safely at my little wooden table, out in the middle of the patch of short grass—a lioness circled and watched. She never came closer than a hundred yards; but when I struck camp she was still there, golden face watching from long, golden grass.

As I drove away I passed close to the bones that were probably all that now remained of the zebra. All that remained, that is, in its old macro-structure. The rest had already been redistributed. The only thing left to be done was for the hyenas to return, after the lions had finally gone. The hyenas would crunch the bones and swallow and digest them and in due course recycle these last remnants of the zebra in their characteristically white, calcium-rich droppings—just as the rest of that recently alive and pulsating animal was already in the process of being recycled to the savanna by lions and jackals and vultures and marabou storks and ants and dung beetles. It was an astonishingly efficient business, this cooperative scavenger service. So efficient that, in spite of the savanna's teeming thousands of living animals, you almost never saw a carcass that had lain long enough to rot and stink and spread disease. So efficient that even stray bones were a rarity.

I drove on across the clean and open grass. My brief inspection of the service in action had taught me, more than anything else, how little I knew about the details of the way it worked. This time, though, my reading could at least provide rather more meaty footnotes. Among other things, I had read that hyenas were undoubtedly guided to carrion by the sight of alighting vultures, and I found myself wondering if jackals were too—and lions. For what I had seen and heard around the dead zebra seemed to confirm something else I had read. A preliminary report of a hyena study in Ngorongoro Crater, just south of the Serengeti, made it clear that the lions there by no means lived up to their traditional billing of lordly hunters who disdained all but fresh, home-killed meat. Neither were the hyenas solely scavengers, mere cleaners-up after the lions. The hyenas often did the killing, particularly at night. The lions then drove them off the prize and appropriated it. At least, that was what often happened

in Ngorongoro. I did not know yet if it also happened in the Mara;
but what I had just seen and heard, night and morning, suggested
rather strongly that even the Mara's well-fed lions were by no
means as particular about their diet as was popularly supposed.
It seemed a bit of a comedown, somehow. But the news that
hyenas often did the hunting meant a degree of rehabilitation for
that mournful, tragicomic species. Rehabilitation, that was, in the
eyes of the human species—which for obvious if dubious reasons
tends to rate killers higher on the moral scale than scavengers.

The hyena study in Ngorongoro Crater was one of a series on
animal behavior and social organization being conducted by Serengeti Research Institute scientists. The full hyena report was not
yet available. But others were. And from them I now began to
catch at least glimpses of the way certain animals passed the days
and nights of their lives.

One report confirmed and augmented the basic facts I had
been told about impala.

The standard impala social setup, though surprisingly variable
from region to region, was indeed a harem dominated by one
male, with a reservoir of replacement lords hanging around
within good girl-watching range. Once a ram had established
ownership of a harem—often by defeating the previous lord in a
fight that might last twenty minutes and end with a broken horn
or foreleg—he maintained his position by an "intolerant and aggressive" attitude toward the bachelors. When his wives' sons
reached the age of ten or twelve months he turned on them too
and drove them from the herd. Such evictions often occurred
when the herd ram was being challenged by an adult male: instead of attacking the strong rival he worked off his aggressive
impulses on the weak youngster—and thereby, perhaps, also demonstrated his strength without risk to himself. Similar "displace-
ment activity" is, of course, common among animals. The bold
vulture at the zebra carcass had repeatedly worked off his fear
and frustration at my presence by threatening innocent bystanders. And *Homo sapiens* has crystallized our own common practice
in the phrase "taking it out on somebody else."

The impala study went into considerable detail about social

organization (harems run from two to a hundred females, bache-lor herds from two to sixty; expectant mothers seek isolation and thick cover), and also explained several things I had seen from my breakfast table at Lemek. The archways, for example—reliably reported as up to ten feet high and thirty feet long—probably helped the impala when they were escaping from an enemy by giving them a good view of him while they continued to flee at full speed. The jumps might also confuse predators whose hunt-ing technique required concentration on a single animal. (Later, a zoologist suggested to me that when an impala herd scatters and individuals jump every which way, the vertical black stripes on the outer edges of each animal's rump add to the confusion because in that moment of panic they look remarkably like horns and just for an instant you may think a certain individual is com-ing when in fact he is like hell going.)

My impala reading also alerted me to things I had not no-ticed before. Whole herds, I learned, were subject to "social moods"—as are many social animals (have you ever watched a chain reaction of cigarette lighting at a party?). Such normal ac-tivities as feeding, cleaning and resting were definitely contagious: when one animal began a new activity others often followed suit—though it was rare for every member of a herd to be doing the same thing at the same time. But for all their necessary herd instincts, impala remained individuals. As in at least one other species, flirtatious females could raise Cain. Sometimes, the report said, "a single female joined a nearby bachelor herd, where it provoked courting behavior and competition among the males."

Once I had read the impala paper I naturally tried, every time I saw a herd of them, to confirm on the ground what I had seen on the printed page. It was the same with other animals too. And as the days passed I began to detect an evolution in the manner of my watching.

At first I had been content when I came across a herd of Tommy to see only their beauty. To smile at the familiar min-now-glint as they turned in sunlight. To note that two males, flashing as they sparred head to head, made me think of paternal sticklebacks defending precious nests. To find, stopping close to a herd in the soft and fading world of dusk, that the contrasting browns and blacks and whites had almost merged, and that when an animal turned it created no more sense of urgent movement than does the stabilizing flicker of a carp's pale fin or the unhurried opening and closing of its fleshy mouth; to find, in fact, that the whole scene had about it that air of serenity you sense in an aquarium when you stand and watch a shoal of aged carp suspended almost motionless in dim and silent depths.

But now I asked, more and more often, the kind of question I had raised just before my orchard lunch with the zebras, the day I Parkinsoned toward the Dawsons: Was the Tommy's social setup the same as the impala's? You saw Tommy groups of all sizes, from isolated pairs to herds of twenty or thirty, and they normally, though not invariably, included at least one male. But you often found a male on his own or grazing alongside a herd of Grant or kongoni or topi or zebras. I had seen several small male herds too, apparently without females nearby. One way and another, the species' whole social setup seemed highly plastic. The only fact about it that I knew for sure—well, almost for sure—was that males established territories.

In Uganda I had watched a male oribi—a small, rather Tommy-like antelope—angle his face over on one side and rub the tops of several widely separated grass stems with a large black gland close to his eyes. Later I learned that he must have been depositing the sticky, scented secretion that marks the boundaries of male oribi territories with the kind of "no trespassing" signs that wolves post by urinating at intervals (a canine practice that I was beginning to suspect might be followed by jackals and that I knew was still performed in vestigial form by domestic dogs, regardless of bladder pressure, when they passed lampposts and fire hydrants and other landmarks). In Nairobi, someone had told me that Tommy marked their territories in the same way as oribi, but I did nothing about checking the hearsay until one morning, not far from the lodge, I found a herd of thirty-seven Tommy— the largest I had yet seen. On the fringe of the herd stood a rather callow-looking male. The rest were all females or youngsters.

I studied the male through binoculars. He was very small. And he kept glancing nervously about him, eyes flicking, muzzle twitching. Then he would pull himself together and take a possessive step or two toward his harem, head held high and haughty. It was impossible, I found, to avoid the conviction that he had been thrown off balance by newfound responsibility and now was torn by alternating pride and panic, like a carefree bachelor, widow-smitten, who finds himself saddled overnight with five half-grown kids. Had he inherited the harem by chance, I wondered—stumbling on it when the old sultan still lay warm under a predator's paws? Or had he proved himself by jousting in the lists of love? I checked him again. He looked very slight, very timid. Perhaps Tommy did not joust for supremacy the way impala did.

At that moment the Tommy made a small head movement that was quite consistent with rubbing a black patch in front of his eyes against a small shrub. I held the binoculars steady. The Tommy continued to move uncertainly around the fringes of his harem, and several times in the next ten minutes he repeated the slight head movement. Each time he could have been rubbing the black patch against a small shrub or tall grass stem, but each movement could also have been coincidental to the act of grazing. I continued to watch. And at last, when the Tommy's head was at just the right angle I saw him, beyond all shadow of doubt, rub the black patch with care and accuracy against the thin topmost branch of a very small shrub.

It was an oddly satisfying moment. But although I had apparently confirmed that this Tommy had established a territory, that only raised more questions. How big was the territory? If the sultan held permanent rights over this king-size harem he would need a considerable area. Of course, the arrangement might be less cut and dried than that. Many animals establish territories from which they exclude other males of the same species, yet still feel free to wander over much wider ranges. Most men, for example, got pretty fired up if strangers wandered around uninvited within the territory established by their garden fences, yet they felt perfectly free to range far beyond that garden.

Later that day, during the doldrum hours, I found my answers. I confirmed from a research paper that male Tommy defended territories—or, rather, that some of them did. But I discovered that when I had watched the callow little Tommy marking his territory I had, in assuming the harem was "his," shown my ignorance of how animal social arrangements worked: defense of a territory and ownership of a harem were "mutually exclusive mechanisms."

The Tommy setup, it turned out, is superficially similar to the impala's, yet critically different. All Tommydom is divided into three parts: nursery herds of females and young, bachelor herds of largely immature males, and a small class of territorial males. A nursery herd, though it may appear to be presided over by one male, is never his "property" (a state of affairs that no doubt explained why the little male had seemed torn between pride and panic). The herd, despite the efforts of each territorial male to detain it within his domain, keeps drifting on across the mosaic of territories into which the males have divided the savanna. Unlike impala, in other words, Tommy do not fight for their females: they fight for territories—and wait.

The mosaic of Tommy territories, although invisible to us, is as clear and imperative to a Tommy as are garden fences to a human city dweller. The boundaries of each domain are marked, primarily, by the method I had seen in operation: the owner selects small bushes or tall, decapitated grass stems on the perimeter of his domain, and by pursing around their tips one of the open glands situated in front of each of his eyes he repeatedly deposits on them a highly scented, pitchlike substance. Over a long period the deposits may build up into globules half an inch across. A typical Tommy territory, perhaps two or three hundred yards in diameter, may be ringed by such deposits at intervals of about twenty feet—and they are reinforced by a series of scatological markers, similar to those put out by wolves but embodying dung as well as urine. This double system of scent posts effectively fences off each domain: it is virtually impossible for any Tommy nose to pass unwittingly across the boundary. Once

I had grasped this system I began to see that the "open" savanna must be "fenced" by a whole series of territorial mosaics. Each system, though binding on participants, might go undetected by other species and would almost certainly be ignored by them. But the mosaics were there, all right, clearly marked and parochially imperative. It made no difference whether they were drawn by Tommy's preorbital glands or by jackals' urine or by map lines called international boundaries.

Not all animals drew such mosaics, of course. Some, like impala, were definitely nonterritorial. Others had evolved social systems that sometimes incorporated the mechanism of personal domain and sometimes ignored it. That, I learned from another study, is how wildebeest function. During the rut, some males establish breeding herds—either on their own or with one or even two cooperating bulls. These bulls defend their herds. But because wildebeest spend most of their lives on the move, trekking to and from water or freshly sprouted grass, the defense involves not fixed areas of ground but moving zones around the herds. So the territorial mosaic that wildebeest impose on the savanna is a constantly moving and fluctuating one. But it is a mosaic, all the same.

Within the confines of this mosaic, wildebeest lead a fluid social life: individuals drift from one loose grouping to another. And outside the breeding season the bonds seem to slacken even further. But the system works. In terms of biomass, wildebeest are the most successful African mammal: they convert more grass into flesh than any other savanna species and can therefore be called the key animal in the savanna community. Yet I found that I hardly ever studied them closely. For one thing, they seemed rather dull creatures. But I think the real reason for my neglect was that they often moved in the company of zebras—and ever since talking to Hans Klingel at the Harthoorns' house and then reading a summary of his recently completed work I had found zebra-watching irresistible. For the species leads a rich and intricate social life.

Burchell's or common zebras, unlike wildebeest, run a tight ship. They organize themselves into two kinds of groups: families and bachelor herds. (Solitary animals are always stallions—or "one-unit-bachelor-herds.") Families consist of one stallion—who is very much lord and master—together with one to six mares and their foals. The total may run to sixteen animals but averages about five or six. Neither families nor bachelor herds defend territories.

Each zebra family is a self-contained, tightly knit little group, governed by protocol and bound by what can only be called affection. Mares, once admitted to the family, normally remain for life. Even if an old or sick stallion is replaced, the family retains its entity. Young males leave on their own initiative when about two years old and join bachelor herds. Young females are abducted by other stallions on one of the early occasions they come in heat, usually at the age of about eighteen months. The family stallion resists such abductions from the zebraglio. Sometimes he succeeds for a while in defending his daughter's honor, but as many as eighteen strange stallions may mill around the family, and while father is chasing one of them across the plain another nearly always manages to slip in at last and drive off the reluctant bride. The abductor rarely keeps his prize. For perhaps six months she does her youthful thing, lover after lover. Then her charms seem to wane. She no longer attracts neighboring stallions. She settles down. If her new master already possesses wives, they are at first violently jealous: they bite and kick and continually harass the newcomer. But the stallion helps protect her from attack and before long she is accepted as one of the family—for life.

A zebra family seems to be a well-ordered and contented little group held together by strong ties of loyalty. Sick and weak animals are not, as in some species, chased from the herd. Mutual grooming takes place between all family members—though everybody has favorite partners. (Mutual grooming was clearly what had been going on when I saw pairs and even quartets of zebras with heads lolled affectionately over each other's backs.) There is time for relaxation too: foals play various running games and the mares sometimes join in. (Among the bachelors these games develop into communal races. The bachelors also play fighting games, but serious fighting takes place only over young mares in heat.) Each family normally ignores all other zebras. But if an outsider, even a lost foal, attempts to gate-crash their ranks they will drive it off. Only the lord and master maintains outside contacts: when he meets other family stallions they exchange a "greeting ceremony" that starts with nose-to-nose contact and ends with at least some movement of the front legs in a kind of ritualized jump.

Zebras may congregate on the open plain by the thousands, but even then the family remains a self-contained unit. (There seems to be no higher zebra organization beyond families and bachelor herds.) If a family member is lost, others search for it, making repeated contact calls that seem to be as individually distinct to zebra ears as are individual human voices to human ears. (Zebras communicate with at least five other vocalizations: two warning sounds, two expressions of pain and one of well-being.) The animals can recognize each other by sight at considerable range—at least in part, apparently, because each individual's stripe pattern is as idiosyncratic as are our fingerprints. Even the human eye, once it knows what to look for, can recognize known individuals. In his paper, Hans Klingel suggested that some such form of conspicuous individual marking was necessary if the zebra's tight-knit kind of organization was to evolve successfully among animals that often congregate in such huge numbers. The less distinctly marked wildebeest, living under very similar conditions, certainly lead a much more Bohemian existence.

There was a great deal more information in the summary I had found of Hans Klingel's research, and as the days passed I became able, more and more often, to detect significance in the kind of group and individual zebra actions that had once—as when I lunched in the "orchard"—seemed more or less aimless.*

---

* It was only later that I had Klingel's full paper translated from the German—and at this point I must make a small confession. By implying that I had during those ten quiet days in the Sanctuary absorbed even the bare-outline detail I have passed on about the zebra's social organization, I may have cheated. I can no longer be sure which facts I knew then about zebras

Other papers and articles answered many questions that I had asked myself earlier. To my surprise and pleasure, two papers by different authors agreed with the conclusion I had tentatively reached about mixed animal convocations: apart from every gregarious species' need for social contact, the only bond holding the groups together seems to be collective security against predators. Sometimes I found answers to questions I had not had the wit to ask, such as: How come there are so many different grazing mammals—wildebeest, zebras, topi, kongoni and Tommy for a start—that all seem to make a living in the same place and in large numbers by eating the same food? Why has not one of them proved so efficient at its job that, as normally happens in the end when different species compete directly, it has come to outnumber the others—or even to drive them elsewhere or into extinction? The answer to both these questions is that, contrary to appearances, the animals do not eat the same food. Often they prefer different kinds of grass. Almost always they tend to eat grass at slightly different stages of growth. Zebras, for example, attack the long, coarse vegetation. Topi tend to eat dried-up stalks. Tommy restrict themselves to short, though not neces-

(and, for that matter, other animals), and which I learned later. But I doubt that it matters much if I have incorporated a few convenient hindsights.

It was certainly not until I had left the Mara that I learned that the large, thinly striped Grevy's zebra of northern Kenya seems to operate differently from the Burchell's or common zebra found in the Mara. Hans Klingel and his wife, Ute, have now completed a parallel study of this species, and they found, among other things, that Grevy's zebras defend territories.

One intriguing aspect of the common zebra's tightly governed little world did not strike me until three years later, when I happened on a biologist studying wild burros in Death Valley, California. These other members of the horse family, it seemed, had virtually no social organization. Some individuals definitely dominated others, but all activities, including sex, seemed to be governed by the rule, "every burro for himself." And when I watched the casual and always changing groups and noted the almost continual bickering and bloody-mindedness that seemed to pervade the lives of these unhappy animals, especially at watering places, and then remembered the contented demeanor of their striped cousins back in the Mara, I found myself unable to resist some heavy anthropomorphic thoughts concerning discipline and anarchy.

sarily new, grass. One morning I drove out from camp with the firm intention of confirming this answer by observation. I failed, utterly. But that afternoon I found in a paper on wildebeest that "it is virtually impossible to determine through observation alone which animal is eating what grass." The only feasible method seemed to be analysis of fresh droppings or, better still, of the stomach contents of recently killed animals.

There was also an even bigger, simpler, more difficult question about the mammals of the savanna: why were they there, in such numbers and such diversity? After all, the world had nothing else like it. I think I had answered this question—without ever quite framing it—by assuming that the wealth was due entirely to lack of depredation by man. But now, from various sources, I built a truer picture. At the beginning of the Pleistocene epoch, about a million years ago, the earth's newest life forms, the mammals, had reached a climax: a rich radiation of species had spread to fill an abundance of "jobs." But during the Pleistocene most of the world's large land masses underwent repeated glaciation; and, between the ice ages, seas and lakes inundated vast areas. Inevitably, many mammal species were snuffed out. But the raised bulk of inland Africa, lying in the earth's warmest sector, escaped both inundation and glaciation. It has escaped them, in fact, since long before the mammals appeared, a hundred million years ago. Its life forms have therefore been free to flourish and expand without the calamitous setbacks suffered by those that evolved elsewhere. So even before man began his recent ravages, the teeming mammals of inland Africa formed one of our planet's unique pageants.

But I do not want to suggest that my reading simply answered old questions and raised new ones. Once, almost at the end of the ten days I spent near the lodge, it structured for hour after hour the very way I watched the animals—and in doing so taught me something new about the nature of a typical Mara day. It happened one afternoon and evening at Saddle Camp.

I did not return to View Camp, as I had expected to do. The day after I watched the eland in the moonlight I met Tipis briefly near the lodge and happened to mention that I would be camping most nights just outside the main gate.

"Oh, but you have no need to go as far as that," he said. There was a perfectly legal place much closer, but although it was outside the Sanctuary he did not for various reasons encourage people to camp there. Still, he felt sure he could trust me to keep the information to myself and he would tell the ranger who would be guiding me that afternoon to point out the place he meant.

It was late afternoon when we reached the lip of a broad, shallow basin. The ranger—not Joshua but an old and amiable if unsparkling man—nodded ahead through the windshield.

"*Hapa tu*," he said. The words meant, roughly, "Here, this is all," and they conveyed a hint of surprise that I should be interested in the information.

In that first moment I tended to share the ranger's surprise. An hour earlier, the day's clouds had fused. Now their gray pall pressed low and heavy, and a blustering east wind cut cold across the leaden grass. The basin, which must have measured more than a mile across, was largely open grassland with scatterings of bush and small trees, and in that first moment its openness depressed me. Or perhaps I am talking about the lack of obvious pattern that this openness imposed. After the balanced complexities of View Camp the place had a barren cheerless look. It promised convenience, but that was about all.

Now I obviously cannot divulge the basin's location; but it was appreciably closer to the lodge than were either View Camp or Waterhole Camp, and whenever I had to pick up a ranger, morning or evening, sleeping there would save me several miles of driving. It had been kind of Tipis to volunteer the information too, and failing to take advantage of it might seem churlish. That night, after I had dropped the ranger back at Keekorok, I camped in the open basin.

I also camped there the next night. And the next. But it was several days before I grasped that more than convenience drew me back.

My change of heart no doubt owed something to the light.

That first afternoon, the basin had stretched flat and sullen beneath metallic clouds. In the days that followed it basked in sunshine, and once or twice, when I had no date with a ranger, I stayed there all day. The hours rang the Mara's daily changes: a vivid morning, all sky and gleaming grass; doldrum afternoon enlivened by cloud shadows; soft evening light regilding the grassland.

But my drift toward affection for the place owed even more, I think, to familiarity. As the days passed I began to grasp the unities. The basin was a single huge paddock, bounded on three sides by low, bush-lined crests and on the south by a hill covered with trees and thick brush. Down the center of this paddock, intermittent at first but consolidating after an abrupt mid-field curl, ran a small donga lined by bush and occasional trees. Because the basin was a place of gentle, open slopes, I at first failed to comprehend these components. But after four or five days I saw when I looked out across the basin not the barren formlessness that had depressed me in that first gray moment but a pattern as balanced and satisfying in its way as the one I had grasped in my first moment at View Camp. There was even, far to the west, a glimpse of the Isuria Escarpment. And when the light was right and my imagination flowing I could make out at its foot a dark and tantalizing sliver of the Triangle.

But the real attraction of my new paddock-basin camp was the passing show.

Almost every evening animals flowed in over the eastern lip of the basin. They came through a barely discernible gap between two arms of bush, and once I had grasped the meanings of the basin's muted slopes I recognized this gap as a low saddle.

After the first night I always camped about three hundred yards east of this saddle. Because I commanded a view down and across the whole basin I could watch the animals after they had come over the saddle and could often see where they went and where they were when darkness fell and what they were doing when the pale light seeped in again from the east. And for the first time I achieved some continuity in the way I watched the life that ebbs and flows across the wide savanna.

My understanding of what I saw, like my comprehension of the basin's components, took time to mature. I did not, I mean, immediately grasp the pattern of the animals' movements. But after a few days I knew what to expect. Zebras and wildebeest made up a majority of the animals that flowed over the saddle, and most of them drifted westward to the expanse of short, open grass that formed the far slope of the basin. By dusk they had massed into a huge assembly—and thereby corroborated the gospel according to Hans Klingel: "At night zebra concentrate in areas of short grass." I could not verify his next rubric—"During resting periods at least one animal per group usually remains standing and alert at all times"—but even after dark I knew the assembly was still there: across the basin floated an almost continuous chorus of flat, midwestern wildebeest grunts punctuated by snorts and brays and other uncouth zebral commentaries. First light found the assembly still there. But by sunrise it had begun to break up and drift eastward. Each group gave me a two-hundred-yard berth and vanished back over the saddle into what I now knew was more broken country beyond.

But I did not appreciate the richness of this daily ebb and flow until I had slept for almost a week at Saddle Camp. Then, one afternoon and evening, I took detailed notes.

I began the notes in midafternoon, casually, as if by acident. I had all along been jotting down short synopses and occasional full accounts of arresting events or impressions; but that afternoon I began to record the minor doings of most animals that came within my immediate ken. And in the end the notes ran to twenty-three closely written pages.

At the time I remained unaware of a change in method, but in retrospect I found it impossible to regard the new structure of note-taking as anything but an echo of the meticulous field records that were sometimes quoted in the animal behavior studies I had been reading. I do not necessarily mean that my notes read much like the researchers'. But they were, I have no doubt, a spin-off.

Their start was suitably doldrum: *3:30. Overcast. Cooler. Note that at the moment 13 out of 17 zebra visible on slope be-*

yond donga are grazing. Only one is lying down. Of 7 wildebeest, none is grazing, 4 are lying down. This should, I'm sure, tell me something. (Thought: Zs sure as hell tend to look fatter and sleeker than Wi. Do they simply spend more time eating?)

At this stage I had time to inject the kind of personal notes that always invade such documents: *Calamine lotion certainly seems ease tsetse fly bites. Half an hour ago put lotion on that one coming up fast on foot. Itching now better. Swelling* possibly *stopped. I hope not one of those bad, sleeping sickness ones. . . . 3:40. In shade just after sunny spell, temp 76°. Sitting in swim suit, in wind, it predictably feels cooler.* (I had swathed myself in the swim suit because, so near the lodge, visitors might surprise me.)

But mostly I monitored the other animals: *4:15. A roughly-counted 83 Wi have wandered in over the saddle in single file and the head of the column has slowed down near the original Z-Wi group and is grazing slowly forward. Four ground horn-bills parading along, also in single file, just to L of Wi parade, not apparently gaining anything from being with them (? insects stirred up). . . .*

The next sixty minutes consume five unremitting pages. Nothing of any great moment occurs, but little event follows little event follows little event. And all the time, out beyond my wooden table, there is flowing movement, slow and unhurried and apparently mindless. A dozen Tommy join the general westward flow on the far side of the donga. A kongoni arrives, then thirty zebras. Group mingles with group, then reseparates. The mingling proceeds without regard to species, color or reputed food preference; yet each group retains its identity, zebra with zebra, wildebeest with wildebeest, hornbill and Tommy with their own. I observe that *Nobody takes any notice of anybody, but anybody.*

For three pages, then, zebras hold center stage. Forty emerge from the bush fringing the hill to the south. Fifteen more wander over the saddle. But the action remains minor. A colt suckles; he is almost as big as his mother. Friendly byplay in one family seems to deteriorate into petty squabbling.

I put on a shirt. *All this time, by the way, so normal that I've forgotten to note it—on slope to W, spread thinly and fairly evenly over the open grassland, are Wi and Z, difficult to estimate quickly with any accuracy, but prob numbering about 1000. All are at least 800 yds away, and I haven't been watching them much. . . . First quick movement to record—a single Z comes braying across line of saddle.*

The passing show continues. A hundred more zebras and wildebeest file through the saddle. Two Tommy. Four kongoni. All go about their quiet business. Nine more zebras, galloping. The lead mare has a distinctive, amoeba-like white inlay in the triangular stripe pattern at her right shoulder (the shoulder is the best place to look for idiosyncratic patterning), and I sketch it so that I shall recognize the family if we meet again.

Now I am aware that none of this sounds like spellbinding stuff. But the notes prove that it gripped my attention: *5:32. Sun behind thick cloud. . . . Wind still blowing. Cold. I put on long pants [and] down jacket.* But it is not until 5:46 that I record: *Actually put on down jacket. (Only had time to* write *it before.) Note that all this long, peaceful time things have been happening so fast that I've had no chance to do anything except scribble down notes as fast as I could.*

And so it goes on, page after page. I record the wanderings of a kongoni that bucks the tide of westward flow, and on his pages appear twenty new zebras, a lone male impala, and a group of seven Tommy that bound and swerve into view, playing God knows what. Their cool-of-evening madness spreads. Two zebra colts run skittish circles. The Tommy run circles too, intersecting those of the zebras. But there is no interaction. I become conscious of birdsong; *but otherwise, except for very occasional Wi grunt and even rarer Z bray, no sound from all the game, which must number about 2000 now, all within a mile of me. . . . A few specks of rain. Ought to put tent up. But I'm afraid of missing something.* I glance over at the western bedroom. The nightly assembly is in place, spread clear across the pale slope. The wildebeest still stand out dark and definite; but now the zebras are almost invisible. They have faded like that every evening, hundreds of them sinking away into the pale grass. Until you have seen it happen you find it hard to accept that a zebra's dazzle pattern can really act as camouflage.

6:52. Light failing fast. I can hardly see the zebras. My writing grows large and sprawling, barely decipherable. *A last look at saddle . . . still empty. No! Motion! Beautiful, fluid motion. Can just see they're Tommy, running fast, now slowing down. 3 of them, or perhaps 4, or perhaps 5. No more than silent, flowing shapes, more spirit than flesh. Had my glasses not been directly on them I'd have known nothing of their passing—and would have been the poorer.*

Now, the grunts on the western slope almost continuous. At this point my handwriting reverts to normal, so I must have been recording it all a few minutes later, by lamplight. The change is confirmed by the unexpected switch in tense near the end of the paragraph. *A last obviously-going-to-be-fruitless look, in the almost-gone light, at the saddle. And there, by God, is another single file of black, silent wildebeest coming over on the milk run. I count to 40, peering, straining. Then I give it up. They're still coming. 150 at least, and no let up. I give up partly because it seems a beautiful and fitting moment at which to stop and partly because the grunt-and-dying-away throb of a lion, far away, reminds me that it is virtually dark and that I am probably not very safe standing there without a light (no longer sitting, somehow, in what were obviously to be the final moments of the day). Soon, hyena noises too. And that wasn't all. This is reputed to be buffalo and elephant country too, and I didn't want to surprise any of them.*

Reluctantly, happily—and warmer now, because the wind had almost died away—I lit the lamp. At once it was black night, out beyond the 20-yard circle of white light. . . .

Lighting the lamp cut me off from the animals. Outside its hissing white dome, the night belonged to them. I opened a small bottle of wine and sat sipping it on an empty stomach.

7:20. No longer Wi grunts from far slope. That may be the lamp shutting it off. Or perhaps lions have disturbed them. That lion-noise seemed a little nearer just now.

About seven-thirty I began to pitch the tent. It was shadowy, out away from the lamp. And the lion sounds were there again, clearer. I went back to the table and took another sip of wine. Then, smiling an oleaginous, Dutchly courageous smile, I took the ax out of the car and carried it over to the tent and put it down on the grass beside me. It helped.

When the tent was safely up, and its blue fly sheet too, I went back to the table. Once more the hissing cut off the nightsounds. *But when I moved out a little way (6 paces perhaps, so as not to be too much out in lion-land) and urinated, looking at the now-familiar shadow of my legs cast out across the grass by the lamp like a caricature of an ad for a western movie, I could hear zebra brayings off to the west and, once more, lion noises, definitely closer now.*

It was about eight o'clock, I think, when I wrote the day's final entry. *I'm not sure how to put this, but: Perhaps the oddest part of all this is that because I wrote down what I saw, as it happened—and because, therefore, I grasped the numbers of animals involved, and the intensity, in its way, of all this slow, incessant movement—I am excited, and recognize that this was a memorable day. And yet I am almost sure that if I had not written all this down—if I had merely sat and done a few things and glanced up now and then and registered that another group of zebras had appeared, or that a line of wildebeest was moving over the saddle, or that there was a kongoni in sight now—then I'd have thought of this as just another typical day on which nothing very much happened. Which, of course, it was.*

But even toward the end of those quiet days in the Sanctuary, my reading often made little difference to the way I watched the animals. It was certainly like that with the lions: our meetings remained raw, immediate, gut experiences, unshaded by book learning.

I had in any case learned precious little about lions. When I met George Schaller in the Serengeti he had naturally been reticent about his provisional findings—though he did mention that a lion territory, or at least the home range covered by a single pride, might be as much as a hundred miles across. By and large, other sources had also supplied nothing more than snippets of information: "The lion lacks full color vision"; "Old females which have passed the breeding age are known as 'aunties' by the hunters, and their function is that of baby sitters to the young breeding females [who are thus freed for hunting]"; "The attitude of lions toward human beings is a sure indication of the quality of the country as game habitat. . . . The well-fed Mara lions are indifferent to man and would be almost the last creatures to cause him any anxiety. . . . There is probably no place in Africa where wild lions can be observed in such numbers and in such mutual confidence." Among the snippets was one statement I found hard to believe: "Lions are said to be able to attain a speed of up to 60 m.p.h. in short bursts." But I had no difficulty at all with: "The species suffers from the extraordinary indolence of the male." This indolence, which hardly seemed restricted to males, was one reason I had made little effort to watch lions since returning to the Mara.

My coolness may also have owed something to snobbery. Most tourists arrive in East Africa with lions at the top of their viewing lists, and until they see one they tend to feel that they have not yet begun to "do" Africa. The bias is natural enough. But it is also natural enough—most people being monstrously human—for residents of any place to scorn mere "tourist attractions." And a corner of me was by now, I think, halfway relabeling myself "Kenya resident."

But my coolness toward lions also reflected, beyond snobbery, a genuine lack of interest. Not long after that first golden morning in the Mara, when the big pride came out of the trees beyond the zebras, I decided that lions did not really repay extended watching. You had to see them, of course, if only to comprehend their dignity and arrogance. But they tended to be dozy creatures: I saw no reason to doubt the statement that the average lion spent only four hours out of every twenty-four in a condition that could be called fully awake.

One morning in the Sanctuary I had found seven lionesses and large cubs sunning themselves on a grass-covered anthill, and had parked close by for more than an hour. But most of that time I watched a distant herd of elephants. For the lions proved a morgue of inactivity. Soon after I arrived the pride began to transfer from the original anthill to another, thirty yards away, and this operation took half an hour: each animal moved at its pleasure, at such time as it happened to come wide enough awake to essay a thirty-yard slouch. Most of the time, the pride dozed with all its collective heart. Three of the seven sprawling animals were so thoroughly tucked in that the grass obscured all detail. Two stretched comfortably out, relaxed to the world. One faced downhill, head hanging awkwardly in midair, apparently too tired to shift into a comfortable position. The seventh body was a mere blur in the long grass; but up from this blur, stiff and ridiculous as one of the legs in a child's drawing of a cat asleep on its back, periscoped a powerful golden paw studded with five black, catlike pads. That paw had put the finishing touch to what I now recognized as an archetypal lion study.

Twice I had been witness to leonine trysts.

Evening, just after sunset. The young lovers meet outside the car's open window, less than four yards from my elbow. As he arrives she rolls over onto her back. He greets her affectionately, nuzzles, seems ready to make love. Then he yawns and lies down behind her. Both animals yawn. Then they yawn again. And again. I take five pictures of the pair and later find that three of them feature yawns and very little else. I do not mean tired, half-hearted, politely-stifled-behind-a-paw affairs. Each yawn is a vast, jaw-stretching, all-white-teeth-and-pale-pink-mouth production. And my final shot shows the lovers still sprawled side by side, eyes shut, ardor zero.

It was Joshua who sighted the other tryst. "*Nafikiri sisi iko na arusi,*" he said as we drove along a track. "I think we've got a marriage here."

We had. Less than ten yards away. The bridegroom was huge and magnificently maned and superbly dignified and very affectionate. The bride was young and slim and sleek, and she lay quietly submissive. They copulated twice. After each orgasm he bit her on the neck, passionately and yet gently. Afterward he got up and closed his eyes and just stood there in the long grass, huge and golden and magnificent, dignified beyond all human dignity. And he went on standing and standing and standing, eyes still closed, with his great shaggy, cat's-nose profile nodding, nodding, nodding. At least, my memory has him nodding. Perhaps, come to think of it, he did nothing so wastefully active. Perhaps he just stood.

Lion's voices had by now become a part of almost every evening. At Saddle Camp I often came half awake during the night to hear them quite close. But I had never seen a lion after dark. Then, on my way back to camp one evening after dropping Joshua at the lodge rather later than usual, Rohosinante suffered one of her regular, thorn-induced flats. By the time I had the spare on it was pitch dark. Almost at once I took a wrong turn on one of the winding tracks. I drove until I felt reasonably sure I was outside the Sanctuary and then, as soon as my headlights revealed an open and almost level stretch of short grass, I stopped and made camp. (To ensure freedoom of movement I struck camp each morning.) As I made final adjustments to the tent's guy ropes I heard, downwind, a small and indeterminate sound. I stood up. No more than thirty yards away, well within my ring of white light, crouched a lioness.

Now I find myself in some difficulty when I write "no more than thirty yards away, well within my ring of light." That is what the notes say and what memory confirms; but other notes and other chords of memory report that my dome of light extended outward for only about twenty yards. The explanation is probably that when there was nothing to see in the circle of white light the openness deceived my eye, and the light was in fact strong enough to illuminate solid objects at far longer range. Anyway, the lioness was there, and I do not think that she can have been closer than thirty yards.

Although she was crouching she somehow did not give the

impression of being about to spring. She just seemed to be watching with interest whatever this curious business was, out in the middle of the dark savanna. No doubt that is why, even in the first moment, I felt little or no fear, only a reciprocating interest. I switched on my flashlight. The lioness's eyes responded with a pale, luminous glow. She moved her head uneasily. I persisted. She grunted, low. Then we faced each other in silence, crouching and standing, for three or four minutes. Or perhaps it was six or seven minutes, or two or three; during such confrontations, time slips its anchors. At last the lioness stood up and swung left and moved smoothly away into the darkness beyond my dome. I swung the flashlight beam after her. Almost at once, an uncertain distance away but probably no more than a hundred yards, a cluster of white eyes was gleaming back at me. I am no longer sure whether the flashlight really revealed any details at that range or whether my imagination filled in the blanks, but I know I formed the impression of five or six small golden faces peering over the top of an anthill. Then the mother had melted away and the cluster of white lights went out and I was alone once more with the darkness and the lamplight. It was only later, I think, that I registered that standing with nothing between me and the lioness had been an altogether different experience from looking out through the car window, safe but cut off.

Two mornings later—it was the last full day of my ten in the Sanctuary—I was eating a very late breakfast at Saddle Camp after a game-viewing drive that had begun before sunrise when I saw a male lion walking slowly across my front, two hundred yards away. It was already past eleven o'clock and hot, and the lion moved through the dazzling sunshine as if in a trance. He walked in a straight and undeviating line, head held low, looking neither to left nor right.

When I first saw him he was in open grassland. Soon he came to the donga that curled down the paddock. He disappeared into its thick foliage. I saw him briefly, just beyond the donga, still hewing to his line. Then a fold in the ground had hidden him again. If he held course, I decided, he would recross the donga beyond its mid-paddock curl. I kept a check on his progress by watching the heads of two rubbernecking giraffes, and as soon as I had finished breakfast I drove around the bend in the donga into the open grassland beyond.

He was dead on course, back across the donga, still moving like a somnambulist. I pulled ahead and waited. He passed less than thirty yards away, holding his line, ignoring me. He was young, but almost fully grown. Shaggy sideburns framed his face. In time they would no doubt merge with the faintly ludicrous ridge of hair along his crown and blossom into a magnificent mane.

We moved slowly onward, the young lion and I, angling up the slope, away from the donga. Out there on the open grass it was hot and bright. Beyond the donga, quarter of a mile away, a dozen buffalo emerged from thick bush. Half a mile to the right, along the edge of the same bush, browsed a herd of twenty or thirty elephants. Otherwise there was just the lion and me and the grass and the sunlight.

We were halfway up the slope when the lion stopped and looked around. He looked in every direction. Then he moved on again. In the next fifty yards he halted three or four times. Each time he surveyed the terrain with care. After the final halt he swung away from his line of march and walked slowly but deliberately to a clump of bush at the foot of two small trees. He circled this clump, then came back through a grassy channel that bisected it and stood at the mouth of the channel, looking out the way he had come. What he saw seemed to satisfy him, for he turned, lay down full length in the shade of one of the trees, and closed his eyes.

He had, I saw, selected an excellent ambush point. Thick bush would hide him from any animals that came up the slope. The animals would be approaching with the wind, too, and would not scent him. And he lay with his head pointing toward the far mouth of the grassy channel, his body at the right angle for instant launch into a short-range attack. Animals approaching from downwind would be able to see him, but they would be forewarned anyway.

I drove into the open downwind arc, eased forward until the right side of the car—the driver's side—was barely nine paces from the lion, and switched off. The lion opened his eyes. They were golden-brown and flecked and expressionless. The line of each lower lid was straight, and it slanted down and in toward the nose. Each upper lid was triangular, like a roofline, and when the eye came open one side of the triangle ran straight up the face, the other straight across. The lion seemed to be making an effort to keep his eyes open, but the triangles of the upper lids looked as if their sides were springs under tension: as soon as the eyes opened, the triangles began to flatten out. Soon, the sides met the lines of the lower lids. The eyes had vanished: there were only the dark, slanting, double lines of the closed lids.

I sat looking at the folded black skin surrounding the closed mouth. Above it, marking the bases of the whiskers, ran four lines of black dots. Irregular black marks on the nose seemed to be old cuts. Black spots moving about the massive face were flies. The lion kept shaking his head to rid himself of the flies. They kept coming back. Every few seconds he would open his eyes and look at me. The eyes were still expressionless. And as soon as they opened they would begin to close, each triangle flattening toward its base. Soon there were once more only the dark, slanting lines of the closed lids and I was waiting for the triangles to lift again and reveal the eyes.

The minutes passed. It was very quiet and very bright and very hot. Down the slope, over beyond the donga, more buffalo drifted out of the bush. Before long, at least two hundred of them were grazing in the open, black and thick and strong against the pale grass. Off to the right, the elephants had moved partway into the bush. A half-grown youngster lay on its side on a big anthill and wriggled happily as it rubbed its gray body against the red earth. But nine paces from my open window, down at the foot of the tree, the lion dozed.

The regular, slow-motion opening and closing of his eyes began to have an almost mesmeric effect on me. I slumped lower in the bucket seat. It had been a long morning and a big breakfast.

And the sun beat down on the stationary car. Even the open side-windows did not help very much. I felt sweat begin to trickle down between the seat and my bare back.

Then an idea had surfaced and I was sitting bolt upright.

I studied the lion again, very carefully. After all, he was at least nine paces away. And he was no edgy female with cubs, just a young male very much on his own. The day was into its doldrums too, and hot. And he had had a long walk in the sun.

The lion opened his eyes again. It seemed to be an even greater effort now. I could still detect no real expression. The upper lids began to straighten. They flattened, flush against the lower lids.

I was bound to see some drastic change in expression, I told myself. Bound to see it long before this sleepy animal could begin to move. Anyway, even if I had to believe sixty miles an hour, his head and body were pointing out through the far end of the grassy channel, away from me.

I started the engine. The lion opened his eyes. They eased shut. I put my right hand on the door lever and pressed. The door clicked. The lion's eyes opened. Still no expression. The eyes closed. Very slowly, I pushed the door open. Halfway, I waited until the next eye-opening and -closing. Then I pushed until the door stood wide. There was nothing, now, between the lion and me. And that, exactly as I had known it would, made a difference.

I waited. The lion opened his eyes. He looked directly at me across the open grass. There was still no expression. The eyes closed. I lifted my right foot out of the car and put it on the ground. The eyes opened. They closed. Very slowly, making no sound, leaving my left foot inside the car, I stood up. My hand still gripped the door.

The lion opened his eyes. I looked down into them. The angle was different now. The grass seemed a long way below. But still nothing in the eyes. Just a sleep-laden blankness. The eyes closed. And as they closed I knew I had won. The standing up, so that my silhouette showed above the car, had been the big thing. There was only the one small move now. Then I would have made it, would be the winner, whatever that meant. And it would be all right. After all, I would still see the change of expression that was bound to come before this sleepy creature could even begin to spring. And the warning would give me time to slip back inside the car and pull the door shut. I lifted my left foot clear of the car and set it on the ground.

The lion opened his eyes.

I do not think I ever saw his expression change. The huge golden body had launched, I mean, before my brain registered the change that must surely have occurred. If he had sprung toward me, perhaps I would never have registered anything. I am sure I would not have had time to slip even partway back into the car, let alone close the door.

But the lion sprang away from me. He launched himself out through the far mouth of the grassy channel, in the direction his head and body had been pointing. He launched himself, from a lying start, at a velocity that I could not possibly put at less than sixty miles an hour. One moment he lay in the shade, eyes closed, the epitome of drowsy indolence; the next, he hung in mid-spring, halfway out of the bush, suspended huge and golden in the sunlight. He landed, bounded twice, and twisted to face me. He stood there for a moment, body half concealed by the bush. The eyes were wide open now, wide awake. They bored into me. Then he had turned and was walking slowly away through the golden grass. And as I watched him go I found that I was at last sitting in the car. The door was still half open.

I closed my eyes and felt my shoulders begin to relax. The engine that was to have carried me to safety if the lion attacked was still idling quietly, just the way it had been idling before I opened the door. At least, almost the same way. Now, I seemed to hear a hollow, futile kind of background ring to it. It was just as well, I thought, that in the course of our error-filled lives most of us are lucky enough to get away with at least one willful, childish, fatuous, criminal moment of plain bloody brazen stupidity.

All through the days at Saddle Camp I kept calling in at Keekorok.

My reasons were strictly practical: picking up or dropping off Joshua or another ranger, filling Rohosinante's tank, perhaps getting a few minor supplies from the little Indian duka beside the gas pumps while yet another flat was fixed; and then driving over to the lodge to buy fresh eggs and bacon from the kitchen, refill my water containers from the tap, and pick up mail from the office.

These brief visits did little to disrupt the quiet days: it was still a pleasure to go to the lodge. The porters still smiled greetings. When I went into the big lounge with the picture windows that looked out onto the swimming pool and the tree-lined donga and the now-familiar sweep of savanna, I sometimes sat down for a drink or a cup of tea with Hans Luther or Steve Joyce. Steve, in particular, seemed to understand what I had found and was trying to pin down. Mrs. Ringberg, the Nor-wegian manageress, had now returned from a long vacation and I began to see why Steve said she was the prime source of the spirit that had prompted me to say, unexpectedly, that the lodge was "a good place." I also began to appreciate the quiet humor of Peter, the Kikuyu clerk, and the wit of Solomon, the barman, also a Kikuyu. Solomon was reputed to have been a big name in Mau Mau and was certainly the kind of man to make his mark in whatever he decided to undertake.

The only sense of disruption at Keekorok came from the news-papers I would sometimes glance at: U.S. ATOM-BOMB WARNING TO CHINA; CZECHS KICK OUT PAKISTANIS; TUNISIANS ORDER OUT CHINESE; ISRAEL—U.A.R. TANK BATTLE; FOUR BIAFRANS EXECUTED BY FIRING SQUAD; SOCCER RIOTERS BURN SHOPS (in Turkey, after at least forty-two people had been killed in a football match riot over a disputed goal).*

---

* So wide was the gap between this world the newspapers reported and my private
I refurbished a statement I had jabberworked on for years:

> All men who turn introspuncible
> In bald and beamish green
> On hearing words like runcible
> Or snark or quince or queen,
> And then flubble about and glee and shout,
> "We're all so yellowish glad!"
> Have worpled it out without a doubt:
> The landscape's painted mad.

On the last of those ten days in the Sanctuary I went to see Tipis.

The county council meeting would be coming up fairly soon, he said. He would let me know as soon as a date was set. Yes, certainly I could take Joshua on my week's trip into the Triangle. "I trust you will find him satisfactory. Oh, will you do me a favor, Mr. Fletcher? Tell me, what did you feel about the capabilities of that old ranger who went out with you one day?"

I confirmed that he meant the amiable but unsparkling man who had shown me Saddle Camp. And at once, almost before I had begun to think, the answer was there, moving out onto the tip of my tongue. It was an apt and just answer, and it said exactly what I wanted to say far more neatly than I could have put it in English. I do not think I held the words back for more than a few milliseconds; even as they teetered on the brink of birth I saw that here at last was the opportunity to overcome the misunderstanding with Tipis about my ability to speak Swahili. I cut the words free: "*Roho yake ni safi sana. Lakini akili yake, sijui.* His heart is very clean. But his intelligence—well, I don't know."

Tipis's head moved back a couple of inches. His eyes opened a shade wider. Then he smiled and gave a little half-sideways nod of approval. "Not bad," he said. "Not bad at all." But then he went on talking in English about my trip into the Triangle. Clearly, he thought I had just begun taking Swahili lessons and had chanced to have these convenient phrases in an embryo vocabulary.

vorld out in the Sanctuary that one evening at Saddle Camp, after a visit to the lodge,

> *From farther and near they pobble and steer*
> *Like Jumblies madder than blue*
> *And carrol and lear for all to hear,*
> *"The world's gone Waterloo!"*
> *And their dedwardlearness and dodgsonness,*
> *Derived from blacker and white,*
> *You grok when you screed the daily press:*
> *My Cheshire Cat, they're right!*

I waited for him to pause. There was still time to explain. But he had launched into a rambling editorial, and with every word the opportunity faded. Before long it had perished.

Tipis was saying that I would unfortunately have to delay my trip into the Triangle because for the next three days Joshua would be busy. "A big party of Masai elders are coming over from Amboseli to see how we run things here. As you probably know, they have had difficulties with their game reserve. And for the day they are here I shall naturally need every ranger." His voice carried a nervous edge as well as a ring of pride, and I knew exactly what was going to happen. Tipis would muster his resources to show off to his neighbors, the way we all show off when we are for some reason raised to temporary model status and the neighbors troop around, sullen but smiling, to learn how things should really be done. For the next two days Keekorok would seethe with preparations. It would be a place to avoid.

So early next afternoon I drove out of the Sanctuary toward the open country that lies to its northwest, just across the Mara River from the Triangle.

I went out by the Talek Gate. And almost at once I passed the manyatta my party had visited our first day in the Mara. That day, I had registered only the sad commercialism we found inside the manyatta. When I drove by two weeks later on my way back from the Triangle to Keekorok I had, I think, been vaguely aware of a difference between the country just outside the Talek Gate, where three manyattas clustered close, and that inside the Sanctuary. Now, my more practiced eye saw at once that the manyattas had killed the savanna.

The grass had been grazed and trampled into a sparse gray stubble. Across this waste, like filaments of a web, ran cattle and foot trails, worn bare and deep. There were vehicle tracks too, branching off from the road. Each gust of wind, sweeping in from the east, raised a dust cloud. Even the trees looked poverty-stricken. On one of them, near an eroded donga, perched a dozen vultures and marabou storks. The tree's branches glared white with their droppings.

Beyond the last manyatta I turned left onto a track that ran westward, parallel to the Talek River. This reach of the river, which flows during the rains but is often no more than a chain of small pools or even a dry donga, forms the northern boundary of the Sanctuary, and as I drove westward I could see that beyond the river course the grass grew long and rich, the trees strong and dark. I saw few animals beyond the river (the land rose sharply, then flattened out of sight), but I had explored that corner of the sanctuary and I remembered the rolling richness of the land and its herds of zebras and wildebeest and topi and Tommy and all the teeming rest.

Now, north of the river, I drove through gray, impoverished wilderness. Cattle droppings spattered the overgrazed stubble. The trees had a ravaged, half-battlefield look. Mile after mile, I saw no wild animals. In the only place the grass grew long—around thick bush in a vlei-like basin—three or four fires were reducing it to a flat, black mat.

This stretch of country, I now knew, had been opened up to cattle in the last few years by the tsetse control scheme based at Aitong. The Masai had naturally moved in without delay behind this new swathe cut by the winds of change. But they had long ceased to be a wide-ranging nomadic people that never stayed long enough in one place to do serious damage to the land: their manyattas often remained in the same place year after year. For the winds had exerted new pressures. You now gained solid advantages, for example, if your manyatta stood beside a road where vehicles would often give you a ride, and especially if it was near a place like the Talek Gate, where tourists would pay, in exchange for permission to take pictures, large sums of the once-despised money—the money that, it now transpired, could buy cattle.

Traditionally, a Masai sees cattle not as producers of meat and milk but as pure wealth. So overstocked land is to him as unreasonable a concept as is an overstocked bank account to a normal European. And a tattered cow bothers him no more than a tattered bank note bothers a Westerner. Furthermore, he naturally strives, like a Western businessman, to pass on to his sons more wealth than his father had passed on to him. The inevitable result of all these things, I now saw, was the kind of ravaged savanna I had found outside the Talek Gate.

I drove on westward. When I looked off to the left and saw the long, gleaming grass beyond the river, inside the Sanctuary, I could not suppress a pricklish understanding of how the Masai cattlemen of Talek must feel. Steve Joyce had said that Tipis was probably the only man who could keep the cattle out of the Sanctuary; now, for the first time, I glimpsed the realities that Tipis must face. I was just conceding that his success seemed nothing short of miraculous when I saw, over on the far side of the Talek, knee-deep in golden grass, grazing greedily, a sizable herd of cattle. And as I watched them it occurred to me for the first time in my life that all wildlife sanctuaries, everywhere, were not, as I had from habit considered them, sanctuaries *for* wild animals; they were sanctuaries *against* men. Not against evil men, of course. Just unaware men.

I drove on across the pathetic plain.

Faced by the new challenges, the Masai would have to change. Throughout human history, whole peoples had been periodically confronted by challenges. Sometimes they succumbed. Sometimes they merely survived. But sometimes they girded themselves and triumphed and thereby honed themselves to greatness. Arnold Toynbee saw each outcome as depending on the severity of the challenge and on the spirit of the people at the time the challenge came. The challenges buffeting Masailand, although severe, did not appear overwhelming. So the spirit would be the thing. The temper of the people would decide whether Western influence will, in Toynbee's words, "evaporate without permanent effect, or whether it will turn the dough sour, or whether it will successfully leaven the lump." In a sense I had known that all along—even before I talked to T-B, even before I saw the wheat-fields slashing square across the savanna. I had grasped, though fuzzily, that the future of the Masai—and of the animals that shared their land—would depend on whether some of the old values and harmonies could weather the nature-dominating, money-centered, Western way of life. And now, as I drove on westward across the plain, it occurred to me that the county council meeting might help me gauge how local leaders were responding to the challenges that had gusted into Masailand at last, through Nairobi, from the world beyond.

The road swung north, away from the Talek. But still, mile after mile, the grass had been stubbled gray or burned to a black and even bleaker barrenness. I saw no animals except a couple of zebras and Tommy and once—on a strip of lush green vleiland—a small herd of wildebeest.

At last, a dozen miles beyond the manyattas, I came to the crest of a low ridge. And suddenly, all around me, the grass grew long and rich. Beyond the ridge the land sloped down, gently and evenly, into a broad valley; and down this valley, north and south across my front, only a mile or two away, ran the strip of forest that lined the Mara River. Beyond the forest rose the Isuria Escarpment. And between treetops and escarpment I could see—clearly, now—the grassland and forest wedges of the Triangle.

I drove slowly down the track. It swung left. I turned down the slope, toward the river. The long grass leaned and nodded. An impala herd grazed quietly, bachelors in attendance. A topi herd stood purple and pewter and perfect. A lone giraffe strode northward like a liquidly graceful derrick. A rift opened in the gray cloudbank above the escarpment and sunlight angled down, diverging beams distinct, and spread a gauzy, luminous white fan. The giraffe strode on, framed by the fan. It slid behind a clump of trees. As if on cue, the fan folded up into the clouds.

And then I saw, emerging from the dark river-forest that was now only half a mile away, a wedge-shaped, battleship-gray convoy of elephants. A large female led. Behind her, flank almost rubbing flank, came five young. The eyes of the smallest barely cleared the three-foot tall grass. Behind these precious charges, her head up in among them, strode another huge female. The grass barely reached her knees. The convoy forged out across a flat and open meadow, away from the forest.

I drove on down the slope, toward the meadow. Soon, the forest loomed tall. Tree trunks and creepers and dense understory gave it depth and richness. Above treetops that now blocked off the escarpment, the gray cloudbank had retreated and the sun was shining, steady but muted, through dispersing haze.

Another wedge of gray shapes emerged from the forest. Two lone elephants appeared, then more small convoys. Soon, twenty or thirty massive gray shapes were drifting northward across the meadow. A lone bull battleshipped south, contemptuous of the tide.

The light gained strength. It bathed the valley in a soft yet startling glow. The pale grassheads in the meadow grew luminous. Above, the cloud haze hung pastel mauve. Along the forest wall, tree trunks stood out against the green and gloom—embossed, tinted purple. The light grew stronger, imposing an eloquent tension on the whole valley.

For almost an hour I sat at the edge of the meadow, watching. The elephants drifted on up an open slope. The huge animals moved slowly, serenely, with immense dignity and indeflectible purpose. They were no longer earthbound gray. I could hear no sound and the eerie light still suffused the valley.

At last the sun slid behind a lingering cloud. The mauve light drained away. The tension slackened and a new and heavier silence settled over the broad valley.

A breeze brushed my arm. I glanced at my watch.

For a moment I hesitated. Tipis had spoken of a good camp-site down in the river forest. But it would take time to find a route across the donga; besides, I did not relish the idea of driving along the edge of the dark forest from which the elephant convoys had emerged. I am not sure whether I acknowledged, before I started the car and swung away from the river, that it would also be a kind of sacrilege to drive across the pale, level meadow where the light and the huge gray shapes had been.

I drove back up the slope, almost to the crest from which I had first seen the river, and camped beside an old anthill. Apart from the anthill and a small thorn tree that grew beside it, the grass stretched open and unconcealing, and for a hundred yards in every direction it grew no more than a foot high. But as soon as I got out of the car I found that the breeze had swung around and was blowing in from the west, directly away from the elephants that were still moving up the open slope, toward me. I knew that the danger of their stumbling on me remained remote, but even before I set up my table I drove to a dead tree a little way off and for the first time for many nights collected firewood. It would be comforting, when I turned the lamp off and went to bed, to leave a hearth of glowing ashes that would telegraph into the night a warning to all involuntary intruders.

After dark, my dome of hissing white light embraced not only table and tent but fire and thorn tree and anthill. All through dinner my eyes kept wandering out toward the anthill. The firelight dug dark caves and canyons in its flanks, then flickered them away, so that instead of standing inert, the way anthills usually did, it had life and movement. And all at once, because of a small incident that had happened earlier in the evening, it occurred to me that ever since I came back to the Mara—ever since I came back to Africa—I had been looking at anthills and failing to make some very simple connections. Often, now, my eye passed over the biggest mounds and barely registered their existence. Even when I did notice them I tended to see only inert, haphazard oddities. Such observations as I made were mostly superficial, largely irrelevant and entirely disconnected: that old mounds often supported star grass instead of the oats grass of the surrounding plain; that in this decaying state the mounds made great gazebos for topi and kongoni, lions, and Welshmen on foot; and that once time and sun and rain and wind had leveled them halfway back to the earth and extinction they could perform much the same function for a Welshman on wheels because when the surrounding grass was too tall for him to emerge safely from his car he could run both its right-hand wheels part way up the gentle lower slopes of the mound and cant the car at such an angle that he sat high above the grass and thereby got at least a reasonably good gaze at the surrounding savanna.

But that was about as far as I had gone. I had failed to see the simple, serious, important, obvious things about anthills. And there was no reason for my failure.

Back home I had several times heard a vivid and poetic radio adaptation of the classic *Soul of the White Ant* by Eugene Marais, the South African naturalist, and the world it revealed had enthralled me. Now I knew perfectly well that the "white ant" was the termite, and that termites were the builders of the "anthills" that I had been seeing every day since I came back to the Mara; but by some involuntary master stroke of stage management I had hung a curtain between the two adjoining compartments of my mind. Not once had I remembered that somewhere inside each living anthill lay a queen mother who, it has been said, "represents the highest natural societal organization known on this planet." I had failed, utterly, to visualize the huge, white, bloated form of the queen lying in her chamber with the king in attendance as she gave birth almost continuously—producing as many as 50,000 eggs a day—while a ring of soldiers surrounded her and masseurs ministered to her body and a stream of workers hurried in bearing food and another stream hurried out bearing away the eggs to the cultivated "fungus gardens" that would feed the eggs when they hatched into larvae. This dark and buried termite world gleamed with unlikely detail and unsolved mystery: the internal protozoans that enabled the termites to digest the cellulose walls of the grass and wood on which they fed—microscopic creatures that had to be passed from generation to generation of termites by a licking of the parental anus; the transfer of the huge and growing queen from one royal chamber to another whenever she became too bloated for the old one—a transfer executed in a palace that seemed to lack passageways big enough to accommodate her; above all, the unknown mechanism by which this huge, white, immobile, egg-producing blimp that was the queen managed to operate as the "brain" of the entire nest—a mechanism so sensitive and all-pervading that if the queen died, then the whole complex life that went on within the nest, embracing thousands of individuals, most of whom never came anywhere near her, would at once undergo a spasm and begin to slow down, and would at length cease to function. When the queen died, that is, the nest died. Marais, after years of observation, concluded that each individual termite nest was similar in every respect to a single animal: the queen functioned as brain; the fungus gardens resembled digestive organs; workers and soldiers operated much as do red and white blood corpuscles; and the sexual flight of king and queen was in every respect analogous to the escape of spermatozoa and ova. This concept had left a vivid impression on my mind. Yet until that evening I had not once since I came back to Africa connected *The Soul of the White Ant* with the Mara's countless anthills.*

The small incident that jolted my mind into making the connection had occurred just after I chose my campsite that evening. In swinging the car away from the main anthill to go for firewood I had failed to notice a very small one a few yards away, half hidden in the foot-high grass. And I had scraped the top of the little red mound with Rohosinante's breastplate. I got out to check that she had suffered no damage. All seemed well. But the plate had sliced about an inch off the top of the anthill. I knelt down—and found myself looking into an exposed gallery. Seething about it, no doubt in utter panic at the disaster that had befallen their community, was a mass of small, white, wriggling termites. But the light was already failing, and after a moment or two I stood up and got back into the car and drove off for the firewood and forgot the termites.

Now, remembering, I got up from the table and took my flashlight and located the decapitated mound. The exposed gallery was a honeycomb of small, dark brown chambers. Most of them had been damaged and all were empty.

On the way back to the table I took my briefcase from the car. And soon, sitting once more at the epicenter of my hissing white dome with the fire glowing red off to my left and the anthill

---

* I find that current expert opinion disagrees with Marais on certain details. But the picture he painted remains fundamentally "true." In any case, the point is that at the time I was in the Mara I knew only Marais's story.

flickering itself into existence to my right and then flickering out of existence, but always there now, I began to read research papers. I read of ants that hunted spiders and termites and other ants; of ants that liked sugar and seemed to be attracted to light; of ants that "milked" captive aphids and plant lice. I read that ordinary termites—Eugene Marais's termites, the Mara's termites—gave communal warning, when their nest was disturbed, by thumping their thoraces on mud plates that acted as resonators.

I leaned back in the chair. Out beyond my dome, the Stilton-yellow moon was levering itself up out of the earth's blackness. It was always appalling as well as wonderful, this business of reading in a new field and discovering that the ramifications stretched back endlessly, alp upon alp, into the darkness of your ignorance. For the microworld of the ants and termites was only a beginning. Anthills, for example, meant ant bears.

The ant bear or aardvark is an elongated but solidly built pig-like creature that may measure six feet from the tip of its long, tapering snout to the tip of its long, tapering tail. It subsists mainly on termites, with occasional side dishes of ants and wild cucumbers. Its powerful curved claws enable it to dig rapidly into the base of a termite nest. It may excavate a tunnel several feet long and wide enough to accommodate its whole body, and as it digs it keeps on moving down the tunnel. When it strikes termites it thrusts its snout forward and shoots out a thin, sticky tongue, a foot and a half long. The tongue darts and flickers through caverns and galleries, collecting termites en masse, the way Billy Graham collects converts. Then it flicks back into the ant bear's mouth and the unfortunate termites have begun a journey that ends—for them, personally—in the ant bear's stomach.

Because ant bears almost always work the night shift, you rarely see them. I had seen none since coming back to Kenya. In all the years I lived there I had sighted only half a dozen, and then always in my headlight beams. But you know they are common in Kenya because ant bear holes are a feature of the landscape. And ant bear holes, I was now beginning to realize, set up a whole new series of termite-initiated ramifications. I rummaged among the research papers again and found, in Darling's ecological study of the Mara, a list of large mammals that used the local ant bear tunnels as homes, or at least as nurseries during the breeding season. Hyenas headed the list. I had known about them: it was into ant bear holes that the two young hyenas had almost certainly disappeared when my headlights surprised the family near the kopje, the evening I camped across the way from the Dawsons. But the list was far longer than I had expected: jackals, warthogs, bat-eared foxes, ratels, hunting dogs, aardwolves, banded mongooses, caracals, genets, and civet and serval cats. And the large mammals were no doubt only a beginning. Rodents and other small mammals probably made use of the tunnels, as well as birds and reptiles and insects. That way, too, the linkages ramified outward, alp to alp.

I began to skim through a paper that investigated the implications of a pattern that showed up clearly on aerial photographs of the Mara as a dense and almost regular mosaic covering much of the open grassland, particularly on the Loita Plains. The pattern was formed by a series of elongated blobs, light at their centers and dark at the edges, like the markings on a peacock's tail, and it turned out that each of these blobs centered on a low, grassed-over termite mound. Rain, washing down the slopes of the rolling plain, tended to collect on the upper side of each mound but to drain quickly from its lower side. As a result, these opposite zones supported different grasses. And the differences, accentuated by the treatment they received from the various animals that lived on them, produced the peacock-tail patterns that showed up so clearly from the air even though they were difficult to detect when you stood beside them.

In itself, this mosaic seemed less than earth-shaking. But then I looked more carefully at the aerial photographs. And I saw that although the mounds averaged only two or three an acre their elongated grass patterns covered something like 50 percent of the plain.

I leaned back in my chair and barbecued this news. The moon had swung high now, but out beyond my dome the night was still black. The fire still glowed red and the anthill still flickered into and out of existence.

Anthills, then, did more than replace the standard oats grass of the open plain with the star grass I had noticed on their slopes. By their very existence they transformed the nature of the grass over almost half the plain's acreage. And that was something. After all, most of the Mara's mammals depended on the grass for their very existence.

I leaned forward again and found a paper by Julian Huxley. I flicked through its pages. It was there all right, as I had half remembered: "The productivity of a habitat depends on its conversion cycle—the mechanism underlying the flux of energy through the animals and plants in a habitat, the metabolic flow of its ecological community. . . . And in our area [East and Central Africa] termites are a dominant element in the conversion cycle." In other words, much of the savanna's seething life depended on the "inert" anthills I had been ignoring.

It was at this point, I think, that depression began to close in on me.

There were more filaments in the Mara's web than I had dreamed of. Some were too fine for the unassisted human eye to see: the microworlds of the cellulose-digesting protozoans that lived in the stomachs of hyraxes and termites and enabled their hosts to make a living. Some were social arrangements easily grasped by social man: impala harems; abductions from the zebraglio. Some of the filaments I had recently read about were broad, overriding concepts that you could easily miss for the trees: the necessity of sheer space for the survival of "a population of large animals which are diurnal and do not inhabit hidden retreats." I had recognized, or thought I recognized, that all these things dovetailed. But I had failed to make the connections, had failed to comprehend the complexities. And the alp upon alp that I now saw stretching away from the "inert" anthills were only a beginning. Their ramifications would stretch away as far as my mind could explore, the way anthills often stretched away across the Mara plains as far as my eye could see.

I leaned back once more in my chair and the huge blackness

of the night pressed in on my little white dome. Off to the left, the fire burned low. I tossed on a new log. The disturbance snuffed out the last flames. But embers still glowed. I sat watching them. At first, the embers would seem to have no effect on the new log. But they would heat it, preparing it. And when all was ready a flame would leap. Within seconds, the whole log would be blazing. It was the same when an idea smoldered in mankind: evolution was in the nineteenth-century air well before a flame leaped, independently, in Darwin and Wallace—and then the idea blazed across the world. It was the same, too, in our individual minds.

Down among the glowing embers, a flame licked up. Within seconds the log was ablaze. But outside the fire and my white dome, the blackness still pressed in, close, heavy.

For one thing, there was the book. Now that I had glimpsed the complexities, it began to look as if I might have bitten off more than I could chew. Hubert Braun, the Dutch grass expert down in the Serengeti, had been daunted by the discovery that his research area turned out to be bigger than his own country. The project I had rushed into threatened to be bigger than my mind.

My depression soon flooded out beyond the book. Because the savanna was infinitely more complex than I had recognized— because the filaments of its life-web depended on each other in a way I had not fully grasped until that evening—it seemed likely that the web was terribly fragile. If the winds of change funneling in through Nairobi broke only a few of its strands then the whole structure might tear apart. The Mara, because of its richness, was terribly vulnerable. And all at once, sitting there very small at the center of my white dome with the fire now burning bright, I saw that the Mara lay in even greater danger than I had thought.*

---

* My reasoning that night involved a fundamental error. I find that current ecological theory sees diversity in an ecosystem as a source of strength, not weakness: the more strands there are, the greater the capacity of the web to withstand damage to some of them. But this error was an integral part of my depression that night, and I shall let it stand. Besides, it does not invalidate my conclusions. Human-dominated ecosys-

I sat on, watching the flames devour the new log. It was pleasant to dream that tourism might offer a solution for the Mara. It might. But the modern African expected to put his regained lands to uses that met African needs; and to the average African, tourism must look very much like setting aside huge chunks of this land so that well-fed white foreigners could drive around it in comfort, gawking. His attitude was certainly human enough. But that was often the trouble: our "humanness." For example, those of us who were passionately concerned with preserving the world's harmonies tended, being horribly human, to get so damned holier-than-thou over our vision that the important things we had to say were likely to stick in any uncommitted craw. And the backlash that inevitably followed often undid any good we might have achieved—and then some. In the Mara, as elsewhere, such highly human happenings would no doubt play their poisonous part. That was a depressing thought too.

But it did not end with the Mara. On such nights it never ends. Out in the wider world, where the cold winds came from, the dominant animal was running rampant, tearing at all the other filaments with its mushrooming numbers and technology and Gross Planetary Product. The only comforting omen, for the world as a whole, was that this cruelly dominant animal—this animal that soiled—had by its expertise initiated a rate of internal change and engineered a degree of complication that it seemed unlikely to cope with. It was therefore showing signs, as a species, of running into trouble. Perhaps into extinction.

But this kind of self-comfort, though somberly satisfying for a while, turns out to be bogus. No matter how aloof and cynical you think you are—and it is very easy to sit aloof and cynical when you are alone at the center of a white dome in the middle of a wide savanna—you still cannot really dissociate yourself from

tems—such as the wheatfields near Lemek and the devastated area around Talek—radically limit the diversity of "natural" local life. So the danger to the Mara does not lie, as I had thought, in its richness but in the threatened reduction of that richness by man. The result, unfortunately, is the same.

the rest of your species. Not for long, anyway. Not totally. In the end, "they" includes "you." And if you are even halfway honest in your imaginings and halfway in command of your sense you have to admit, once you have savored the thrill of doomsday clairvoyance, that you cannot go gentle into that good night of decline.

I pushed back the chair and stood up and lifted the hissing lamp from the table.

If you are used to living on your own, far from the crutches of the human world, you relish and even come to depend on the freedoms that such a life lavishes on you. But there is one sense in which you become vulnerable. All of us, I assume, suffer moments of cosmic despair. In a city you can drown out your sorrows, or you can escape from the man-world and seek solace in more profound realities. In wilderness, moments of cosmic despair do not come very often; but when they do you are alone and naked with the earth and the huge darkness, and there is no defense.

I walked to my little tent and crawled inside and reached out and turned off the lamp. The fire still glowed its red and piffling warning to the minor dangers of the darkness. I slid back into the tent and lay down and pulled the sleeping bag over me. And eventually I fell asleep.

But the sun always rises, and it did so next morning. By that time I was conducting a small elephantine experiment.

I had struck camp at first light and driven down toward the river. Most of the elephants were still there, scattered in groups across the open slope. In the flat gray light they looked from a mile away like blobs of spilled mercury. They did not have the gleam and fluidity of mercury, though, and at that range there was something faintly comic about them.

I drove down the track toward the nearest group. Like the rest, it was drifting toward the river-forest. Its members browsed as they went. Long before I came close to them the mercury illusion had rolled aside and I had grasped once more the realities of size and bulk. T-B's voice was there again, under the floor-boards: "It's the cows you've got to watch, especially when they've got calves." And I could see, etched across my wind-shield, the comment Fraser Darling had made in his survey of the Mara: "Quite the shyest elephants I have met with in Africa." Two hundred yards from the first group, I stopped.

There were nine of them: three big cows, each with a small calf; one larger calf; and two near-adults that tended to keep together, a little apart from the others. One of the cows turned to her left and through binoculars I found myself looking full onto her huge, sloping, wrinkled and still somehow surprising rear end. A small calf moved up alongside her and laid his trunk back along the top of his head and thrust his mouth up and for-ward between her forelegs. There was still a puff of surprise about that too, even though I had long ago learned that an elephant's teats, unlike those of most mammals except us primates, are placed up near its forelimbs.

The group continued to browse slowly forward. They ap-peared to ignore me; and yet, although I am no longer sure what actions signaled the information, I felt sure they were aware of my presence. I checked the faint easterly breeze. The track had brought me in at an angle that meant the group would not yet have caught my scent. (An elephant's sense of smell is acute, its hearing good, its eyesight poor.) I drove closer. A hundred and seventy-five yards. A hundred and fifty. Still the elephants ig-nored me. But the cows had begun to look very big. I hesitated. Then I swung Rohosinante around and started to back slowly down the track toward the elephants. I drove with chin on shoulder, eyes fixed on the cows, and hand resting on the gear shift so that with a flick of foot and wrist I could, at any change in their demeanor, take off. The elephants continued to ignore me. They drew a little closer together perhaps, but that could have been coincidence.

A hundred yards. Eighty. Sixty. I stopped. The elephants browsed peacefully on. Once or twice a cow lifted her head in my direction. Nothing more. I switched off the motor.

Through binoculars I could see that the adults were not, as I had assumed, eating grass: they were pulling up thorn trees so small that the grass nearly always hid them from my eye until they came up, roots and all, in the curled tips of the trunks and swung back and up into the waiting mouths. A flag of foliage or a web of roots might protrude briefly from a corner of the mouth. I might even see earth crumbling away from the roots, sat waiting. The sun came up over the crest of the slope and the last of the little tree would vanish.

The group continued to drift down the slope. Their advance, angling in toward the track, brought them closer and closer to the broad line that I knew flowed directly downwind of me across the open grass—the invisible line of my scent that would be as clear and unmistakable to an elephant as a stream of marker dye would be to a helicopter pilot hunting for a splashed-down spacecraft. I watched attentively. The elephants drifted on. I sat waiting. The sun came up over the crest of the slope and flooded across the pale grass, transmuting it to gold.

The lead cow came to the edge of the marker line. She continued to browse forward. I could detect no change in her demeanor. The others moved quietly along behind her. As they crossed the line the whole group made, perhaps, a mild swing away from me. But it was at most a kink in their line of advance; and otherwise the whole group of immense gray animals continued to ignore my presence. At one point, when five of them were within fifty yards of me, one of the near-adults moved out from the general line of advance, directly toward the car. She raised her trunk, nostrils facing me. The tip of the trunk waved and quested. But she seemed only curious; I felt no sense of being threatened. When she was barely thirty-five yards away I started the motor. She backed off, still without hostility, and turned and rejoined the group. Soon all nine animals had crossed the invisible marker line that flowed across the now golden grass.

The group continued to drift down toward the forest. The track swung right, then resumed its original line, and I could see that if the elephants held their course they would cross it about two hundred yards ahead of me. I could pass them, of course, by detouring as widely as I wanted across the open grass; but now I saw that by moving on down the track I could complete a little experiment that I had, almost without knowing it, already begun.

I swung the car around and eased forward in low gear. The vivid, invisible, marker-dye flow of my scent moved with me, out to my left front, out across the open grass. It swung closer and closer to the elephants.

I think the uneasiness began to spread through the group even before my scent reached them. I know that by the time it was flowing directly into them the uneasiness had crystallized. There was no sudden movement, and no concerted movements that I detected; but all at once the scattered group had fused into a solid phalanx. And then the phalanx had swung a little right of its original line and was angling toward me.

The three big cows formed the wedge of the phalanx. The rest had bunched in tight behind them, just the way the younger animals had bunched in behind their leader the evening before, when the convoy emerged from the dark river-forest. I continued to drive slowly down the track. The phalanx continued to close on me. Forty yards. Thirty.

The elephants were also moving slowly now, almost tentatively. At first they seemed to pose no direct threat. But all at once the three cows were huge and towering. And then the only thing in the world outside the car was the biggest and nearest cow, and I saw, as if I had never known about them before, the ringed caterpillar-pattern of wrinkles on her upper trunk and the smudges of dark soil on her tusks where she had been digging. Suddenly she swung her huge ears forward, wide and menacing, and I could see that they were smooth at the center and deeply veined around the edges. Then, before anything else could happen, I had passed the critical point and was beginning to draw away.

The phalanx halted. I kept going for ten or fifteen yards, then stopped. The elephants seemed to suffer a moment of indecision:

the whole phalanx did a kind of on-the-spot shuffle. Then the big cow took a couple of strides forward. Her ears were still spread wide. And even before my foot began to come up from the clutch pedal she had lowered her huge barn of a head and then flung it backward and upward with a quick, eloquent tossing motion. Her trunk swung up and poised, high, like a gigantic nightstick. I had seen elephants make this motion before; but even the first time you see it, there is no doubt about what it means. It means: "Get the hell out of here!" And all at once Rohosinante was very small and as fragile as paper and I was a trapped insect and without any further ado whatever I got the hell out. In my driving mirror I saw the cow's trunk come down and her ears drop back to their normal position. And then the phalanx was moving forward again. It crossed the track and continued on down toward the river.

I drove a little further, then stopped. My breathing slowed toward normal. The little experiment seemed to suggest, very tentatively, that if you had established a position and elephants moved toward you they would yield the right of way; but that if you were unwise or unlucky enough to move in close when they had in some sense established position then you should be prepared for trouble. Such a theory certainly seemed to explain why even the unpredictable Mara elephants did not seem to molest people's camps.

The phalanx of elephants crossed a donga that bordered the meadow. They moved on toward the forest. I sat watching them.

Now that I stopped to think about it, I realized that my reading had produced remarkably little information about elephants. There had been notes on their value to the savanna community as cross-country trailmakers, as plowers and aerators of the soil (when they pushed big trees over or pulled up small ones with their trunks), as reseeders of forest (through their droppings), and as well diggers (in some places, a large local population ranging from rhino and buffalo down through gazelles and monkeys and birds to butterflies may depend for survival on the waterholes that elephants regularly dig with tusks and trunks in dry, sandy watercourses). But I had found few solid facts. In Nairobi, when Toni Harthoorn and I were discussing proposed elephant control plans, he had said, "The fact is, you know, that we're talking about big-scale programs that'll mean shooting hundreds of elephants when frankly we know precious little about them— about either their physiology or their behavior." Toni had also said, "Elephants seem to be the only animals apart from us with a comprehension of death." And there had been a sudden warmth in his voice, so that I felt his sense of comradeship with the huge gray beasts that he had so often tranquilized with his flying syringes and meticulously prepared drugs.

Toni was not alone, of course. Elephants, Asian as well as African, seem to hold a special place in men's minds. It is a place that by no means depends on sheer size or even on the aura of mystery created by our lack of knowledge. André Maurois has quoted a Buddhist text: "The elephant is the wisest of all animals, the only one who remembers his former lives; and he remains motionless for long periods of time, meditating thereon." The Masai are said to regard elephants with "respect bordering on awe." If a herdsman sees one near his manyatta as he brings the cattle home at dusk, or if he hears one trumpet at that time, he pays it "a kind of tribute" by "ringing cow bells or holding an ax." And any Masai who finds an elephant's afterbirth is regarded as the recipient of the highest good fortune. Such an event is rare, and a complicated ceremony must take place before the good fortune matures. But it seems that "only one family in the Narok district is known to have found an afterbirth, and it is now certainly one of the wealthiest."

Most people who have much to do with elephants seem to share the Masai's feeling. A hunter on elephant control duty in western Kenya once wrote of "an extraordinary display of animal loyalty." He and some game scouts had shot three elephants of a herd of about thirty. The surviving animals—no more than sixty yards from the human party but directly upwind and apparently unaware of their position—milled around the corpses, trumpeting and shrieking and throwing up showers of grass and stones. Then they tried to lift their dead companions. They pushed and butted at the inert forms. They pawed frenziedly at them with their forefeet. By entwining their trunks with those of the dead animals, they tried to lift the carcasses. Their efforts continued for more than half an hour, and all that time they showed no interest in other matters, no trace of fear for their own fate. The hunter's account went on to describe how a large cow knelt beside one dead animal—an adult female that could hardly have been her calf—put her tusks under the belly, and tried to stand. She tensed in tremendous effort. Then, with a loud crack, her right tusk snapped off. It arched through the air and landed about thirty feet away. The hunter kept the account strictly factual. But it rang with his respect, bordering on awe, for those other animals that a part of him felt obliged to "control."

My group of elephants reached the far side of the meadow. They vanished into the forest. Further north, the last of the other groups had already moved down into the meadow. I looked up across the open slope. A mile away, almost at the crest, half hidden in a fold, a handful of buffalo had drifted into view. It looked as if they might be the advance guard of a big herd, still hidden in the fold. I started the car and swung back up the track, toward the buffalo.

Off to the left, the last of the elephant groups melted away into the river forest. Without them, the meadow looked very ordinary. Facts, I decided, were not what mattered most about elephants, anyway. Their essence lay in their presence. In their bulk. In their dignity. In their astonishing delicacy of touch and movement. In their huge, sloping, wrinkled backsides. In the way the sunken temples of older animals, set just behind the eyes, sometimes made you see those barnlike heads as belonging to frail old professors emeritus whose learned lives had left them replete with kindly wisdom. The eyes themselves, though too small for the colossal heads, were in no way piglike: they confirmed the impression of wisdom. They were also wary, weary and more than a touch sad.

I was still a quarter of a mile from the buffalo when the track breasted a shallow rise and I found that I was looking across a broad fold in the savanna. The buffalo herd was only twenty or thirty strong; but it formed the flank unit of a mixed congregation of animals scattered over something like a square mile of grassland. The core of this congregation was the biggest topi herd I had yet seen: a loose, drifting assembly that must have numbered close to three hundred. I eased forward along the track. When I was well into the congregation, I stopped. The topi stretched across my front in a diffuse crescent. Off to the right, beyond the crescent's tip, the buffalo stood watching the car, all curiosity and distrust. I could see now that they were not far from the anthill camp I had left only an hour or so before. Behind me, a large impala harem I had just passed was still grazing peacefully. Spare lords waited. A dozen Tommy attended. Off to the left, half a mile away, a lone rhino was lumbering a straight, unheeding line to somewhere. A pair of ostriches moved respectfully aside. I watched the rhino sink away into another of the shallow, rolling folds that can turn empty, open savanna into a place of surprises. Only then did I see, directly ahead of me, close beside the track, a warthog family indulging in family business.

Very slowly I drove to within fifty yards of them. The three half-grown piglets were rootling for breakfast. The adults had other things in mind. She led. Wherever she went he followed in articulated tandem, his outstretched head resting on her plump black rump. Conjoined in this ludicrous linkage, they trotted around and around in aimless, irregular circles. Occasionally she would stop. He would try to mount her. She might turn and nuzzle him briefly; but then she was off again, and back would go his head on top of her rump.

Once, he stopped of his own accord and began to sniff the ground, as if he had had enough of her teasing. She, being feminine, stopped and waggled her rear end at him. He, being masculine, rose to the lure. And off they went again.

I glanced to the left. The rhino had resurfaced, still on course; but almost at once he lumbered out of sight again, over the crest.

I looked around. The buffalo still stood and stared. The impala sultan still mounted regal guard over his harem. The bachelors waited. The Tommy grazed and metronomed. A tendril of the topi crescent had drifted down toward my anthill camp. Away to the left, the two ostriches were grazing south, honorary mammals to the hilt. And all around us the grass gleamed golden in the sunlight. I decided, although it was still early, to stay for breakfast, there in the center of my congregation.

I made every movement slowly and I left the car where it was, rear door facing away from the warthog family. But when, in sliding out the table, I banged it against metalwork, the adults broke off their tandem circling. For an instant they stood staring at me. Then the whole family, children and all, was warthogging away, tails held stiffly and resentfully erect. The other animals went on with their various businesses. The nearest of them tended to drift away from me, but that was all.

I began to cook breakfast. Rummaging in the car for something, I came across my little transistor radio tucked into a food box. It was at least a week since I had used it, and without really thinking—perhaps to make sure the batteries still worked, or to find out if Nairobi would still reach me over on this side of the Mara—I switched on. From the little leather-covered box there came, faint and attenuated but still unctuous, the Nairobi-Oxford voice of a newscaster. "Today," it said, "the vice-president of Kenya, Mr. Daniel arap Moi, will attend prize-giving at K——— High School. The students will sing the Kenya national anthem. The vice-president will speak of the necessity for political unity at this time. Afterwards he will . . ." I switched off.

The tea water boiled. I sat down and began to eat.

It was surprising how rarely you got a good look at warthog. You saw them often enough, but they always seemed to hightail away before you got close. It was surprising, too, how little I had learned about them. I had read that they lived in old ant bear holes, or at least raised litters there; but beyond that I knew precious little. They were yet another of the Mara's filaments that remained, for me, detached from the web.

The thought generated a twinge of depression—the same kind of depression as had swamped me the night before at my camp beside the anthill. I looked over there. The tendril of topi had almost reached the place. Between us, the long grass glowed in the sunlight. A breeze came down over the crest and the grass rippled. Something about its motion, or perhaps about its color or its richness, struck a chord from that first morning near Keekorok when the lions came out of the trees beyond the zebras. I listened. All around me the grass was rustling, very faintly. I could smell it now, with its blend of dust and life.

I leaned back in my chair. Perhaps I had grown too used to this life in the open savanna where I could eat my breakfast in the company of a congregation five hundred strong, could lunch among zebras, might find a lioness crouching inside my dinner dome. Perhaps that was the trouble. Perhaps I had lost sight of the things that mattered, the things that had set my mind stirring that first morning near Keekorok. As with the elephants, it was not the facts that mattered. Not really. Its essence lay elsewhere.

Perhaps I had had my head buried too deep in behavior studies and the like. Facts were a part of it, of course. An essential part. Still, I could learn enough of them when I came back for the six months of solid research. But even then, although I must grasp the patterns of the Mara's web, I must not let myself be bamboozled by the chimera of "solid fact." If you were not careful you began to think you were out-Hamleting Shakespeare if you wrote, "What a piece of biomass is a man!" I must aim for a different kind of understanding, something closer to "grokking." If I did that it would be all right. For my job was to write what I found: the good things and the bad things and all the other things too, whether I liked them or not, whether I knew what they meant or only grasped that they were in some way important. So once the county council meeting was over and everything was official, all I had to do was rake up enough money to come back for six months, the way it always seemed possible to rake up enough money at the last moment for something you wanted badly enough. Yes, it would be all right. I need not have let myself get depressed about the book, over beside the anthill.

Out in front of me, a breeze set the grass rippling again. It was almost a wind now. I watched the ripples move westward across the slope. The rest of the depression was a different matter, of course. But when you were sitting alone in the sunlight like this, with the Mara spread out in front of your breakfast table, you could not really believe in threats to the existence of the place, let alone to the continued dominance of your own species. Everything looked too sure and right, too permanent.

I stood up and began to clear away the breakfast things. There was a lot to do, anyway, before the council meeting. For a start I had the meadow where the elephants and the light had been. I turned and looked toward it, down the slope. Here near the crest, I was once more high enough to see, above the treetops of the river-forest, the alternating fingers of pale grass and dark trees that reached out toward the river from the foot of the Isuria Escarpment. A few miles to the south, close beside the river, rose the low, black, flat-topped hills I had seen from View Camp and other places. With luck I would in two days be camped somewhere down there with Joshua. Meanwhile I had the meadow. It promised to be an interesting place. And the Triangle, over beyond the river, where men rarely penetrated, would wait for me.

I stowed everything into the car and drove back down the slope. The track made an unexpectedly easy crossing of the donga and then ran northward through the center of the meadow. On either side, the grass grew tall and thick. Off to my left, the forest loomed dark. I drove deeper and deeper into the meadow, thrusting aside the last hints of sacrilege.

After two miles the track forked. I swung left, toward the river. The forest parted ahead of me and I found myself driving into a grassy salient dotted with thorn trees. The salient cut back to the very bank of the river. And beside the river, tucked into the edge of the forest, I found a little group of neat green safari tents, a supply truck and three cheerful African servants. The

Africans said the *bwana* was out in the Land Rover with his two clients; but they were sure he would not mind if I camped over on the other side of the clearing.

When I had pitched my tent I walked down to the river. There beside the brown and turbid water, cut off from the clearing by a steep muddy bank, it was a new Mara world—a world that would be knit together, I knew, by its own web of complexities. Complexities I had not even begun to see. But as I stood there in the sunlight, listening to the soft, gurgling silence, it was not the swirling river that held my eye, or even the hippo tracks that pottered up through thick mud toward my tent, fresh and four-toed and huge. It was the forest. The lush, green, billowing forest that pressed dark and impenetrable to the very lip of the high banks. A forest on which the brilliant morning sunlight shed no purple evening mystery; but still the forest from which the elephant convoys had emerged, and the forest into which they had that morning retreated.

I climbed back up the muddy bank beside the hippo tracks, got my camera from the car, and then walked slowly and reluctantly and eagerly along an elephant trail to the edge of the clearing.

At the point the trail went into the forest the foliage had grown over and sealed off the entrance. I halted. The foliage was very dense. On my side, birdsong and the hum of insects and the pumping of my heart. Beyond the green curtain of foliage, silence.

I pushed aside the curtain.

Leaves. Green leaves. Green leaves and green shade and dappled green sunlight. Green leaves and green coolness and green silence. Motionless green leaves forming a carpet with an uneven, five-foot pile. Above this carpet, space. Space filled with the shade and the coolness and the silence. Space broken only by mottled gray tree trunks and by sprays and galleries and scattered pagodas of motionless green leaves. Above the space, more leaves. And this final green canopy, high above my head, cut off the sky and filtered the sunlight and created within the forest its shade and coolness and silent, cathedral privacy.

I stepped forward.

In my preview through the curtain I had seen the understory as an unbroken, deep-piled carpet, almost at eye level; but now I found that the elephant trail, which had swung left and out of sight, cut through the carpet, thrusting aside its green pile. I moved tentatively forward. The trail wound away in front of me. Its surface, barely a foot across, had been trampled into a hard, impervious pan. Almost at once I came to an igloo elephant dropping. It was at least a week old. Allowing for slow evaporation in that shaded place, it might have been a month old. But there on the dead leaves, almost spanning that hard and pounded trail, it looked very big and very immediate. I moved forward, beyond it.

After half a dozen paces I stopped beside a climbable tree. Except for my heart, complete silence. No matter how I peered, no gray or black bulk looming ahead. I moved on another half-dozen paces, to the next climbable tree. And then, after a further security check, to the next.

Thirty paces into the forest I stopped and looked back. The last hint of the clearing had vanished. There seemed no point in going further. I might have been a hundred miles from the nearest savanna.

But as the minutes passed my heart pounded rather less violently. I began to wander up and down the trail, investigating. I even ventured a few yards along a minor, non-elephant side trail. I began to notice the way many of the trees rose in graceful curves, no doubt because they had reached toward some shifting patch of sunlight. I saw that their slender trunks often grew in multiples of three or four, apparently from the same roots, and so formed sturdy, sculptured columns that had at first conveyed an impression of single thick trunks. I even registered that the sunlight was not really green after all. Only the shade was green. Where the sunlight penetrated, it built columns of gold.

Once, a flash of green and scarlet. Then the bird had settled again on another branch. It sat very still. Only its head moved, swiveling in wide arcs, extremely slowly, like the head of a soldier scanning his front through binoculars. The bird must have been at least a foot long, and its plumage was a dazzle-bag of vivid green and scarlet and white and black and gray. And yet, although it had perched barely thirty feet from me, it remained almost invisible against the rich, mottled background. Unless I had seen it fly I would almost certainly have overlooked it. The minutes passed. At last the bird took flight again. It vanished into the dense foliage.

I do not think I spent more than twenty minutes inside the forest. At no time did I penetrate deeper than about fifty yards. And except for the bird, nothing happened. Nothing at all. But the greenness and richness of the place, and the shade and dappled light and golden sun columns and the way the foliage concealed and kept you wondering, all these things are with me still, as if I had lived in the forest for a year of sunlit mornings. I do not think I shall ever quite lose them.

When I had walked back down the elephant trail and pushed aside the curtain and emerged once more into the clearing—breathing a little more freely at last, though I did not like having to admit it—I went to the car and picked up the bird book and found that what I had seen was a Narina's trogon.*

---

* When animals are given the proper names of humans, the stories behind their christenings tend to be uninspiring. It was only later that I found, in an article by Charles Guggisberg in *Africana* magazine (Vol. 2, No. 4 [June 1965]), an account of how Narina's trogon came by its name.

"The bird was discovered in the Knysna forest area of Cape Colony, South Africa, by François Levaillant, a French 18th-century traveler and ornithologist.

"At that time, Knysna was inhabited by the Gonaquas Hottentots and Levaillant, being a gallant Frenchman, fell in love with the prettiest girl of the tribe.

" 'Her figure was charming, her teeth beautifully white,' he wrote, 'her height and shape elegant and easy, and might have served as a model for the pencil of Albane. . . . I found her name difficult to pronounce, disagreeable to the ear and inapplicable to my ideas.

" 'I therefore renamed her Narina, which in the Hottentot language signifies a flower, desiring her to retain this name for my sake. She promised to keep it as long as she lived.'

"The day came when M. Levaillant had to part from the fair Narina, in order to continue on his travels. But he gave her name to the most beautiful bird in his collection."

As I put the bird book away, a Land Rover carrying three people drove into the camp on the far side of the clearing. I waited a few minutes, then walked over.

The hunter was sitting alone outside his tent. He was young-ish, mahogany skinned and amiable. He introduced himself as Bunny Ray.

"Don't give it a second thought," he said. "Plenty of room for both of us."

I mentioned certain matters still prickling around my mind.

Ray smiled. "Yes, I find it a bit scary in there too. Frankly, getting up a tree might be all right for buff but I don't think it would do you much good with elephant. What I do is keep right along the edge of the bank, and if I was charged I'd jump into the river. The bank's so steep and high that I don't think any-thing big would follow you down. Oh yes, there's plenty in there. I was crawling through some really thick stuff once when I saw a family of giant forest hog."

I asked if this was indeed the Governor's Camp that Tipis had told me about.

"No, actually that's downstream a mile or so. Beautiful place too, if you want to camp there some other time." He gave me directions. "Wait a mo'—you've only got two-wheeled drive, haven't you? Yes, I know those little Rohos are good, but . . . Look, you say you'll be going this afternoon? Well, I'm taking my clients down that way about four o'clock, so I'll just drop in and make sure you get through okay. Oh, no trouble at all."

A little after three o'clock I drove downriver toward Gover-nor's Camp. On the way I ran into several routine Mara delays: a lone bull impala posing proud and statuesque on an anthill; a rhino ambling across the track less than forty yards ahead, appar-ently unaware of my presence; a lilac-breasted roller that tried to perch on a topi's horns but was peremptorily head-tossed off and then slanted away, blue and electrifying, over a male water-buck sitting regally beside the topi herd—and thereby gave me a photograph that I think I prayed for as I squeezed the shutter re-lease. By the time I had found a meadow that Bunny Ray had told me about, cutting back into the forest, it was close to four o'clock.

A faint track cut diagonally across the meadow. I drove along it. The grass grew taller, thicker. Soon it rose like a four-foot wall on either side of the track. I could barely see over it and I drove slowly, sitting bolt upright and peering about me.

The track cut between two arms of forest, then launched out across a second meadow. It was an enclosed place, this inner meadow, ringed by dark forest. And it had an air about it. But now that I have written "had an air about it," I am not too sure what I mean. The afternoon sun beat down hot and unmysterious, and driving into the meadow was not, this time, a question of sacrilege. But from the moment I began to move out into the open, beyond the two arms of forest, I had the feeling that there was more to see in the place than my eyes reported. The whole enclosed arena was very flat and the grassheads tossed in a gentle breeze, so it may be that all I am trying to say is that as I eased forward through the waving grass I felt rather as if I were sailing out into a very big lake in a very small boat that drew almost no freeboard. On the other hand, it may be that my feeling of unease only surfaced after I saw the elephants.

I saw them almost four hundred yards ahead, over on the far side of the meadow. There were only two. But they were cow and calf. I stopped. The gray shapes melted back into the forest. I drove forward again, very slowly. The track sagged into one of the meadow's almost invisible undulations and soon I could no longer see over the grass to the place the elephants had been. A few feet to the left of the track stood an old anthill and I swung off and ran my left-hand wheels up its lower slopes. It would have been better to run my right-hand wheels up the slope and so cant the driver's seat high, but that would have meant driving blind through tall grass into an area that might be pockmarked with deep, wheel-snaring ant bear holes. When I had stopped on the slope of the anthill I found, as I had hoped, that by leaning over and sticking my head out of the passenger window I could look across the meadow to the place the elephants had been. There was no sign of them. I eased the car down off the anthill. It was just as I began to drive forward again along the track that I saw, off to the right, the charging elephant.

I am still not sure whether I saw the elephant first or whether I heard its trumpeting and then looked to my right and saw it. As a matter of fact, I am not a hundred percent sure that this elephant did trumpet. But there was no doubt about its charge. It was coming for me head on. Its ears spread wide and huge and menacing. Its tusks, pointing directly at me, gleamed white and sharp. And as each gigantic stride carried it closer, so the towering head and great outspread ears rose and fell, rhythmically. Now that I can calculate with cool hindsight, I am surprised to reach the conclusion that when I first saw the elephant there must have been something like two hundred yards of open grass between us; but at the time all I knew was that the beast was already too damned close by far, and that its great galumphing, rhythmic strides were eating up the distance between us, and that it was high time for me to get the hell out of there.

I do not think I even glanced ahead or to the left. Ahead, the dark, encircling forest promised no exit; there was the cow with her calf, too. And to the left of the track, a few yards behind me, rose the anthill: if I swung that way to turn around I might find it blocking my path not only with its obvious bulk but with possible satellite ant bear holes waiting to snare a wheel and leave me sitting there, helpless, while the elephant pounded Rohosinante to a wafer. So I looked only to the right of the track, toward the charging elephant. Between us, the grass seemed to stretch flat and unblemished.

I swung the wheel hard right. The hood burrowed into the golden grass. For a long, etched instant the elephant and I were closing fast, head on. The ears looked enormous now, the tusks thick and brutal. And the rhythmic rise and fall of the huge gray bulk had become mesmeric as well as menacing. Then Rohosinante's white hood had swung right and the elephant was slipping out of sight behind my left shoulder and all I could see was the grass parting before the hood like the sea before a ship's prow. Seedheads sprayed back over the hood. Some of them lodged on the windshield wipers.

For what seemed like an ocean of time, all I could see was the parting grass and spraying seedheads. Then the grass fell away and a space opened up in front of the hood and I had swung the wheel left and then straightened Rohosinante up again and my foot was doing its best to push the gas pedal clear through the floorboards and we were barreling to safety down the track between its enclosing walls of grass. I glanced back over my shoulder. The elephant was swinging away. The terrifying, rhythmic rise and fall had begun to slacken. I allowed my foot to ease up on the gas pedal. I looked ahead again. A hundred yards down the track, stationary, just beyond the point where the arms of forest pressed close, stood a Land Rover.

Soon I was pulling up alongside it. "Just been mildly charged by an elephant," I said. There have no doubt been times when my voice held steadier.

Bunny Ray was grinning. "So we saw," he said.

A neat, white-haired woman sat beside him. Behind her, a man in shirt sleeves and a well-worn soft hat was cleaning the lens of a movie camera. Both man and woman wore spectacles and both had an indefinable American look about them. I put their ages at around sixty. Beside the man sat a well-built African with binoculars slung around his neck. We all smiled greetings.

Bunny Ray nodded down the track into the meadow I had just vacated. "Perhaps we should go back in," he said. His voice, I am sure, had never sounded calmer.

I stared at him. "In *there?*"

"Yes. Perhaps we can get them to move off."

He seemed to be serious about it, so after a while I said, "Okay. I'll follow."

We drove slowly along the track, out into the meadow again. I kept a good thirty yards behind the Land Rover.

We were far out into the meadow when the African tracker in the back of the Land Rover turned and grinned at me and pointed off to the right in the direction my elephant had come from. I craned an inch higher. Over near the edge of the open grass, two cows and two calves were moving away from us, toward the forest.

We rolled on across the meadow, still thirty yards apart.

And then the Land Rover was accelerating and the tracker was pointing off to the right again. He was no longer grinning. I craned up and peered over the grass. The calves had vanished and one of the cows was charging. At that moment the second cow, which had been standing half concealed on the edge of the forest, pivoted around, spread her ears, raised her trunk high, and trumpeted. Then they were both pounding across the meadow toward us, ears spread wide. The second cow trumpeted again. It was a wild, brassy, martial fanfare.

I glanced ahead at the line of black forest barring our path. It was comforting to realize that Bunny Ray must know the way through. I looked right again. The second cow had passed the first. She was still trumpeting. And she was gaining on us, fast.

The two elephants were now aiming at a point some way ahead of the racing Land Rover, and because I was still well behind it I had a half side view of them. I could see the whole vast bulk of the bodies rising and falling, rising and falling, rising and falling, like factories in some nightmare, roller-coaster earthquake. With each colossal stride, their huge gray feet swung up clear of the four-foot-high grass. I accelerated and pulled up almost level with the Land Rover, to its left. I think my idea was to encourage Bunny Ray to go faster; but it may well be that I just felt safer in his lee.

At the time, our formation seemed to hold for hours: the racing Land Rover; Rohosinante and me tucked to leeward; and the two huge, galumphing elephants angling in from the right. Mostly I had to look ahead, but I could still hear the trumpeting. With each fanfare it seemed to have drawn closer; and whenever I glanced to the right the two cows were still coming, ears wide, huge gray feet still swinging up clear of the grass with every stride. At last, one of my hurried glances showed that the elephants were losing ground. And then they had dropped back far behind and the trumpeting had died away and the Land Rover had begun to slow down and there was still plenty of room between us and the dark forest.

We reached the forest. The track cut through an arm of it. Its channel was narrow and winding, its surface rough and rutted, and we had to drive very slowly. But soon we broke out of the trees into another sunlit meadow. The track swung right. The Land Rover stopped on the edge of the high, open river bank. I pulled alongside.

"Hm," said Bunny Ray. "Really quite a determined charge." His voice had the sort of vibrant ring to it that you would expect in the voice of a man ordering fish and chips. He jerked his head toward the arm of forest we had emerged from. "Governor's Camp is back in among those trees," he said. But neither of us seemed particularly eager to go back and investigate.

We all got out to stretch our legs and enjoy the moment. Ray introduced me to his clients. Their name was Silverson and they came from Minneapolis. The tracker was Malai, a Mkamba. Everyone basked in the warmth that shared danger always generates.

We stayed on the river bank for ten or fifteen minutes, talking a little and wandering about in the sunlight and looking at the river and the grass and the dark forest. Just before we left, Bunny Ray took me aside. "The Silversons say they'd be very happy if you would join us for dinner tonight. They're extremely nice people and I hope you'll come. Good. Just give us half an hour after we get back."

Dinner was fresh steak and wine and a tablecloth and servants and mosquito netting on the open side of the big dining tent. As a change it was very good. And the bond forged by the charging elephants was still there.

Over dinner we relived those racing moments in the inner meadow. Mrs. Silverson had been amazed at the way Malai, the tracker, who was normally ice calm, had kept screaming at Bunny Ray to go faster.

"Did he?" said Ray. "I didn't notice. But I'm not really surprised. Once I had to shoot an elephant that charged us when we were on foot and it came down so close that the trunk clipped Malai's leg. Since then he's never been too happy around elephants. Can't say I blame him, really. They're not exactly reassuring creatures when they charge, are they? Still, they don't have very good eyesight and you're supposed to be able to lose them by throwing down something that will have your scent on

it, like a piece of clothing. The idea is that the elephant'll think
it's got you and will stop and trample the clothing into pulp
while you make yourself scarce. I'm always meaning to try it
out." Ray smiled. "But somehow I always seem to forget."

A little hesitantly, I mentioned my theory about establishing
territorial rights when you are close to elephant.

"Yes," said Ray. "That seems to be about the way it works."

I mentioned the route through the forest on the far side of
the meadow. While the elephants were charging it had been
comforting to feel that he would know the way through; but
when we reached there I had wondered about the rough and
narrow track and the way it wound so tightly. If the elephants
had still been close behind, would we really have been able to
get through fast enough?

"Frankly," said Ray, "I'd never been through there before.
But I think we'd have been all right."

Silverson smiled at me over the top of his glasses. "I don't
think you need worry," he said. "Down the years, we've learned
to trust Bunny. This is our third photo safari with him, you
know."

He and his wife began to talk of their past experiences. When
they learned that I hoped to write a book about the Mara they
seemed to understand, without discussion, what had attracted me.
But after some obvious hesitation Mrs. Silverson asked if I knew
yet just what the book's theme would be. The question, she said,
was not idle. Back home they were trying to put together a movie
—a strictly amateur little thing, I must understand—from all the
footage they had taken. The difficulty, they had found, was deciding just what they wanted to say with it. For the rest of dinner we discussed what the human animal was doing to the Mara,
to Africa, to its planet, and long before we moved outside for
drinks beside the campfire I understood that these two unassum-
ing people had taken home much more from their visits to Africa
than a stock of stills and movies and a fund of factual knowledge.

Near the campfire, a pressure lamp stood on a table and built a
familiar white and hissing dome around us. At the edges of the
dome, mottled tree trunks rose pale and mysterious. The firelight

kept flickering them into sharper existence, then letting go. Above us, a saucer of black, starlit sky broke the blacker canopy of the trees.

We sat sipping our drinks, talking a little, falling silent, talking again.

After one of the longer silences Silverson said, "Yes, we've been all over with Bunny—Tanzania, Uganda, most parts of Kenya." He had taken off his glasses and was cleaning the lenses with a handkerchief. The lamplight fell full on his long, sunburned face. "But after all of it, no matter where we go, my favorite is still the Mara." He gave an embarrassed little smile and I knew that, because he was finding it difficult, he would mean every word he managed to lay hands on. "And yet," he said, "even now, somehow, I couldn't for the life of me tell you just why I feel this way about the place."

Next morning I drove back to Keekorok. Outside the lodge I found T-B standing alone in the sunshine, massive shoulders hunched forward against the world. As we shook hands I realized with some surprise that it was the first time we had met since we shook hands at his office door. The visit of the Amboseli Masai had gone well, he said. He seemed glad, in his abstracted way, to hear that things were going well with me too. The council meeting had definitely been scheduled: Tipis would be able to tell me the details.

I met Tipis coming out of his house. The meeting was set for four mornings ahead, in Narok, at nine o'clock. I would have to appear, but it would not take long and there was nothing I need worry about.

For a moment I considered postponing the Triangle safari. Then I remembered that from Narok to Mara Bridge was only sixty-odd miles. If it was still all right to take Joshua, I said, I would leave for the Triangle in the morning. I would drive out for the meeting and then go back in for the balance of the week.

Tipis said that Joshua was at my disposal.

I asked about tipping. I did not want to spoil the market by giving Joshua too much, I said. Or to disappoint him with too little.

Tipis looked solemn. "Please give him nothing, Mr. Fletcher. I would rather my rangers did not get the idea that they always get tipped. After all, they get paid. And of course there is no question of you paying the normal guide fee. As I told you, this is on the house."

I thanked him and went and made final arrangements with Joshua. He still seemed eager at the prospect. I got the feeling that he too regarded the Triangle as the heart of the Mara.

Next morning I picked him up at his hut and after some delay we drove out through the Talek Gate and came to Aitong and turned west toward the Triangle.

DISCOVERY

We came to the edge of the plain. At the opening in the bush that gives you your first view out over the valley, the opening I had stopped at the first time, I stopped again. Only one weak pillar of smoke rose from the Triangle. But through binoculars I could see fingers of burned grassland reaching out, black and dead, between the river and the Isuria Escarpment. Above the escarpment, the day's clouds banked gray and heavy, veiling the sun.

I drove on. The flat gray light made it seem more like dusk than midafternoon. The grade steepened. I found myself looking off to the right, where the land sloped down to the river and I remembered grass waving rich and golden. The slope was bare, black earth.

The road curved right, flattened out, became bridge. I drove onto the bridge, stopped in the same place as before, and looked upstream toward the overhanging bush where the otters had paused while they cleaned each other with deft paws before arching back into the river in quicksilver unison. There was no bush. Fire had swept down the open bank and consumed it. Only a blackened stump remained.

I forced my eyes upstream, away from the stump. There, greenery still clothed the river.

Joshua, sitting in the passenger seat on my left, shotgun clamped upright between his knees, leaned forward and peered past me. "*Hii ni inchi safi, kweli*," he said. "This is clean country, in truth."

I drove on. We began to angle up the skirts of the escarpment. Soon we came to the track, unmarked on the map but seeming to lead down into the Triangle, that I had noticed the first time.

"This one?" I asked.

Joshua leaned forward and studied the track. "It will be good," he said, "if we go up the road first."

"Oh, is there another track that goes down there?"

"I hear there is only one."

I looked at him. "But you do not know?"

Joshua shook his head.

"But . . . you said you knew the Triangle well."

Joshua shrugged his shoulders. He was still studying the track. There was a faint smile on his lips. "I have seen it from up there on top," he said. "But I have not yet been down into it."

Just for a moment I considered turning around and going back to Keekorok. Then I drove on up the road. Joshua continued to smile his faint, triumphant smile.

From the top of the escarpment I could see the Triangle much more clearly than the last time. Below us, the meadows looked less burned over than our first glimpse had suggested, but to the south, down toward Tanzania, where there seemed to be little or no forest, almost half the flat and open grasslands lay black, and a second pillar of smoke was now rising to meet the cloudbank. Joshua advised me that the smoke to the south almost certainly came from fires lit by poachers to make the game concentrate in places it would be easy to catch them; but the meadows below us, he said, had probably been burned by the Masai group that lived on top of the escarpment and sometimes grazed sheep and goats down in the Triangle and therefore wanted the fresh green grass that would sprout on the burned land as soon as rain fell.

We had seen no other tracks leading off the road, and I turned the car around and we came back down to the track near the foot of the escarpment.

"It is this one," said my guide. "It cannot be any other."

I turned onto the track. Our view of the Triangle had flattened almost to zero but off to the left we could see a meadow stretching flat and open to the dark line of the river-forest. Only one corner of it had been burned.

The track meandered down the curving hem of the escarpment. It looked very little used. At first the grass on either side grew tall and rich and the track surface was smooth, root-bound soil. Then the grass thinned and the track grew stony; a quarter of a mile, and we came to a shallow but rocky donga. Water seeped along its bed. A few big stones had been shepherded together to form a rough crossing, adequate for Land Rovers.

"*Nafikiri gari hii hawezi*," said Joshua. "I think this car is not able."

I got out and inspected the crossing. Joshua joined me. I said we would try.

Joshua went over to the far side of the donga and packed a few stones at the foot of the rock-slabbed exit. He did a perfunctory job but the stones looked as if they would do very little harm, and as I walked back to the car I told myself that at least the man seemed to be trying to make amends.

Rohosinante bucked and slithered over slippery stones, faltered, lurched, scraped bottom, recovered, clawed her way up the rock slabs, then surged forward onto level ground.

Joshua got back in. "I see as if this car has strength," he said.

Another layer of me thawed.

The track swung around the crest of a spur. Below us and to the left, a strip of bright emerald green would be marsh. Ahead, the forest had begun to look very tall, very dense, very dark. And then, standing on the left of the track, there was a man.

I pulled up beside him. He was quite an old man. Under his gray shuka he wore a pair of khaki shorts. I greeted him in Swahili but he ignored me and spoke to Joshua in Masai. They talked for several minutes. When we drove on Joshua told me that they had met many years before, when he was still in the police and the old man was in the army.

"In the army? So it is necessary that he knows Swahili."

Joshua smiled. "Yes. But he does not like to use it. These days he is a man of the manyatta."

We came to the foot of the escarpment's last, gentle slope and the track swung south across flat meadow. The grass grew tall and golden and I could no longer see any burned land. But the forest ahead looked even taller, denser, darker. It threatened to block our path.

I found myself trying to imagine the kind of adjustments a man would have to make when he went back to manyatta life after serving in the army. Or, for that matter, in the police. Or even after being a ranger. I asked Joshua how he liked being a ranger.

"Oh, it is not bad," he said. "But there is not much pay. And they do not teach you anything."

I asked if he ever considered going back to manyatta life.

"Me?" he said. "*Hapana!*" The negative spouted out, dripping with scorn. Then he added something in Swahili that included two words I did not understand.

I asked him what the words meant.

He repeated the whole sentence in English: "When a man has seen the light, how can he return to darkness?" The words sounded mission-perfect.

We were getting close to the forest now. Dark arms reached out on either side of us.

Joshua had often dropped stray English words into our conversation. On one drive near Keekorok he had picked up a copy of *Africana* magazine lying in the car and read the first couple of paragraphs of a commentary on the wildlife management conference I had attended in Nairobi. When he put it down he said, "*Kumbe ninyi Wazungu iko na* understanding *kushinda yetu kabisa.* You Europeans certainly have an understanding far greater than ours." I had been impressed by his ability to read and also by his humility (it is, of course, diabolically difficult to remain unsoft-soaped by this kind of humility), but I had paid little attention to his occasional use of English words. The syndrome is common among those who want to demonstrate that they know at least a smattering of a foreign tongue. Europeans learning Swahili are highly prone. But Joshua's mission quote had flowed very smoothly.

The track swung left, directly toward the forest.

"But it must be," I said in Swahili, "that many soldiers and policemen go back to their manyattas."

"Only those who cannot read," said Joshua, also in Swahili. And again the scorn was there, even more withering than before. I glanced left. He sat very straight, face set, nose up. And for the first time I recognized in his profile the chip-on-shoulder Nairobi look, the defensive arrogance of those first sad products of Western lobotomy, the semiliterate. He slid me a look. "Do you know," he said, "that of all the rangers at Keekorok only four of us can read? Most of them, such as that sergeant, cannot read even a little!"

A gap had opened up in the forest. The track cut through it. The gap was wide and grassy and the trees never pressed in very close. And then we were out in the open again. But now the earth stretched black and naked. A remembrance of burning lingered in the air.

Another line of forest loomed. The track slid through another gap. Beyond, the grass once more grew tall and pale and whole. Three zebras lifted their heads and looked toward us. Except for half a dozen baboons and vervet monkeys, they were the first animals we had seen since we came down into the Triangle. When we were still two hundred yards away, the zebras turned and trotted out of sight behind a line of bush.

The country began to open up. The last swathe of forest swung away to the left, toward the river. Sometimes we drove through pale grass, sometimes across scorched black earth.

After two or three miles we found, parked beside the track in one of the unburned sections, two Land Rovers. Around them sat half a dozen Europeans, eating out of cans. I stopped.

The nearest man was about forty. He wore a black shirt and khaki shorts.

"Afternoon," I said.

The man nodded. The others looked at me.

I asked if there was really a good camp, as I had been told, down at the bend in the river, where it swung east.

"Down here you can camp anywhere," said the man in the black shirt.

"Sure. But do you happen to know that camp by the bend in the river?"

"Down here you can camp anywhere," the man said again. He stared at me over his food can, eyes blank.

I drove on.

As soon as we were out of earshot Joshua said, "Those were people with bad souls."

"True."

"I think it was a matter of me," said Joshua. "Because I am a ranger. I do not know what they had done but I am unable to think it was a good thing. It is very hard for us to protect the animals down here."

In the next hour we saw only a distant group of eland, one male impala, a small topi herd, and a lone wildebeest far off to the right. But the stretches of burned land grew less frequent and eventually we drove only through grass. The grass was shorter now, and thinner. The plain stretched flat and featureless. The sole landmark was the escarpment towering up to our right, tall and suddenly impressive. The map showed the whole area between river and escarpment as a blank.

The track grew progressively fainter. From time to time it forked. At each divergence I looked down both tracks as far as I could and then, lacking any useful advice from Joshua, took the one that looked more traveled by and hoped that would make all the difference. But the track continued to grow fainter and several times I had to stop to make sure we were still following it. Joshua's contribution to the route-finding was a lengthy explanation that this was just the kind of track that T-B liked to follow, so we were undoubtedly going somewhere important. The idea seemed to delight him. Every time the track threatened to vanish he would say, with appalling cheerfulness, "*Hii ndio ni njia ya Temple-Boreham.* This is a real Temple-Boreham road!" And every time he said it he made a performance of "Temple-Boreham" and then looked at me, apparently to make sure I grasped that he, Joshua, unlike most rangers and especially ranger sergeants, could pronounce the name in full. Because there was no escape, I made an effort to respond to his mood. But I do not think I did too well.

We continued to push southward. All afternoon the cloud-bank suspended above the escarpment had been building. By five o'clock the light was leaden, the air heavy with threat of rain. At last, out in the middle of featureless nowhere, our track tapered to extinction.

"Yes," said Joshua with glee. "This is a *real* Temple-Boreham."

I looked left, toward the river. As far as I could see, no marsh or donga barred our way. I rechecked the map: still a blank between escarpment and river. I estimated, with marginal confidence, that in the two hours since leaving the road we had covered about six straight-line miles. I tried to match the map with irregularities along the wall of the escarpment, but the results remained ambiguous. Through binoculars I studied some low, flat-topped hills to the east: they seemed to be those I had seen from the far side of the river, near my anthill camp, and I knew that if they were, then their northern shoulder would lie close to the bend in the river. Eventually I decided, very tentatively, that we were probably no more than two miles from the bend, west of it and perhaps a touch north. From the map I worked out a rough compass bearing to the bend and found a conspicuous tree in the river-forest more or less on this line. Then I swung the car left and drove directly for the tree.

It was like steering a course over water. Across our front ran the river-forest, low and dark, like a shoreline. Behind us, like a thousand-foot coastal cliff, rose the escarpment. And all around stretched pale, featureless grass.

No marsh or donga rose up to bar our way, but we had hardly started when Rohosinante's breastplate thumped hard against some hidden obstacle. I backed off. We had grounded on a small anthill. It had not yet risen above the eighteen-inch-high grass or caused any discernible change in the vegetation and so was invisible to the driving eye. Soon we scraped a second anthill, and after that I either drove very slowly or detoured into areas where the grass was too short to conceal anything we could not clear. But I held close to the line of the conspicuous tree.

It took us about half an hour to reach the river. We hit it only a couple of hundred yards north of the big bend and it pleased me to see that Joshua was impressed. I did my best to look as if such accuracy was nothing more than I had expected.

Parallel to the river ran a faint vehicle track. I turned right along it and drove to the bend. The place was bare and rocky, with none of the rich, sanctuary feel I had found three days before in the meadow where the light and the elephants had been, the meadow on whose edge I had camped next to Bunny Ray and the Silversons. We got out of the car and walked toward the river. There was no sign of a camp. As we came up onto the open bank a huge crocodile splashed off a rock in midstream.

"*Ile mamba ni kitu kuua tu*," said my game ranger. "Crocodiles are something to be killed, that's all."

We went back to the car and drove on downstream. Almost at once we came to a little basin with thirty or forty vultures perched on riverside trees. Beneath them the bare rock was white with droppings. The track faded away. There was still no sign of a camp. I turned the car around and followed the track back past the bend and past the point we had joined it. There was forest on our right now, lining the river. It was not thick and rich the way it had been beside the meadow, three days before, but it helped.

A shaft of sunlight slanted through the gloom. I looked left.

The cloudbank suspended above the escarpment had begun to break up. The flat grassland was already tinged with gold.

The track gained definition. Soon it swung right, into the trees. And then we were in a grassy clearing and along its margin there were marks where vehicles and tents had stood and at its center was a small black circle where a campfire had been. I switched off. It was very quiet. The sunlight, slanting in through the trees, painted zebra stripes across green grass. There was a stretch of open bank too, and beyond it swirled the river.

For a while then, it was better.

I pitched my tent. Joshua collected firewood. The sun sank behind the escarpment.

Down by the river, a hippo snorted. We walked over, together, to the bank. For a moment we saw, less than twenty feet out from the bank, bulging pink nostrils and bulging pink eyes and pointed pink ears and the top of a straight black profile, awash in the muddy water. Then the hippo had submerged. We saw it come up for air once, far upstream. It seemed to take a long look back at us. Then there was once more only the swirling brown river.

We walked a few yards up the bank. Immediately below us, half submerged, snagged among tree roots and held tight against the bank by the current, were two dead wildebeest. I checked upstream through binoculars. Within a I hundred yards I saw three more corpses, similarly trapped.

Joshua frowned. "I had heard that there were many dead wildebeest in the river," he said. "But I do not know what thing killed them." *

---

* Later I came across reports that suggested an answer.

One of them described how, in the Serengeti, "a herd of about 5,000 wildebeest rushed to water in the Seronera River, the pressure of those behind forcing those in front into the water one on top of the other, sometimes three deep. When the herd had left, [a game warden who had been watching] found 19 dead wildebeest in the mud."

And the March 1969 issue of *African Wildlife News* reported: "On 21 August [1968], over 300 dead wildebeest and 1 zebra were found drowned 5 miles upstream from the Bologonja/Mara junction over a stretch of about 6 miles of the Mara. These deaths in the river are caused by the stampede in

We walked back to our clearing. Out beyond the trees, pale grassland stretched quiet and mysterious toward the dark escarpment. I opened two bottles of beer and for a while we sat beside the fledgling fire. Dusk enveloped us. The night eased forward, tree trunk to tree trunk.

I asked Joshua what kind of reading he liked best.

"*Kitu napenda saidi,*" he said, "*ni kusoma ile kitabu ya Allan Quatermain.* The thing I like best of all is to read the books of Allan Quatermain."

I think I managed to hide my astonishment. Allan Quatermain is the English hero of a series of novels about Africa, written around the 1880s by Rider Haggard. The best known is *King Solomon's Mines.* I was still digesting the new information when it occurred to me that reading Rider Haggard demanded more than a smattering of his language. "What do you like best about the Allan Quatermain books?" I asked in English.

Joshua sat still, staring into the fire. It was a long time before he spoke. I can no longer remember what his answer was when it came at last, but I know the words emerged slowly and that they were so clumsily connected that their meaning hung in doubt.

Remembering how I had been struck dumb when Tipis spoke to me unexpectedly in Swahili and how the lack of an immediate chance to clear up the misunderstanding had erected a potential barrier between us, I continued to speak English. And because it seemed possible that the broad scope of my question might have created difficulties, I tried to deal in specifics. But it was more than thirty years since the Haggard books had been read to me

crossing the Mara and is a factor in the wildebeest mortality of which little is known. At one place on the river, in some rapids, the carcasses formed a solid line across the river."

It is easy to see how something of this sort could happen anywhere the Mara is steep-banked, as it is for most of its length along the boundary of the Triangle. The stampede reported in *African Wildlife News* took place just eleven months after Joshua and I found the dead wildebeest in the river, and only fifteen miles downstream, so perhaps such deaths occur almost routinely during the regular wildebeest migrations between the Mara and the Serengeti.

and I found the going hard. Joshua tried to explain something about Allan Quatermain's ax, apparently called Inkosikazi, but my memory failed to stir. I guided our talk toward other matters, but Joshua remained almost tongue-tied. I could not decide whether it was lack of knowledge that blocked off the springs of speech, or the unexpected opportunity, or resentment at my condescension in switching suddenly to English. But we continued to get nowhere. And when we began to talk about dinner we slid back into Swahili.

Although the abortive language experiment hardly helped, it was not, I am sure, the reason things did not stay better for very long, that first evening by the river.

All day, inch by reconnoitered inch, Joshua had been edging forward, testing the limits to which he could go. Now it is necessary in any new relationship to establish mutual rules. Most people, though, once they have grown up, do so with understanding, or at least with subtlety. But ever since we drove away from Keekorok, out on our own, Joshua had pushed. Frankly, I can no longer recall specific incidents. Each of them was minor and in itself eminently overlookable. But they added up. And at the end of that first evening Joshua reached his limit.

My little tent, though reputedly designed for two men, could house only one in comfort. And I value privacy. So I had all along planned that Joshua should sleep in the car, as I had often done. When I explained the position to him on one of our drives near Keekorok he assured me instantly that the arrangement was fine by him. But that first evening, when the time came to go to bed and I stood beside the tent cleaning my teeth and Joshua was standing with his head inside the car, six or seven paces away, I became aware that he was going through some kind of elaborate pantomime with his blankets. He supported the pantomime with a muffled, recurring commentary, semi-sotto voce: "*Hii hapana kitanda kwa mwanamume*. This is no bed for a grown man."

I went on cleaning my teeth.

But when I had crawled into the tent and zippered the netting shut and pulled the sleeping bag loosely over me, the com-

mentary still whimpered on, out in the darkness. And at last I
blew. *"Sikia, rafiki,"* I said. *"Kama kitanda ile hapana tosha kwa
wewe, nitatumia. Na unaweza lala hapa kwa hama yangu.* Listen,
friend, if that bed isn't good enough for you, I'll use it. And you
can sleep here in my tent."

For a long moment there were only the nightsounds and the
soft swirl of the river. I began to wonder if the wretched man
would have the gall to accept.

Then his voice came out of the darkness. It sounded markedly
chastened. *"Hapana fikiri, bwana,"* it said. *"Nitalala hapa. Takuwa
mzuri tu.* Don't worry, bwana. I'll sleep here. It'll be fine."

I pulled the sleeping bag closer around me. Outside, Rohosinante voiced a mild protest as Joshua turned over. Otherwise I
could hear only the river and the nightsounds' raucous silence.
But for once the nightsounds failed to soothe me. I lay looking
up at the blackness that I knew was the orange fabric of the tent.
I was angry. I was also angry with myself for being angry, and
that always makes it worse. But the stubborn fact remained that,
although I knew not why—in any truly sufficient sense—and could
not quite tell, I suddenly and unexpectedly and with precious
little hope of reversal, just plain did not like thee, Dr. Fell. And
that boded ill for our stay together in the Triangle.

Now I am wearily aware that in today's world, with human
sensitivities whipped raw by the winds of change, I shall probably be accused of racism. I have already admitted that I am
irreparably British and an ex-colonial. And I am inclined to cock
a cynical eye at crowd-pleasing but biologically nonsensical decla-
rations like "all trees are created equal." But I would deny the
impeachment. I doubt that my expectations in the Triangle were
really much different from those of anyone halfway honest with
his feelings who has ever gone out with a professional guide. And
I look forward with rich hope but slim confidence to a day when
you can like or dislike a man of a different race, heartily and
openly, without having him and most other people assume that
the cause is the color of his skin. That would be something.

Later, when I looked back on those last days before the

council meeting, it was tempting to lay all the blame on Joshua for the way things turned out. His presence certainly did not help. But my loss of solitude no doubt took its toll—and that had nothing to do with him personally. A similar intrusion had scarred a trip for me once before. Still, there was more to it than that. I do not mean that anything calamitous happened. As a matter of fact, very little happened at all. Perhaps that was the core of the trouble.

We spent most of the second day looking for springs. I could develop no great thirst for muddy river water flavored with rotting wildebeest; besides, I could think of no better way to begin our exploration of the Triangle than a five-mile drive across the flat and then a southward reconnaissance along the base of the Isuria Escarpment, where a series of wooded gullies suggested a good chance of surface water.

When we left camp before sunrise, heading on a beeline for the most northerly gully, I drove eagerly, with the kind of shining hope that early morning starts can generate. But eight hours later, when we struck back toward camp across the open plain, I found myself sagging in the driver's seat. It is true, of course, that on any day in any place, let alone in a hot climate, you are less likely to be bouncing at two o'clock in the afternoon than you were at six that morning, especially if you have in the meantime done a lot of driving and next to no eating. As we drove back riverward from the escarpment, it was hot in the little car, even with the windows wide. And on my left sat Dr. Fell. But I also sagged under a different kind of load.

Our outward drive across the plain that morning had taken us south of the open, oceanlike route by which we had reached the river the evening before. There were patches of bush to break the monotony, and clumps of thorn trees and occasional gardenia trees and candelabrum euphorbia. We crossed only two minor patches of scorched earth. But the unburned grass did not grow tall and rich, the way it had done on the far side of the river, in the meadow where the elephants and the light had been. Above all, we saw no animals.

Still, the morning produced its moments.

There was no water at the first gully or at the second, but at the foot of the third we found a trickle of a spring. We reconnoitered slowly south, found another even less productive, went on for another couple of miles, found nothing better, and came back to the first spring. And as I lifted the two half-empty jerricans out of the car I told Joshua that while he filled them I would take a look at something, just a few hundred yards back, beyond the last protruding slope of the escarpment.

As soon as I was out of his sight I stopped the car and got out and sat on a rock. The plain was in front of me and the escarpment behind me. Everything was very wide and open. And after I had sat there for a while with the openness and the silence and the wind blowing steadily across the plain, full in my face, there began to be a coming together of the things I saw, the way it had been during the ten quiet days in the Sanctuary, the way it often is when you sit quietly in a beautiful and unspoiled place, alone. But all around me the grass stretched sparse and pale. Out across the plain I could see swathes of blackened earth. Beyond them, down toward Tanzania, two columns of smoke rose into graying sky. Nowhere could I see any animals. And that was the way it had been almost all morning.

After about twenty minutes I drove back to the spring. Joshua had only just begun to fill the first jerrican. I walked twenty or thirty paces from him and sat down on another rock.

It was astonishing, really, the way we had seen so few animals. Out on the plain we had seen none at all. At the first wooded gully, a handful of buffalo had showed briefly, well up on the escarpment's apron. But almost at once they had faded away. I looked out across the open plain. Nothing moved. I checked with binoculars, swinging across the whole wide expanse from south to north. Nothing. And then, just as I was about to lower the binoculars I saw, coming down from the north, close under the escarpment, a straggling line of zebras. They were five or six hundred yards away. A low spur hid Joshua from them, and they would be able to see nothing of me except my head. I sat very still. The zebras continued to approach. And then, when the lead animal was still almost four hundred yards away, it stopped dead in its tracks, thrust its head forward, and peered directly at me. Then it whinnied, pivoted and galloped back northward. The rest of the line panicked after it.

I went back to the spring and told Joshua about the zebras. They had, I said, much better eyesight than I had imagined.

He nodded and smiled mysteriously and led me to a small bush near the spring. I had passed it on the way down to my rock. But now, looking closely, I saw that it was not just a bush. Fronting it was a rough structure of interwoven branches. The foliage had withered and fallen off but I could see that it had once formed a screen. And the little patch of grass between screen and bush had been trampled flat. In this hideout, said Joshua, a poacher had lain in wait for the animals that used the spring. When they came close enough he speared them or shot them with poisoned arrows. That was why the zebras had been so alert.

Joshua went back to the spring. I remained standing beside the poacher's hideout. In itself, this hideout was a very small project. But as I stood looking at it I grasped for the first time the reality of more ambitious undertakings. And I remembered what Fraser Darling had written of zebras in his Mara report:

> I have sometimes thought them silly creatures of which there are plenty, but when you have seen them in the charnel houses of the poachers' hiding places, severed heads grinning hideously alongside those of wildebeest which look sadder than ever, and striped legs all atumble to the sky, a fetlock cut to the bone by the wire of the noose and guts lying strewn, or if you have seen them lying alive but hamstrung because the noose line has been too successful for immediate clearance, the heart is touched for the species.

Another report told of animals deliberately hamstrung or left with their legs broken "so that they will remain alive until hunters care to dispose of them at their leisure."

I walked back to the car. One tended to look with tolerance

on poaching by Africans. After all, it was their land. And they needed all the meat they could get. I leaned into the car and found the little book I had been reading before we left Keekorok. Sir Julian Huxley had written:

> Killing for meat is a minor menace. Most poaching is frankly for money. . . . All too often it takes the horrible and wasteful form of merely taking the valuable trophies, such as rhino horn, wildebeest tails, or elephant ivory, and leaving the slaughtered carcasses to rot. The abolition of this shocking trade is becoming just as compelling an aim in the Africa of the present as was the abolition of the slave trade in the Africa of a century ago. Like the slave trade, it is profitable, highly organized, extremely cruel, and quite ruthless.

I rechecked Fraser Darling's Mara report. He made it more specific:

> [In the Mara] the general problem [is] of a fairly small but prolific game area being conserved, with the pressure of pastoralism on one side and of African commercial gang poaching on the other, and the insidious, slow degradation of the habitat. . . . As so often happens . . . the problem is not a clean-cut one of plant and animal ecology, but of human ecology as well, and once that is admitted the world of human politics is found to be a considerable ecological factor.

The morning's best moment came soon after we had left the spring and were driving north again along the foot of the escarpment toward the first wooded gully so that I could strike out across the plain on the back-bearing of the outward drive.

The antelope stood alone, almost three hundred yards away, up on the escarpment's sloping apron. It was my first glimpse of a roan. But even before Joshua had identified it there was no doubt in my mind about those thick, curving horns and that long, black-and-white face. There was no doubt, either, about the beast's beauty and strength and dignity. For perhaps ten seconds it stood staring at us. Then it moved quickly behind thick scrub.

But even that silver moment had its cloud. Fraser Darling had reported that the roan antelope of the Triangle—in part because they rarely moved far from their home ground—stood in grave danger of extinction from poaching.

Soon after we struck eastward toward camp, out across the open plain, I stopped to urinate. And as I stood beside a little bush, recycling to its roots, the wind brought me a faint, familiar smell. It was vaguely minty. I looked to my left. Among the foliage of another small bush grew several spindly green plants with distinctive, pointed leaves. When I had finished I walked over and crushed one of the leaves and held it to my nose. No doubt at all: Mexican marigold. And that was wrong too. Back when I was the young farm manager who lived near Nakuru, Mexican marigold had been a damned nuisance of a weed. I had read somewhere that it had been introduced into Africa during the Boer War by Mexicans who brought it in sacks of horse fodder. A plant that immigrated through the agency of a human war and then spread to choke human fields at least struck a note of diabolic justice; but growing wild in the middle of a plain that I had thought of as pristine, as the epitome of unspoiled Africa, it tolled only a sad and sinister dissonance.

By the time we got back to camp it was almost three o'clock.

After lunch I suggested we take a walk in the river-forest.

Joshua looked up at the sun. Then he stroked the barrel of his shotgun, which he had been cleaning. "*Hii hapana saa mzuri kutembea,*" he said. "*Badai, takuwa nyama saidi.* This is not a good hour for walking. Later there will be more animals about."

Soon afterward I noticed that one of Rohosinante's tires was flat as a cobra's hood. Wishing I could as usual wait until I got back to the Keekorok garage but knowing that it would be asking for trouble to cruise around the Triangle without a spare, I took the wheel off, located the inevitable thorn, and patched the tube. Now there are people who can put a tire back on a wheel without loss of dignity, temper and two hours' sweat. I am not one of them. Neither, it turned out, was Joshua. And for a while our mutual incompetence forged a kind of bond.

But Joshua took the opportunity to exact a measure of revenge for my attempt to get him to talk English. At least I think he did.

I happened to mention that I could not understand the "clean" Swahili in which government announcements were couched. I had learned my Swahili on farms, I said, where very few people, African or European, understood its fancy version.

Joshua, whose turn it was with the tire, paused in his labors. There were two things, he intoned, that ruined Swahili. One was the Indian duka. The other, the farm. "*Mahali yote mbili wanatumia ile Kiswahili naharubika, sawa sawa yoko.* In both places they use fractured Swahili, like yours."

I examined the middle distance.

A little later, when I was back wrestling with the tire and Joshua sat watching, he regaled me with a long story of how, years before, he and a friend had killed an elephant calf and been chased by its mother. They had taken refuge in a narrow crack between two rocks. The elephant could not get her tusks into the crack and every time she reached in with her trunk they hit it with a heavy stick. After several hours they managed to slip away when the elephant was downwind. Two days later she was still standing beside her dead calf.

I asked why they had killed the calf.

"Well, that was before I understood that all animals are to be preserved."

"All animals?"

"Yes."

"Including crocodiles?"

"Oh no, not crocodiles."

By five-thirty we had the tire back on. To celebrate, we took a short drive. We went downstream. At the dead place where the bedrock was white from droppings, the vultures still waited in the trees. A hippo snorted, and we heard it splash into the river. When we went to look, there were two more dead wildebeest snagged among tree roots, half submerged. They had begun to smell. On the way back to the car Joshua found a foot trail running parallel to the river. It was, he said, a poacher's trail. "*Hawezi kuwa kitu ingine*. It cannot be anything else."

We tried to follow the trail downstream in the car but the narrow corridor between the river and the first flat-topped hill was full of half-hidden boulders. Just after we had turned back I discovered that the tire we had repaired was going down again.

On the way back to camp we passed a big male lion who stalked by less than ten paces from the car, ignoring us. He looked so pervasively preoccupied that he hardly seemed to belong there. He was the only mammal we saw.

Back at camp I found that in replacing the tire we had pinched the tube. As I began to repair it, I remembered our walk.

Although Joshua did not seem especially eager, we went. We went with Joshua leading, gun at the ready. I followed, gripping my ax, which Joshua now insisted on calling *Inkosikazi*. At the place the really thick forest began, fifty yards from our clearing, Joshua stopped. I moved up beside him. The forest was very dense. You could see no more than five or six yards into it. And it was a place of shadows—not, this time, of greenery and filtered sunlight. I glanced at Joshua. He was staring ahead, face taut.

"*Hii hapana saa mzuri kutembea*," he said. "*Karibu usiki sasa*. This is not a good hour for walking. It is almost night now."

So we went back to camp. I wish I could say that my contempt was untinged by relief.

Next morning we had the tire back on within two hours and after breakfast we drove southwest, toward Tanzania, toward the daily smoke columns—toward the Lamai Wedge.

The words "Lamai Wedge" appeared in every report I had read on game preservation in the Mara. East of the Mara River, the northern boundary of Serengeti National Park coincides with the southern boundary of the Masai Mara Game Reserve. But west of the river the Serengeti's boundary does not continue, like the Mara's, to the Isuria Escarpment. Instead it swings further south, following the river. As a result a hundred-square-mile wedge of land, in which animals remain unprotected, drives deep into the flank of the Serengeti-Mara. The Wedge is remote savanna country, tsetse-infested and unsuitable for cattle raising or agriculture. No men live there. But it is prime game country. Huge herds of zebras and wildebeest and other mammals pass through it on their regular migrations—perhaps because the river south of the Tanzanian border offers easier crossing places than in the Triangle. And poachers, mainly from the neighboring Watende tribe, take a heavy toll. Fraser Darling called their predation "an intensive industry." He found some of their hiding places on the Kenya side of the border.

That morning we drove down toward the Lamai Wedge I had no great hope of stumbling on a poacher's hideout or any other dramatic find. Apart from anything else, we had no time to go very far. The council meeting in Narok was scheduled for nine o'clock the following morning, and although a pre-sunrise start would in theory get us there in time it would leave no margin for car trouble. So I had decided to start the drive back in midafternoon. All the same, the map suggested that we should be able to penetrate at least a little way into the Triangle's most remote sector, and I was looking forward to the reconnaissance.

As far as I could judge, we went five or six straight-line miles, or about halfway to the Tanzanian border. There were no tracks, even of Temple-Boreham grade, but most of the way we crossed open savanna that made for easy driving. The country was gently rolling—and so featureless and repetitive that I began to understand why people said the Triangle was a great place to get lost in. I also kept thinking that it was the kind of country that should have teemed with game. But the only animals I remember seeing in our whole six-hour tour were three ostriches.

Other things were missing too. The light may have had something to do with it. The evening before, the cloudbanks over the escarpment had again failed to attain their orgasm of rain. But they had not broken up, the way they usually did. In the morning, as sometimes happened after such frustration, a thick cloud screen shrouded the sky, and as we drove southward, skirting the western flank of the first black, flat-topped hill, the grass stretched away flat and pale and lifeless in the flat gray light. The scattered thorn trees cast no shadows.

We drove on. The grass was short and thin, the thorn trees stunted and straggly. Then the grass ended and we were crunching across black earth and black stubble. Far ahead, a smoke column spiraled upward and spread a gray pall along the border. The pall had begun to merge with the gray clouds. We drove back into grass, then out again onto scorched earth. The further we drove, the less living grass we crossed, the more black deadness.

It was almost a relief to turn back at last and run for camp on a compass bearing.

By the time we turned into our little clearing among the trees it was close to two-thirty. We had some tea, then began to pack everything away into the car.

When we were nearly ready to go I picked up my camera and walked a few yards out of the forest. In spite of the clouds it was hot, out there away from the trees. I shot a general view of the plain and the escarpment. And as I stood alone, with the silence around me again and the grass rustling and the scent of its dryness rising up into my nostrils, it occurred to me that in our forty-eight hours in the Triangle I had taken no more than six or seven photographs and written barely half a page of notes. Disenchantment, whether with a companion or a place, can kill even an ingrained habit of keeping records.

Near the crest of the escarpment a fire was burning. Above it, the cloudbank lowered gray and leaden. The wind had died away and the air hung heavy and still and the smoke from the fire drifted slowly down the slope of the escarpment and spread out in a pall over the plain. Far to the south, the pall that lay along the border had almost absorbed the individual smoke columns. And it had merged, now, with the cloudbank.

I stood looking out across the plain. For two days the companion had tended to overshadow the place; but I could not blame it all on Dr. Fell. Perhaps I had expected too much. It could easily be that. But in two days we had, as far as I could remember, seen only the roan antelope and the buffalo and the zebras near the escarpment, three ostriches and a lone lion, one hippo sauntering out from the forest at dusk, and a rhino doing the same. Back near Keekorok you would expect to see more than that within an hour. And as I stood looking across the plain I remembered for the first time since I sat facing T-B across his office table that he wanted to build a lodge in the Triangle. When he told me, I had been appalled. Perhaps that was why memory had swept the idea under a rug. But now I understood. This remote place that I had seen as the heart and essence of the Mara stood, because of its very remoteness, in immediate danger from the world's most dangerous animal.

I turned and walked back into our clearing.

Just before we got into the car, Joshua looked around the clearing. Then, for the first time in two days, he spoke in English. "Good-bye, good camp," he said.

Now I have often said these same words, out loud to the open sky, on leaving a camp that I know I will remember with affection. But I found myself flouncing into the car, asking myself whether Joshua had parroted the phrase from some previous tourist or from Allan Quatermain. I think I knew at the time that from any man but Joshua I would have approved of the farewell. But it was no good. You cannot fight Dr. Fell with cool reason.

I swung the car out onto the track, turned north along the edge of the forest, and settled back for the seventy-mile drive to Narok. The time was a few minutes past three-thirty.

We had gone all of thirty yards before the dynamo warning light on the dash flashed red. I got out and lifted the hood. One of the two fan belts had snapped. When I had finished cursing my inefficiency at traveling without a spare, I got some nylon parachute cord from my pack and made a mock-up belt. It slipped like a banana skin. And none of my wrenches would budge the bolt that secured the adjustable pulley. After twenty minutes of it I blessed Rohosinante for having a pressurized water-cooling system and drove on.

The track swung away from the river, out across the open plain. But it was still second-gear work at best. Two miles, and the red "overheating" light came on.

I stopped. Less than a hundred yards away stood a herd of buffalo, thirty strong. It hardly seemed an appropriate time to meet our first big herd of animals in the Triangle. I eyed the buffalo distrustfully. When I got out and opened the hood they stood their ground, eying me back. I put my head in under the hood. Once or twice I pulled it out again and checked the buffalo. They still stood quietly, placid looking as Angus cattle. Reassured, I went back under the hood. But in the end I gave up. We would have to keep stopping to let the engine cool down. It would be better once we reached the road, where I could change into high gear and get air rushing through the radiator fast enough to help cool it. By then, the heat of the day would be past too. I straightened my back and came up out of the enclosed, man-made world under the hood—the world of hot metal and grease and the useless length of nylon cord—and found myself out once more in the open, living world of the savanna. The buffalo had begun to drift away. As I watched them go, conscious of my relief, it occurred to me that although they were the largest concentration of game we had seen in the Triangle I had been looking at them as nothing more than a hazard that might interfere with a solution of the fan belt problem. And I saw that, in spite of everything, the slow rhythms of the savanna had, at least in part, governed our hours in the Triangle; but the moment the light flashed red on the car's dash, the jar and jangle of the mechanical world had taken over.

And that was the way it stayed. When I drove on again, my mind remained riveted to the slope and roughness of the way ahead, to speedometer and odometer and wristwatch—and to the place on the dash where the little light might flash red again, any minute now. There was no time to look beneath these flat, enumerated surfaces.

But at least I won. The ten miles of low-gear driving across the Triangle were the worst of it. By six o'clock, with the heat of the day a memory and a cool wind blowing from the east, we had crossed Mara Bridge and eased up out of the valley and were cruising in high gear across the open plain, and Rohosinante's pressure system was keeping its cool the way no ordinary car's would have done. To avoid wasting the battery's precious charge on headlights, we camped soon after dark, near Lemek.

At first light we took to the road again. Soon afterward we must have passed the wheatfields, but I do not remember them. The air was cool, even after sunrise, and we made good time and the red light did not come on. By seven-thirty we were within a mile of Narok village. The meeting was scheduled for nine o'clock. I pulled off the road into a little clearing in the bush.

As I cooked breakfast, Joshua told me that before we left Keekorok all the rangers had assured him we would never make it back out of the Triangle. The place was death on vehicles. We would find ourselves swimming the river and walking to the lodge across the Sanctuary, the way another ranger and visitor had had to do a month earlier when they went down into the Triangle alone. They had been in a Land Rover too, not a ridiculous little Renault.

Joshua smiled and nodded toward Rohosinante. "But now," he said, "I see that your car truly has strength. And I did not believe it."

Once again, an outer layer of me thawed. Just for a moment, I almost liked the man.

After breakfast and a comprehensive wash I drove into Narok village, dropped Joshua at the main duka with instructions to meet me there in an hour, and went on up the hill to the government compound. As usual, I had managed to cut things Fletcher-fine: when I pulled in under the trees in the small and almost empty parking lot, my watch said nine-five.

I hurried into the compound's main quadrangle. The place was very quiet.

A large and smiling policeman appeared, and I asked him if the meeting had begun and where it was being held.

Oh, no, he said, it had not begun yet. But the council members would start arriving any time now. And the meeting would be held in that building over beyond the trees.

I walked over to the building. It was a long, wooden structure with a deep veranda and green corrugated-iron roof. The sunlit courtyard in front of it seemed even quieter than the main quadrangle. I waited in the courtyard. From an open window came the laborious, intermittent tappings of a typewriter.

About nine-fifteen T-B arrived. He wore his usual khaki drill slacks and bush jacket. We exchanged a few words but his mind was clearly on other matters and before long he disappeared into the meeting room, massive shoulders still hunched against the world. Even at that hour the air of tiredness had hung about him, as if the shoulders had not quite worked and he was struggling against something huge and irresistible.

Tipis arrived soon afterward. He wore a thick gray business suit, innocent of creases, with pants that sagged like a gunnysack, and a good pair of brown suede shoes. His khaki shirt was open at the neck and frayed at the collar. On his head perched the gray, piratical sock cap. The meeting would soon get under way, he told me. There were a couple of matters to be disposed of first, but my turn should come within half an hour. It shouldn't take long, either.

By this time the courtyard had begun to fill with council members and Tipis introduced me to one or two of them. A few wore neat business suits. Three were of the open savanna: instead of shukas they wore blankets or army coats and old felt hats, but they remained dirty and dignified. Most of the members dressed somewhere between these two extremes but almost all of them, as they stood around the courtyard in small groups, looked stiff and self-conscious. Tipis, bustling from group to group with his beard bouncing as he poured out sentences that might tumble from English through Swahili to Masai and then back again within a dozen words, stood out as a man of drive and character. And as I watched I felt renewed respect for him. He was, T-B had said, a nervous man, and his easy manner, which gave no sign of being forced, must have been achieved through considerable self-discipline, after many internal battles. If any questions cropped up when I was before the committee, it would be good to have men like T-B and Tipis on my side.

Soon after nine-thirty the members filed into the meeting room, near the center of the long building. The door closed behind them.

I waited in the courtyard. Occasionally, people went in or out of the other rooms in the building or passed along the shady veranda. The slow, intermittent tappings of the typewriter still came from the open window. It was pleasant, I found, to stand in the morning sunshine doing nothing. There was nothing I could do, now. My appearance before the meeting promised to be a formality, anyway. During breakfast I had reread the carbon of the letter I had given Tipis to pass on to the council and it had still seemed to cover all the bases: an outline of what I hoped to write about, an explanation of the publicity a book could offer, and a request for free camping and waiving of Sanctuary entrance fees. All I would have to do, probably, was answer a few questions and remember T-B's advice: "Don't offer them money. They'd only smell a rat."

I began to stroll around the courtyard. On my two brief visits to the compound I had not seen this corner of it. And all I had carried away was the vague impression that nothing much had changed since colonial days. Now I had time to inspect things more closely. Two grassy patches covered most of the courtyard, and I saw that the grass had once been surrounded by a knee-high fence of whitewashed posts joined by whitewashed rope. Most colonial compounds had featured something of the kind. The neat little fences, kept gleaming white, produced an effect that was military and unimaginative, but they fitted in with the general air of no-nonsense, no-more-than-moderate-bumbling efficiency. And I had always found that the line of the white rope, with its regular, shallow dip, carried your eye along in pleasing fashion. Now, strolling around the edge of the courtyard, I saw that most of the rope lay on the ground, rotting. You had to look close to find flecks of whitewash. The whitewash had lasted better on the posts but several of them were down too and they lay where they had fallen in the rank, uncut grass.

Across the two patches of grass cut three or four footpaths, worn bare by feet that could now pass without hindrance over the disintegrating white fences. But a new fence seemed to be going up along the border nearest the building. Four rough-hewn cedar posts, each seven or eight feet high, had been set in the ground. I checked the tamped red earth around their bases. It was very fresh. I was still wondering about the new fence when two men arrived carrying a large section of ironwork. In the next ten minutes they brought several more sections and stacked them off to one side, against the building. I can no longer remember whether the sections were old iron gates or pieces of sheep fencing or cattle grids or a mixture of all these, but I know they were heavy and rusty and battered and unlovely. The men began nailing and wiring them to the huge cedar posts. But before long a council member came out of the meeting room and told them they were making too much noise. The men sat down on the grass. They displayed as much grief at the recess as workmen would have done anywhere in the world. I walked over and asked one of them what the fence was for. The man looked up. His face was thin and pale, Kikuyu rather than Masai. To stop people crossing the grass, he said. The answer was curt, astringent. He clearly regarded me as a fool for asking such a question and saw no reason to conceal his opinion. At least, that was one explanation.

As I walked away I glanced at my watch. Ten o'clock. Tipis's "half an hour" was about up. It was getting hot, anyway, out there in the sunlit courtyard. I went in under the veranda and stood near the entrance to the meeting room.

Further down the veranda, the sound of the typewriter still floated out of the open window. I was getting used to the rhythm now. Or, rather, to the lack of rhythm. The taps came irregularly, painfully, with long hunts between each peck. Out in the courtyard, the sun beat down.

From time to time people came along the pathway between the veranda and the huge cedar posts that would anchor the new fence. Most of them had thin, pale faces. None looked typically

Masai. Almost without exception, they avoided my eye. I found
that by nodding at them and smiling I could often, but not always, induce at least the flicker of a more genial response. One
lean individual wearing a dirty, crumpled business suit responded
by moving his eyes in my direction but then looking through me
with the kind of icy cut that lies beyond the reach of almost
everyone except the British and the Kikuyu.

I began to patrol up and down the veranda.

After about twenty minutes a neatly dressed African came out
of the meeting room and invited me, very pleasantly, to wait in
his office. I would find it cooler in there, he said. He ushered me
down the veranda, stopped at the third or fourth door, unlocked
it, gave me the key, and hurried away.

His office door said TREASURER. Inside, it was cool and dim. I
sat down. My eyes began to adjust to the gloom. On one wall
hung the obligatory portrait with its standard inscription: MHE-
SHIMIWA MZEE JOMO KENYATTA. RAIS WA KWANZA WA KENYA
(*"His Excellency Jomo Kenyatta. First President of Kenya"*).
(*Mzee* means "old," but applied to a man is normally a term of
respect, akin to "elder.") On a bookshelf stood a long line of box
files, and on the desk, beside a red Thermos flask, a tray marked
IN VOUCHERS ONLY. Over everything hung the aura—bleak and
moribund, thin yet interminable—that seems to permeate the offices of parochial bureaucracy all over our world.

I took out my pocket notebook and began to catch up with
notes on the Triangle.

About eleven o'clock I went into the next-door office, marked
DEPUTY TREASURER, and bummed a cigarette from the Asian who
was its only occupant. He was a small, neat, amiable man with an
air of busy efficiency. Masai beads decorated his wristwatch strap.
He had been two and half years with the council, he told me, but
he was probably about to leave. He rather thought they were
deciding it that morning. Like everybody else, they were thinking in terms of Africanization, and he was the last non-African
with the council. Except for T-B, of course.

We discussed the future of the wildlife.

"As long as T-B is here," said the deputy treasurer, "we can expect a lot."

"And after that?"

The Asian shrugged his shoulders.

We talked until I had finished the first cigarette and bummed another. "No, not too many of the Narok people are really Masai," the deputy treasurer said at one point. "For years now, most of the wives have been Kikuyu, you know. And these days a lot of the men come from Nairobi too."

I went back to the treasurer's office. Time passed, paced by the laborious tappings of the distant typewriter.

About eleven-thirty I got up and went outside and locked the door. A runty little man was passing by. He had been around the place all morning and seemed to be some kind of messenger. He had carried chairs into the meeting room before the council went into session, and later I noticed him carrying files. He wore sagging blue jeans and narrow, pointed shoes. The backs of the shoes were folded down under his heels but he had perfected a smooth, sliding shuffle that somehow succeeded, without destroying all suspense, in thwarting the shoes' constant threat to launch out on their own.

When the messenger came level with me I said, "Is there a *choo* near?"

I had chosen my words with care. If the man spoke English he would probably feel offended at being addressed in Swahili. On the other hand, I wanted to make sure he understood my question. So I had compromised: *choo* is the Swahili word for "toilet" and is used by almost everybody in Kenya when speaking either Swahili or English.

The messenger stopped and looked me up and down. "Oh," he intoned. "You mean a lavatory?"

He turned away, motioned me to follow him, and slide-shuffled down the veranda. When we came to the office at the far end he reached inside its open window, lifted out a key, gave it to me without quite throwing it, nodded down the side of the building without looking me in the eye, and then slide-shuffled back along the veranda. I watched him go.

"It's just around the corner, that way," said a voice.

I looked in through the window. An African girl sat behind a typewriter. She was smiling and pointing. She was a large, round, beaming girl, singularly uninspired but the kind of person you cannot help liking. I thanked her and went around the corner. Behind me, the girl resumed her painful hunt and peck.

The ring-seat of the toilet had been broken off. Half of it lay on the floor. The rest was missing. Heavy paper clogged the bowl and the flush did not work. It was a very long time since the place had been cleaned.

I went back outside. As I came to the window the girl stood up, smiling, and took the key. I thanked her again and she beamed. I walked on down the veranda. The girl went back to her typewriter.

I walked slowly along the veranda. The sunlight beat in against its avenue of shade. Out in the glare, the two workmen sprawled beside their unfinished fence. Beyond them, a small post still streaked with white lay half obscured by rank grass. A length of rope protruded from the grass. Its frayed end snaked limply out onto a dusty red pathway.

I went on down the veranda with the glare and heat of the courtyard at my right shoulder, and unlocked the door of the treasurer's office and passed into its cool, dim sanctuary. I sat down. The slow, erratic tappings of the typewriter still reached me, faintly. There was no other sound. Outside the window, beyond the shaded veranda, the sunlight streamed down. I looked away. My eyes began to adjust once more to the dimness of the room. The red Thermos flask still stood on the desk beside the red tray labeled IN VOUCHERS ONLY. On the bookshelf, the backs of the box files announced, in unison and painstaking freehand, REPUBLIC OF KENYA. I sat on in the cool, dim silence— unexpectedly knowing something of how a Roman visitor to Britain must have felt after the legions had begun to withdraw and the Britons to fumble away the trappings of alien but civilized Rome and to start their slide and crumble into a dark age that would last a thousand years. President Kenyatta bigbrothered benignly down from the wall. The typewriter tapped slowly on.

My watch hands crept toward noon, eased past.

At last, footsteps hurried down the veranda. The door opened. Tipis and another man came in.

The moment Tipis saw me, he stopped. His eyes opened wide. One hand went to his forehead. "Oh, oh, oh!" he said. "I'd completely forgotten you." He was very apologetic. But the meeting had only broken off for a brief recess, and he would see to it that I was called in just as soon as it reconvened. He introduced me to his companion, a slight, reserved, faintly bearded Masai named Sloma. He was clerk to the council. They both drank from the Thermos on the treasurer's table, then hurried out. I followed.

Ten minutes later, the last of the council members filed back into the meeting room and the door closed. I waited on the veranda. Out in the sunlight, the two workmen still lay sprawled on the grass beside their ugly, unfinished fence. I found myself squinting into the glare, trying to picture how the fence would look when all the sections of heavy ironwork had been anchored to the massive cedar posts. I was still peering when I heard the meeting room door open behind me. I turned. There hardly seemed to have been time for anyone to read out my letter. But Sloma stood in the doorway and he nodded at me and moved aside. I walked past him into the meeting room.

At first I could see almost nothing. After the sunlight, the room was a block of shadow with only a white and glaring window in the far wall and a vague central squareness and bareness that seemed to hang suspended at a distance, screened off by a gauze curtain. The darkness immediately in front of me was so blank that I checked my stride. I checked, I suppose, for no more than a second. But in that brief interim the gauze screen began to dissolve and I saw that the center of the squareness was an empty space and that around its edges sat dim figures. As soon as my eyes had registered this tentative and still unreal scene, memory thrust up from thirty years deep a picture of our debating society at school where we used to sit around the edges of a room just about this size, all of us ill at ease, all of us much more concerned about the way we would play our own little parts in the charade than about the merits of the airy proposition we were supposed to be debating.

The blankness immediately in front of me resolved into a man sitting at a large table. I stepped forward. Sloma introduced the man as the chairman. We shook hands. The man was no more than a silhouette against the white glare of the window, but I could see that he had broad shoulders and a big, square head. Sloma motioned me to one of two empty chairs set just to the right of the table. I sat down. Sloma sat down on my left, blocking off the chairman's silhouette.

When I looked directly ahead I no longer faced the window. The gauze screen had almost gone now and I could see that the council members sat in chairs set flush against the walls, just the way our chairs used to be set for debates. The only break in the square was to my right, where T-B and Tipis sat side by side, a few feet out from the wall, with a small table in front of them. They faced the window and I could see their faces clearly. T-B looked very tired. Even Tipis seemed to have deflated in the minutes since I had last seen him. The pair of them, coupled behind their fragile table, looked curiously powerless in that encircling assembly. Even a little daunted.

A voice on my left said, "We have read your letter, Mr. Fletcher. But please tell the council in your own words just what it is you want." I think the voice was the chairman's, but it may have been Sloma's: I cannot honestly remember. And that is unusual. At pivotal moments my mind tends to record detail with granular fidelity and to play it back without serious loss. Recall is always an uneven process, of course, with vivid peaks and hazy valleys; but when I looked back later at the council meeting I found that everything that had happened remained obstinately diffuse, as if I were still peering through the gauze curtain that the sunlight had hung before my eyes. Perhaps I never shook off that initial impression of unreality. I know that after a while an almost dreamlike, standing-outside-myself quality descended on the scene in that shadowy meeting room.

It was Sloma who spoke next, I am sure of that. "Some of the council members do not understand English, Mr. Fletcher, so please pause after each sentence and I will translate."

I looked around the room. Except for T-B and Tipis, the members sat in such a way that the harsh light from the window screened off their expressions. I took a deep breath and began talking. Oddly enough, I did not feel nervous—the way you often do at such moments of launch, the way I had felt in T-B's office—and although I had come unprepared for a full statement and had never before suffered the disconcerting interruptions that a translator imposes as he spigots your speech, I do not think I did too badly. Still, you can easily be wrong in such judgments when your audience is almost invisible. Naturally, I was less explicit than I had been in my letter—I assumed that Sloma or the chairman had just read it out loud—and I concentrated on fleshing out some of its salient points.

A couple of these attempts lured me onto uncertain ground. I said that I wanted to write about the animals because they were "the unique contribution that East Africa has to offer the world"; and the phrase was out before I saw that such a sentiment might go down like a load of cement. I also suggested that my book, if successful, would publicize the Mara the way *Serengeti Shall Not Die* had publicized the Serengeti; and that was out too before it occurred to me that most of the council had probably never heard of the Grzimeks' book. But some of my flourishes may not have reached the non-English-speaking members: Sloma's brief translations often suggested paraphrase by puncture. I concluded by saying that provided the council agreed to my proposition I would come back the following year for a full six months' research.

When I had finished there was no clear reaction. I do not mean that I sensed hostility. The council simply seemed to be waiting for more.

The first question came in Masai from the far wall. My eyes

were doing better in the shadows now and I could see that the questioner was one of the men of the open savanna. He wore an army greatcoat and a vast, wide-brimmed hat. Sloma translated: "The member would like to know just what kind of book it is that you will be writing."

That, I said, was a difficult question to answer. A book was like a child: you could never tell what it would grow into. I had launched on this analogy before it occurred to me that the average Masai child was still destined to grow up into a morani and then a herdsman and then an elder. But I think I wriggled clear by waving an arm vaguely around the room and saying, "When a child is born you have no idea whether he will become a herdsman or a ranger or a warden or a district commissioner or something quite different."

There was another unsatisfied pause, a further uncommitted waiting.

A man in a neat business suit broke the silence. He sat directly under the window, and because of its glare I could see only that he wore glasses and that his head was the large, square kind typical of the Luo and other lakeside tribes rather than of the Masai. "I am inclined to think," said this man, "that what worries the council is whether you will be writing, as some people have written, that we go about naked—or other bad things like that." He spoke politely and effectively.

For the first time I remembered something that I now saw should have been in the forefront of my mind: the trouble between Mwangi and the woman who wanted to write about *The Last Tribe in Africa*, the woman who had made even Tipis angry.

I assured the council that I would write only what I saw, only the truth.

A free-for-all discussion followed, partly in English, mostly in Masai, and I gathered that the council would not be satisfied unless I told them exactly what I would be writing. But I could only repeat that at this stage I had no idea how the book would turn out, except that it would be primarily concerned with the animals. More discussion followed. Members kept coming back to the idea that I might write "bad things."

In the end I said that I could not possibly promise to write only things that everybody would consider "good." But, I repeated, I would write only the truth. I was afraid they would have to take my word for that.

There was a brief silence. Then the square-headed, bespectacled man sitting under the window spoke again: "I think the fact that Mr. Fletcher came to us openly shows that he is working in good faith." I could not be sure, because of the window, but I think the man smiled. He certainly spoke with a touch of warmth. It was the first time since I walked into the room that I had heard in anyone's voice a note that was not impersonal, almost clinical.

There was another pause in the proceedings. I began to think that perhaps the council had tacitly approved, as if there had been only this one point of doubt and that now, given no alternative, they had reluctantly decided to trust me. But something still hung in the shadows, waiting.

It crystallized in English in the mouth of a man sitting against the far wall. He was an extravagantly casual dresser and his carefully idiomatic phrasing suggested that the question was also a product of forethought: "I take it you are not doing this for love, Mr. Fletcher?"

I think I must have looked blank. Anyway, my questioner quickly added, "I mean, you will be making money out of this."

"I hope so. Eventually. I live by writing."

"But you may make a lot of money."

"Yes, it's always possible. If I manage to write a good book. And if I'm lucky."

"Then how much can you pay us if we agree to let you write the book?"

I glanced at T-B. He was leaning back in his chair, still as a statue, studying the ceiling. But other members were stirring. I do not think I mean that anyone actually leaned forward. There was probably just a general crossing and uncrossing of legs. But I sensed that the members' attention had sharpened, as if the waiting was over at last. And from that point until the end we never again talked of anything except money. At least, not on the surface. That first question about money also marked, I think, the point at which the dream quality began to invade our scene.

Now my grasp of financial matters—though it can tighten in miserlike spasms, especially if I suspect I am being "taken"—tends to be uncertain. But I doubt if finance had much to do with my growing sense of unreality. It is more likely, I think, that at this point in the meeting I began to be thrown off balance by the turn of events and by the way the council escalated matters so fast that I hardly had time to get a grip on one rung before we were confronting on the next. But whatever the cause, it was round about now that I began to view the scene in that dark and crowded room with a kind of shadowy double vision: the man sitting beside Sloma remained unquestionably me; but at the same time I was also halfway hovering outside him, so that he became in a sense one of the figures that my eyes could now pick out more clearly from the general gloom—a graying, bearded individual whom I recognized from many mirrors.

I went out to meet my questioner halfway. After all, a financial arrangement had been part of my original proposal to T-B. And at that stage of the meeting I think I was still suppressing the doubts about what I wanted to do—the doubts that had stirred, just before we left camp, when I walked out from the river-forest and stood looking at the smoke pall that lay over the Triangle; the doubts that had stirred again, but still had not quite surfaced, when I sat alone in the cool, quiet treasurer's office and looked at the sunlight streaming down beyond the veranda and listened to the tappings of the distant typewriter. So I made my original offer: 5 percent of all royalties on the book.

The council wanted to know what that would mean in hard cash. I explained that royalties could range from a pittance to a small fortune. Then I tried to do some calculations out loud on 5 percents of sample dollar sums, with rough conversions into East African shillings at the going rate of seven to the U.S. dollar. It is not the kind of thing I do well and I do not think I did it well. The council did not seem to think so either. Someone asked if I could not pay a specific amount. I agreed. How much? For a moment I felt at a loss. Then I suggested two thousand shillings.

I rather think I chose this figure because it sounded a nice round sum. Although I had been back in Kenya for nearly four months, large sums in shillings still tended to confuse me, and I am almost sure that when I spoke I had not translated "two thousand shillings" into the more meaningful sum of "three hundred dollars." I am almost sure of the vagueness in my mind because this was one of the moments at which I became acutely conscious of hovering outside myself, and as I spoke the words I looked down at the bearded figure sitting beside Sloma and wondered what the hell I thought I was doing. Later, I found this recollection interesting. It suggested that even then a part of me knew that the shillings we were talking about could not really be converted into dollars.

I gained no clear impression of whether the council found my offer adequate, but I suppose they must have done because we promptly passed on to the question of when payment would be made. I said that judging by my past performances the book would be published in five or six years. The first royalties would fall due six months after that and I would be happy to make full payment then. The shadowy figures around the wall sat silent. Would I not pay at publication? I agreed. And then, almost before I had finished telling myself that such an arrangement would work out all right because if the book was any damned good at all I would by that time have some kind of an advance, the demand had escalated from "when you finish writing the book" to "when you come back to do your research" to "now." I agreed to the first two without much hesitation. I think I told myself that if I was going to travel back to Kenya and then support myself without income for six months I would certainly have to rustle up some outside money—from a foundation or something—and that an extra two thousand shillings (which I suppose I had by now translated into dollars, at least roughly) did not seem likely to make all that much difference. But at the request for payment "now," I balked. And for the first time my irritation surfaced. Surfaced, I mean, in my own awareness. The bearded figure sitting beside Sloma showed no emotion.

The council must understand, I said, that I could not yet be sure that the book would ever be written. Like a child, it might die in infancy. I could not even be sure I would indeed come back to research the book.

Later, I found that an interesting remark too. Perhaps the doubts had begun to surface at last, along with the irritation.

I do not think we ever resolved the question of when payment should be made. After I had said my piece about not yet knowing if I would come back, there was a pause. I am not sure how long the pause lasted. Time did not really work for me in that shadowy meeting room, a world away from the wide grasslands of the Mara. Even now I am not sure how long I was inside. I suppose the answer is "no more than twenty or thirty minutes."

The pause ended when somebody, probably the chairman, said, "You will naturally have to get written permission from the Ministry of Tourism and Wildlife and from the Office of the President."

"Of course," said the figure sitting in the chair beside Sloma.

But still the shadowy room held no sense of decision.

I cannot remember just how we got onto the next rung. The proposition may have been put to me direct. More likely, it spun off from one of the free-for-all discussions into which the meeting's formality periodically dissolved. Anyway, the suggestion was suddenly there, out in the open, explicit: during my researches I would pay normal camping fees of thirty shillings a day.

I remonstrated. My letter, I said, had specifically asked for a waiving of the camping fees. I could not possibly afford them, not for six months.

Now I know that I did not even begin to work out, there in the meeting room, how many shillings the camping fees would amount to, so it seems I must have grasped by this time that, no matter what the council might imagine, the shillings we were talking about represented a currency unconnected with money.*

---

* It is only now, as I write these words, that I have at last bothered to do the arithmetic. Camping fees for six months at thirty shillings a night

Almost at once somebody said, "Then there will also be entry fees into the Sanctuary."

"I shall have to consider that," said the man sitting beside Sloma. But the sector of me that remained inside him knew now, on some rapidly emerging and increasingly angry plane, that he would not really consider the matter at all.

"Will there be photographs in your book?" asked someone on the far wall.

Although my feelings were fast catching up with events, there must have been a sense in which I still only halfway understood what was going on, for I gave the question serious attention. "I'm afraid I really can't say yet. It's far too early."

"But there may be?"

"Yes, there may be."

Somebody, I think it was the chairman, said that if there were to be photographs then naturally I would have to pay the normal professional photographer's fee of a thousand shillings a week.

"That is another thing I shall have to consider," said the man beside Sloma. The half of me hovering outside him heard the sudden British starch in his voice. The half of me inside him knew he no longer cared a damn.

And that was where it ended. Nobody seemed to have any more questions, and I wanted only out.

The graying, bearded individual beside Sloma stood up—and the movement shifted all of me back inside him. I found myself shaking hands with the chairman. Then I had turned to the room at large and was saying, "Thank you gentlemen." My voice sounded almost elaborately civil. But the council had, after all, been unfailingly polite. As I turned to go I nodded to T-B and Tipis, coupled behind their little table. For the first time I realized that since I came into the room neither of them had said a word.

Then I was outside on the veranda, and then out in the harsh noonday sunlight. On my left, stacked against the building, stood

amount to fifty-four hundred shillings, or seven hundred and seventy dollars. Although a sizable sum, that is hardly enough, in financial terms, to have stopped me from going back to the Mara.

the ugly ironwork for the new fence. Beside it, the two workmen still sprawled on the grass. And then I had crossed the uncut grass with its fallen posts and loose ends of rope and was walking under trees into the dusty red parking lot.

By the time I drove into Narok village, five minutes later, I had grasped at least the surface of what had happened in the dark meeting room.

Joshua was not at the duka. It took me half an hour to find him. At last I saw him sauntering out from a cluster of huts at the edge of the village. Four or five women escorted him and he was taking pains to show them he was in no hurry. He got into the car clumsily. He reeked of beer. I drove down the Keekorok road, fast. I think I told myself that I had to drive fast to keep air flowing through the radiator because if I went at normal speed in the afternoon sun without a fan belt even Rohosinante would boil.

We were three miles beyond the fork at which the roads to Keekorok and the Triangle diverge when Joshua sat upright and bleared out at the scenery. *"Sisi hapana rudi katika Triangle?"* he asked. "Aren't we going back to the Triangle?" For the first time I realized just how much had changed since I stepped into the meeting room.

I said that we were not going back to the Triangle because of the fan belt. It seemed easier that way.

But Joshua, now roused from his stupor, was in a conversational mood. The beer had hardly improved him. I was in no mood to suffer, and before long I snapped, in Swahili, "You think that because you can read you are better than the other rangers, don't you?"

Joshua focused on me. *"Ndio,"* he said. "Yes."

"Kwa mutu mazima," I advised him, *"ni shauri ya roho, hapana ya akili.* For a whole man, it is a question of spirit, not intelligence."

I do not think he opened his mouth again.

But the outburst did me little good. I continued to drive stupidly fast, just the way I had driven after the talk with

Mwangi, three weeks earlier. It was difficult, I found, to believe that the meeting with Mwangi had taken place so recently. It seemed a long time ago now, that other time I had been angry in the Mara.

All the way to Keekorok my mind raced. I do not think I saw a blade of grass, let alone any animals. I could still grasp little more than the surface facts of what had gone on in that bare and crowded meeting room where the whole thing had come apart, but I knew that what it amounted to in the end, goddammit, was that they had said they might graciously grant me permission to write a book provided I paid all normal camping and entrance and professional photography fees plus two thousand shillings. If I had only had the sense to keep quiet and go about my own business I could have saved myself two thousand shillings and God knows how much a month as well as a whole lot of horse-shit. That would teach me to "work in good faith" and "go to them openly," as the pleasant man under the window had said.

I did my best with the anger. It may even have been during the drive back to Keekorok that I raised the question of why I should expect special treatment. At first I could lay hands on nothing better than the ancient and paltry one: "because that's how it's always done, everywhere." If people were willing to let you write, I had found, then they "let you in free." In the U.S. I was at least as much a foreigner as I was in Kenya, but when I wanted to write a book about walking through the wild regions of a national park the only assurance the authorities had ever sought was that I would take reasonable precautions against dying on them. Once, when I sent a superintendent a rough draft that included harsh criticism of certain park policies, he said he disagreed with me, and left it at that. So it had not, surely, been unreasonable for me to expect the usual kind of writer's arrangement in the Mara. Come to think of it, T-B and Tipis had accepted the idea from the start, without discussion. Anyway, I was offering a lot. The council lacked vision, that was all—the vision to see that the publicity I offered could bring in much more money than I could possibly rake up on my own.

When I considered the matter I found I was by no means sure what the council had finally decided, if indeed it had decided anything. But I was almost sure what I had decided. For I was beginning to see that those shillings in the meeting room represented the currency I had been handling ever since I came to the Mara. Its coin was the harmony between land and men and the other animals, the beauty of golden, rippling grass, and the spirit of a people who when they first encountered Western mores and money would have none of these things. And while I talked in the dark meeting room with these same people, or their modern representatives, something in that currency had died.

But my anger would not die. As soon as we reached the lodge I dropped Joshua like a stone. Then I radio-phoned Nairobi and arranged for a fan belt to be shipped on a tourist plane that would be flying in two days later. And then I drove out to Waterhole Camp. It seemed the natural place to go: if I could sit quietly for a day in that little sanctuary of a clearing I might be able to find the kind of calm I had found there after the meeting with Mwangi.

When I drove back out of the main gate and turned right up the track through the bush I found that once again everything was just as I had left it. The trunk of the clearing's main tree still twisted up like a meld of many columns. The donga cut deep and dark and mysterious and definitely not mine. And avenues still radiated out into the dark foliage, never leading anywhere and never quite stating anything but always hinting and suggesting.

In a way, it worked. By the evening of the next day my anger had subsided. But it did not work the way it had worked after Mwangi.

Once the anger had cooled I could see that the council members probably knew what had been decided too. They would see it rather differently from me: they would no doubt feel content at the way this minor nuisance had been nipped. And now I could see that it was the old difficulty: not evil men, just unaware men. And by "unaware men" I meant, of course, men who were unaware of things I now judged important. I did not mean men unaware of things that the farm manager from Na-kuru might have judged important. For the council members were men who might very well say, "But you can't farm in a menagerie." They were men who, naturally enough, did not yet understand the appalling wrongness of the bleak, gray, concrete world that can surround bus stops, the world that was already reaching out toward them on the wind that blew from Nairobi. But above all they were men who could not yet see beyond their shillings. They were men, in other words, who were behaving as we men have nearly always behaved.

But when a cusp has passed, rationalizations are no good. I still knew what had been decided while we wrangled over shillings.

So it would not turn out the way I had dreamed it. I would not be coming back to the Mara to live for half a year as close as I could, in my earnest but untutored way, to the golden grass and the great herds of glorious, unknowing animals and the tall red men striding across their open plains. I felt spasms of sadness at the things that would be left undone. I would never explore the mission turnoff or the hyena burrow where the cubs had peered into my headlights. I would not play soccer again at the lodge. I would never learn the Masai language or begin to know the Masai people. I would not even come to know T-B or Tipis, the men I had thought would be my symbols.

It was difficult to believe that only five weeks had passed since I drove into the Mara looking for T-B. Less than forty days. Yet every day had been sharp, etched—the way the hours and minutes and wrenching seconds of a love affair can be. Perhaps that was it. That first day in the Mara, even before I stood beside the swimming pool and understood, it had been love at first sight. And our affair had been "too hot not to cool down."

That is always the danger with love at first sight. Without knowing it, you build an insurmountable expectancy barrier. And in the end something has to give. She is bitchy, or you think she is. You are a bastard, or she thinks you are. Or chance reveals an impossible discord. And because you had expected too much, scales fall from eyes. Neither of you knows just what has happened, but both of you know it is over. Because of the memories, though, you cannot just let it slip away. So you go on trying. Or a layer of you does. Or, saddest of all, a layer of one of you does. But now, down where the music was, only silence. And no amount of straight, logical, heart-to-heart talk can ever rekindle the fire.

Perhaps that was how it had been with the Mara and me. The first night, when I stood beside the floodlit swimming pool and stared down at the intricate and harmonious vein pattern of the brown leaf deep in the pale water, the harmony was all I had heard. Now I came to consider it, I knew that the seeds of discord had been there all along. They had even been there that first afternoon, when we visited the manyatta. And once or twice I had glimpsed the expectancy barrier. Each time, I thought I had passed through. But now the affair had gone sour on me. Now, down where the music had been, only discord. It was no good administering straight, logical, strictures. The fire was out. And without a fire there could be no book. No matter what the council had decided in that dark meeting room—if indeed they had decided anything—it made no difference. I could not go on. You cannot do a perfect thing in a place you are no longer wanted: the thing is no longer perfect.

And yet, as I sat sadly in my little clearing at Waterhole Camp, I knew that I could not run away from the book. Now that I had found the sunlit plains and the herds of free, unknowing, threatened animals, I could not desert them. I sat hour after hour, looking out along the green avenues that led nowhere but still hinted and suggested. I saw no way out of my dilemma. But I went on hoping.

Next day I drove in to the lodge and found the fan belt waiting. It turned out to be the wrong size, and I had to wait for another three days.

I spent the three days in the Sanctuary. An eland herd wheeled in unison, then trotted away in formation across a paddock—and the black top-of-the-sock markings on their legs made me think of a good soccer team's forward line moving to the attack. Two very young Tommy broke free from their herd, chasing each other with the kind of pointless and glorious exuberance that often erupts among kittens; but when they invited a passing secretary bird to join in and the bird flapped its huge gray wings and then stalked off in huffed, schoolmasterish solemnity, the youngsters tiptoed back into the fold as if ashamed of what they had done. A rhino, presumed female, astonished me by urinating in a hoselike stream that jetted out aft for at least fifteen feet. But such scenes were no longer enough. I know they were not enough: on the third afternoon I was talking to Steve Joyce at the lodge when he suddenly said, "I don't know what happened at the council meeting, Colin, but I can see that you feel quite differently about it all now."

I tried to explain.

"You say it isn't the money that bothers you?"

"Christ, no! At least, not *my* money. The council's attitude to money—yes. That spoils the whole thing. Maybe it doesn't sound logical, but there it is."

"And now?"

"I really don't know."

On the fourth day the proper fan belt arrived. When I drove away from the lodge at last, late that afternoon, I said no good-byes. Tipis had not been back since the council meeting, but I did not say good-bye, either, to Steve or Hans or Peter or Solomon or to the porters. It was partly, I suppose, because I hate good-byes. But mostly it was because I still hoped.

I know I hoped because half a mile down the road, at the first donga, I stopped and photographed a tree in which a pair of hammerkops had a few days earlier begun the huge task of building a new nest beside their existing mansion. I assumed that the job would take several weeks or even months, and as I focused the camera I told myself that I wanted to take these first photographs because it would be interesting to have a record of the work in various stages of progress. I understood the irony of the thought. But I took the photographs. So I must have been hoping.

I went out through the main gate, passed the track to Waterhole Camp, and drove steadily north, toward Narok.

Soon, two tall red figures strode down the road ahead, owning it. The sun glinted on spears carried high across red-smeared shoulders. Red shukas swung rhythmically. The men were talking earnestly as they walked, and they clearly did not hear me coming. I bore down on them, feeling like an intruder. But when I tapped my horn at last and they jumped aside, they stood beside the road laughing at the way they had been surprised, and as I drove by they waved their spears in salute.

I passed a manyatta. Another mile, and a small herd of calves grazed along the shoulder of the road. Three of them stood in the road itself. I slowed. The child who was tending the calves appeared. He wore khaki shorts and tennis shoes. When I came level he ran alongside the car, ignoring his charges, scattering them in front of me. As he ran he held one palm outstretched. I drove on, forcing a passage through the calves, and soon I could no longer hear the young voice crying, *"Shillingi! Shillingi! Shillingi!"*

I camped at dusk, not far from the place the cheetah had killed the Tommy. I camped a mile off the road, beside a ridge that sheltered me from the east wind. I set up my table and chair and lamp and tent. I cooked dinner. Outside the hissing dome it was very dark. I sat listening to the thunderous silence. By the time I went to bed I had drunk a large bottle of wine.

Some time during the night, lions passed within a few yards of the tent. Their roaring threatened to touch off an earthquake. In the morning I woke to see a flock of guinea fowl clucking in nervous procession across the grass outside the tent entrance. I got up. Four hundred yards away, out on flat grassland, a herd of topi was grazing. Nearby were three zebras. I checked them through binoculars. The zebras were all males and the two younger ones were doing something I had never seen before but which was clearly what Hans Klingel had called "play fighting." They were jousting, neck against neck. But they pulled their punches. And between bouts they nibbled each other affectionately. Once, they rolled together on the ground, still playfully grappling. I watched until they drifted into thick bush.

The sun rose. I sat down to breakfast. From the crest of the ridge behind me came the sound of breaking wood. A dozen elephants were feeding on low trees and scrub. All through my breakfast they moved slowly along the ridge, silhouetted against the shining eastern sky, feeding, ignoring me. Out on the grassland, the topi grazed closer. The three zebra bachelors reappeared. A Tommy herd drifted in from the left.

After breakfast I packed away, with the inevitable wave of sentiment, the table and the chair and all the other things that for five weeks had built home wherever I chose to stop. Then I drove slowly across the trackless savanna. For a mile there was no tarnish of man's hand, nothing but the grass and the trees and the bush and the sunlight and the animals to whom this land belonged. Then I came to the road. I turned left, accelerated past the mission turnoff, and drove on toward Nairobi.

Man: Manyatta

Postlude

I suppose I ought to leave it at that, knotted off, dead. But I stayed in Kenya for two more months. And I went on hoping.

I spent the two months doing things I thought I wanted to do. For a week I clambered around Mount Kilimanjaro on my own and sustained—while making tea at 16,000 feet and two o'clock in the morning—a sizable earthquake. Then I drove down to the coast and rediscovered the silent, flickering underwater world that ebbs and flows around the coral reefs. And I enjoyed myself, I suppose.

Back in Nairobi, I went—because I was still hoping—to the Office of the President and got my letter of clearance. I began trying to extract one from the Ministry of Tourism and Wildlife. But all around me the papers were still at it: CIVIL WAR TO

GO ON, SAY BIAFRA LEADERS; ATHLETIC BAN ON NON-KENYANS (Kenya Athletic Association debars non-Kenya citizens from meetings it organizes); a small, un-headlined paragraph about a British M.P. who asked the British government to intervene in the case of two British seamen jailed in Mombasa for calling President Kenyatta a dictator; and—from down in Tanzania, where the alien influence on the Masai was now Chinese rather than British—"The Arusha Regional Commissioner, Mr. Aaron Weston Mwadang'ata, has banned the wearing of animal skins, smearing the body or clothes with red ochre, walking about half-naked or wearing mini-skirts."

I went back once more to the Mara.

This time I was leading another group of Americans on an airborne safari of East Africa's game area spectaculars. When our planes touched down on the little grass airstrip at Keekorok, topi and kongoni and zebras were grazing out beyond the wingtips. We taxied up to within a hundred yards of the lodge, and when the porters came out to collect our baggage and saw me there was much laughter and shaking of hands. And then I went inside and Steve and Hans and Peter were all in the office and Steve said, again, "Good to see you back, Colin," and for a while it was the way it had been at the start of everything.

We drove out game-viewing. The grass stretched rich and golden. We found a big pride of lions and the cubs played romp and my people were enchanted. I rephotographed the nest that the hammerkop couple were building nextdoor to their old one, where the road crossed the donga. It was several inches taller than it had been the day I drove away. But when we visited a manyatta—a different one this time—nothing had changed.

As I was dressing for dinner a knock sounded on my cottage door. It was the ranger whom I have, for his sake, called Joshua. He had been sent by Tipis, he said, to tell me that I owed a hundred shillings in ranger's fees for the ten days he had guided me, first near the lodge and then into the Triangle. A hundred Kenya shillings amounted to barely fifteen U.S. dollars; but de-manded verbally like that, at second mouth, and after all that had gone before, these shillings had no more to do with dollars than had the council-meeting shillings. I told Joshua that there had been a mistake and that I would see Tipis next morning.

In the morning I went to Tipis's office. He was busy, he said; but that evening he would be less busy, and perhaps I could return then. As soon as we came in from our evening game-viewing I went over to the office again. Tipis was not there. He would not be back, said the clerk, for at least two days.

During dinner the head ranger—a tall sergeant who apparently could not read and who clearly disapproved of me, but whom I could not help liking—came to the lodge to dun me for the hundred shillings. I wrote a note to Tipis. Obviously, I said, there had been some mistake: he had explicitly stated that the rangers who guided me were "on the house." But if any doubt remained in his mind I would rather pay than leave a bad taste behind. I gave both my Nairobi and home addresses.

Next morning we flew south into the Serengeti.

All through the rest of those final two months in Kenya my mind kept picking up little barbed burrs of conversation—the kind that you feel snagging on the fabric of your memory, so that you know they will cling for years.

"Oh dear, I'm afraid you've been here too long, Colin," said the wife of an old friend. "It was wonderful talking to you when you first came back. You were so full of hope. It's always like that with newcomers, or people who've been away for a long time." She sighed. "But it never seems to last."

Then there was a British research biologist who drew graphs to show me how many elephant should be shot to bring the herds into balance with his computation of what their habitat could support. We hardly saw eye to eye. But when we discussed the human situation we began to communicate. After a while I mentioned a way that I had begun to see out of my dilemma about the book.

"Now *that* sounds like sense," said the biologist. "Planeloads of people come out here these days, brimming with hope and hell bent on writing books. Most of them go home disillusioned.

But they write their books anyway. The original books. It's damned dishonest, and it does an awful lot of harm. But if you went home and wrote the kind of book I gather you're talking about—wrote it honestly I mean—you'd be doing Africa and the Africans a good turn. Not to mention the game, of course, which is the main thing. The government people here are so damned pompous and so sensitive to criticism that a breath of truth would do them a power of good after all the hot air that's been pumped in from the outside world since Independence. Yes, you're right, it might well mean that you wouldn't be allowed back in the country afterwards. Still, I should think the price would be worth it."

The edge to his voice rekindled my own petulance. But even after the sadness had flowed in again, I remembered.

Toward the end of those two final months, Rohosinante and I went on a 1500-mile safari through northern Kenya and Uganda, up as far as the Sudanese border. That was a good safari too, in its way. But on its last afternoon, on the last lap into Nairobi, we came—as I had known we must, eventually—to the road that cut westward across the floor of the Rift Valley toward Narok. A car had just turned onto the road. Beyond its dust cloud rose the blue escarpment that marked the beginning of the Mara.

We passed the turnoff.

Five miles down the Nairobi highway I pulled in at a gas station. An African waiting beside the pumps asked for a ride into the city, and I found room for him. He had a big, square head, just like the man who had sat under the window at the council meeting, the only man there to show any sign of human understanding. This one too, I told myself, looked like a Luo. He turned out to be a Masai from Narok. He spoke excellent English and he was a most reasonable man. When we discussed the game and I got on my high and self-righteous horse and read the riot act about the wheatfields—saying that his grandchildren would blame him for the loss of the game just as much as would my grandchildren—he did not seem to agree, but he took no umbrage.

We passed the little Italian chapel, climbed the escarpment, swept by the sad Kikuyu hawkers and sheepskin vendors. And all the time, we talked.

"Yes," said the Masai as we reached the fringes of Nairobi, "I know it is bad here for Europeans now. And worse for Asians. But it is bad for us Africans too, you know. Especially for non-Kikuyu. No one is allowed to criticize. And these politicians we've got are not interested in the people at all, only in lining their own pockets."

We turned onto the broad, tree-lined thoroughfare that is now called Kenyatta Avenue and I asked the Kenya question of the day.

"After Kenyatta?" asked the Masai. He looked ahead down the crowded street and sighed. "I am very much afraid that we shall have our Biafra."

That evening I bumped into T-B in the New Stanley Hotel. In a business suit he looked even more like a huge, sad, faithful St. Bernard.

"Yes," he said, nodding down at me, slowly. "I can understand how you felt after that meeting."

We talked for only a few minutes. I remember thinking again that he looked tired in a way that had nothing to do with sleep. But I could hardly know that eighteen months later, just before he was due to retire—on the very day he was being presented *in absentia*, in San Antonio, Texas, with the major award of Game Conservation International—this huge, honest, dedicated man would, in that same New Stanley Hotel, without warning, keel over and die.

Three days later, very early, I parked Rohosinante outside the garage from which I had rented her. It was raining. The street was deserted. A cold wind blew. I got into the car of the friend who was taking me to the airport and we went away and left Rohosinante standing there in the wet, gray street.

At the airport it was still raining. I said good-bye to my friend. I found my seat in the plastic maw of the jet. We taxied out onto the dismal gray tarmac. We pounded down it. We took to the air. Almost at once, the light outside my window began to grow brighter. We broke free into dazzling sunshine. A few last cloud filaments sped past. And then there was only sunlight streaming down onto the billowing mountaintops and folded valleys of a white, untrodden world.

BIBLIOGRAPHY

As I have indicated, this list serves both to acknowledge my reference debts and to suggest avenues for further exploration. Most of the books should be obtainable from good libraries and the right kind of bookstores. For the more technical papers, the best bet is probably a college biology library.

I have kept the list as short as possible. Explorers who want to keep going have only to browse through the bibliographies of a few of the listed works and press on from there, alp to alp.

GENERAL

Books

GRZIMEK, Bernhard and Michael: *Serengeti Shall Not Die*. Translated by E. L. Rewald. New York: E. P. Dutton & Co., 1961. 344 pages. Paperback: Collins, Fontana Books, 1964. 256 pages.

MABERLY, C. T. Astley: *Animals of East Africa*. Paperback: Nairobi: D. A. Hawkins, 1965. 221 pages. (Until the publication of John Williams's *Field Guide to the National Parks* [see below], this was the only convenient popular guide to the East African mammals. It still has its uses.)

SIMON, Noel: *Between the Sunlight and the Thunder*. Boston: Houghton Mifflin, 1963. 384 pages. (A background to the wildlife situation in East Africa.)

WILLIAMS, John G.: *A Field Guide to the Birds of East and Central Africa*. London: Collins, 1963. 288 pages. (The standard popular local bird book, the equivalent of Roger Tory Peterson's American series.)

——: *A Field Guide to the National Parks of East Africa*. London: Collins, 1967. 352 pages. (More than the title suggests. Part I: Brief descriptions, sketch maps and complete mammal and bird lists for all parks and game reserves in Kenya, Uganda and Tanzania—including the Masai Mara. Part II: Field guide to the mammals. Part III: Field guide to the rarer birds.)

Papers and articles

GLOVER, P. E.: *Wildlife*. 27 pages. (Undated mimeographed booklet.)

GLOVER, P. E., and GWYNNE, M. D.: "The Destruction of Masailand." *New Scientist*, No. 249, August 24, 1961, pp. 450–3.

HUXLEY, Sir Julian: "Serengeti: A Living Laboratory." *New Scientist*, Vol. 27, No. 458, August 26, 1965, pp. 504–8.

KENYATTA, President Jomo: *Nairobi Manifesto*. Washington, D.C.: African Wildlife Leadership Foundation. (2-page pamphlet in English and Swahili.)

Proceedings of the Symposium on Wildlife Management and Land Use, Nairobi, July 5th–8th, 1967. Nairobi: Government Printer, 1968. 297 pages.

THE MARA

DARLING, F. Fraser: *An Ecological Reconnaissance of the Mara Plains in Kenya Colony*. Washington, D.C.: The Wildlife Society (Wildlife Monograph No. 5), 1960. 41 pages.

GLOVER, P. E.: *An Ecological Survey of the Narok District of Kenya Masailand. Part I* (Geology, Topography, Climate, Hydrology, Soils). Nairobi: E.A.A.F.R.O., 1966. (Mimeographed booklet, 72 pages.)

——: *A List of Mammals from the Mau-Mara area of Masailand*. Nairobi: Kenya National Parks, 1968. (Mimeographed booklet, 141 pages.)

GLOVER, P. E., and TRUMP, E. C.: *An Ecological Survey of the Narok District of Kenya Masailand. Part II* (Vegetation). Nairobi: Kenya National Parks, 1970. (Mimeographed booklet, 167 pages.)

GLOVER, P. E., et al.: *A List of Birds from the Mau Mara area of Ma-sailand. Part I (Struthiones, Coraciformes). Part II (Passeres).* Nairobi: Kenya National Parks, 1970. (Mimeographed booklets, 137 and 188 pages.)

TALBOT, Lee M.: *Land Use Survey of Narok District.* Narok, Kenya: 1960. (Mimeographed booklet.)

TALBOT, Lee M., and STEWART, D. R. M.: "First Wildlife Census of the Entire Serengeti-Mara Region, East Africa." *Journal of Wildlife Management,* Vol. 28, No. 4, October 1964, pp. 815–27.

SPECIES

This is where the alps rise steepest. And they are still building up, fast. But this is where explorers must go if they want to mine the richest veins of current knowledge about how the other half lives on the sunlit African savanna.

Grant's Gazelle
ESTES, Richard D.: "The Comparative Behavior of Grant's and Thomson's Gazelles." *Journal of Mammalogy,* Vol. 48, No. 2, May, 20, 1967, pp. 189–209.
(Unfortunately I failed to obtain: WALTHER, F. R.: "Verhaltensstudien an der Grantgazelle im Ngorongoro-Krater." Z. *Tierpsychol.,* Vol. 22, 1965, pp. 167–208.)

Elephant
LAMPREY, H. F., *et al.*: "Invasion of the Serengeti National Park by Elephants." *East African Wildlife Journal,* Vol. 5, August 1967, pp. 151–66.

Hyena
KRUUK, Hans: "A New View of the Hyena." *New Scientist,* June 30, 1966, pp. 849–51.

Hyrax
TURNER, M. I. M., and WATSON, R. M.: "An Introductory Study on the Ecology of Hyrax." *East African Wildlife Journal,* Vol. 3, August 1965, pp. 49–60.

Impala
SCHENKEL, Rudolf: "On Sociology and Behaviour in Impala." *East African Wildlife Journal*, Vol. 4, August 1966, pp. 99–114.

Rhino
GODDARD, John: "Mating and Courtship of Black Rhino." *East African Wildlife Journal*, Vol. 4, August 1966, pp. 69–75.

Termites
MARAIS, Eugène. *The Soul of the White Ant*. Translated by Winifred DeKok. New York: Dodd, 1937. Reprinted Toronto: Kraus, 1969. 184 pages.

(For more up-to-date scientific information, see: WILSON, E. O. *Insect Societies*. Cambridge, Mass.: Harvard University Press, 1971.

GLOVER, P. E.: "Further Notes on Some Termites of Northern Somalia." *East African Wildlife Journal*, Vol. 5, August 1967, pp. 121–32.

GLOVER, P. E., *et al.*: "Termitaria and Vegetation Patterns on the Loita Plains of Kenya." *Journal of Ecology*, Vol. 52, July 1964, pp. 367–77.

Thomson's Gazelle
See Grant's Gazelle, above.

(Two papers that I failed to obtain are clearly relevant: BROOKS, A. C.: *A Study of Thomson's Gazelle in Tanganyika*, Col. Res. Publ. No. 25. H. M. Stationery Office, London, 1961. 147 pages; and WALTHER, F. R.: Einige Verhaltensbeobachtungen an Thomsongazellen im Ngorongoro-Krater. Z. *Tierpsychol.*, Vol. 21, 1964, pp. 871–90.)

Tsetse Fly
GLOVER, P. E.: *Relationship Between the Tsetse Fly and Its Vertebrate Hosts*. Booklet No. 6 (New Series), *International Union for Conservation of Nature and Natural Resources*, 1965. 84 pages.

Wildebeest

TALBOT, Lee M. and Martha H.: *The Wildebeest in Western Masai-land, East Africa.* Washington, D.C.: The Wildlife Society (Wildlife Monograph No. 12), September 1963. 88 pages.

Zebra

KLINGEL, Hans: *Soziale Organisation und Verhalten freilebender Steppenzebras* (The Social Organization and General Behavior of Free-Living Plains Zebras). Z. *Tierpsychol.,* Vol. 24, 1967, pp. 580–624. (In German, with 1-page summary in English.)

Some early biological information arising from Dr. Klingel's research appeared as: "Notes on the Biology of the Plains Zebra." *East African Wildlife Journal,* Vol. 3, August 1965, pp. 86–8.)

A NOTE ON THE TYPE

This book was set on the Linotype in Janson, a recutting made direct from type cast from matrices long thought to have been made by the Dutchman Anton Janson, who was a practicing type founder in Leipzig during the years 1668–87. However, it has been conclusively demonstrated that these types are actually the work of Nicholas Kis (1650–1702), a Hungarian, who most probably learned his trade from the master Dutch type founder Dirk Voskens. The type is an excellent example of the influential and sturdy Dutch types that prevailed in England up to the time William Caslon developed his own incomparable designs from them.

Composed, printed, and bound by
H. Wolff Book Manufacturing Co., Inc.,
New York, N.Y.
Typography and binding design by
Virginia Tan

Illustrated by Tom Harris

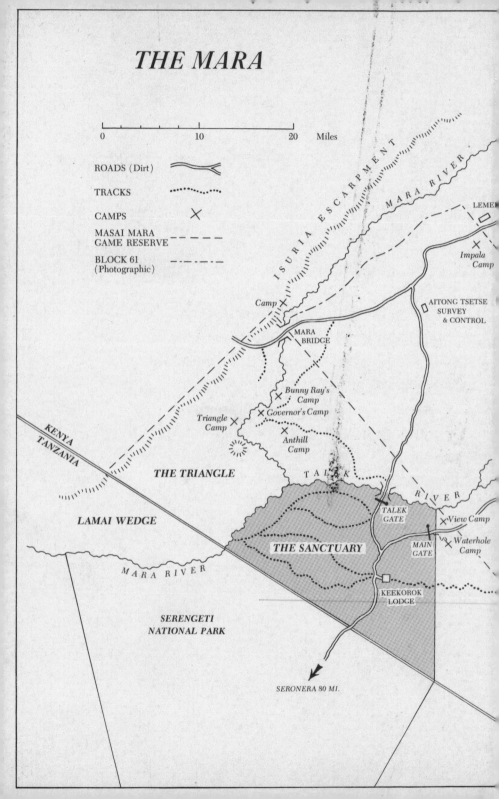